ROUTES TO SLAVERY

Studies in Slave and Post-Slave Societies and Cultures

Co-Editors: GAD HEUMAN
JAMES WALVIN

THE SLAVES' ECONOMY
Independent Production by Slaves in the Americas
Edited by IRA BERLIN and PHILIP D. MORGAN

THE ECONOMICS OF THE INDIAN OCEAN SLAVE TRADE IN THE
NINETEENTH CENTURY
Edited by WILLIAM GERVASE CLARENCE-SMITH

OUT OF THE HOUSE OF BONDAGE
Runaways, Resistance and Marronage in Africa and the New World
Edited by GAD HEUMAN

THE BUSINESS OF ABOLISHING THE BRITISH SLAVE TRADE, 1783–1807
JUDITH JENNINGS

AGAINST THE ODDS
Free Blacks in the Slave Societies of the Americas
Edited by JANE LANDERS

UNFREE LABOUR IN THE DEVELOPMENT OF THE ATLANTIC WORLD
Edited by PAUL E. LOVEJOY and NICHOLAS ROGERS

RECONSTRUCTING THE BLACK PAST
Blacks in Britain, 1780–1830
NORMA MYERS

SMALL ISLANDS, LARGE QUESTIONS
Society, Culture and Resistance in the Post-Emancipation Caribbean
Edited by KAREN FOG OLWIG

From Chatte　　　　　　　　　　*ngland*

ROUTES TO SLAVERY

Direction, Ethnicity and Mortality in the Transatlantic Slave Trade

Edited by

David Eltis and David Richardson

FRANK CASS

LONDON • PORTLAND, OR

First published in Great Britain by
FRANK CASS & CO LTD
Newbury House, 900 Eastern Avenue
London IG2 7HH, England

and in the United States by
FRANK CASS
c/o ISBS
5804 N.E. Hassalo Street, Portland, Oregon 97213-3644

Library of Congress Cataloging-in-Publication Data

A catalog record of this book is available from the
Library of Congress.

British Library Cataloguing in Publication Data

A catalogue record of this book is available from the
British Library.

ISBN 0-7146-4820-5 (hb)
0-7146-4390-4 (pb)

This group of studies first appeared in a Special Issue on 'Direction, Ethnicity and
Mortality in the Transatlantic Slave Trade' in *Slavery and Abolition*, Vol.18, No.1,
published by Frank Cass & Co. Ltd.

Printed in Great Britain by
Antony Rowe Ltd.

Contents

The 'Numbers Game' and Routes to Slavery

DAVID ELTIS and DAVID RICHARDSON

Despite a major research effort in the last few decades, less is known about the movement of African peoples to the New World than the much smaller movement of their European counterparts before the mid-nineteenth century. Given that the record keepers were Europeans who regarded Africans as outsiders, it is likely that we shall never have as much information on the personal lives of individual Africans making the Atlantic crossing as we do of Europeans. But on the identities of large groups entering the African stream as well as the size and demographic characteristics of these groups, the picture is much less discouraging. Indeed, in a few years it may well be the case that in these areas, and in the early modern period at least, we will actually know more about these aspects of African than of European transatlantic migration. As knowledge of the patterns of the trade is basic to evaluations of the cultural implications of long-distance movements of people, this is an exciting prospect. One of the developments that has made it possible is, of course, the computer revolution and the related, but ultimately more important, explosion in archival research that has occurred since the late 1960s.

Historians are sometimes prone to exaggerate the significance of published works, but the largest single influence over the exploitation of the archives was arguably the publication in 1969 of Philip Curtin's *Census* of the Atlantic slave trade.[1] It was a landmark in the historiography not just of the slave trade but in the larger fields of slavery and migration. Drawing almost exclusively on previously published work, Curtin provided the first detailed assessment of the overall volume of the transatlantic traffic in enslaved Africans between 1500 and 1867. His estimates of the trade – up to 11.8 million slaves embarked at the coast of Africa and 9.4 million arrivals in the Americas – was substantially lower than most of the figures previously assumed by historians, some of which were several times greater than those calculated by Curtin.[2] Curtin's book provided, however, more than a reassessment of the overall dimensions of the Atlantic slave trade, valuable though that was. In the course of producing his census, he also generated data on temporal changes in the scale of the trade in slaves; on mortality levels of slaves in the Atlantic crossing or middle passage; on the numbers of slaves carried by different national carriers; and on shifts in the geographical distribution of slave departures from Africa and of slave arrivals in the Americas. In each of these areas, Curtin's findings represented a major advance on existing knowledge of the transatlantic slave trade.

The radical nature of Curtin's revision of the most frequently cited of the earlier estimates of the magnitude of the Atlantic slave trade provoked a lively and, at times, heated debate.[3] Most discussion centred on the last two centuries of the trade, for which records are most abundant and when the movement of African slaves across the Atlantic was unquestionably at its height. Disagreements continue over estimates of the scale of slave shipments by some countries.[4] Consequently, the 'numbers game' relating to the volume of the Atlantic slave trade is likely to remain a significant historical industry for some time to come. The latest estimates tend, nevertheless, to corroborate Curtin's overall assessment of the trade, at least for the period from 1650 to 1870, though they also suggest that he probably overestimated slave shipments before 1700 and underestimated them in the nineteenth century.[5] On the basis of the most recent surveys, it appears that some 10.1 million people left Africa for America in 1660–1867, most of them carried in British, Portuguese, and French ships. This is close to Curtin's assessment which suggested that between 1650 and 1870 some 10.5 million entered the transatlantic traffic, with some 8.9 million surviving the Atlantic crossing. Assuming that, at most, one million slaves were shipped from Africa before 1650, then the most recent evidence suggests that perhaps 11 million Africans were forced to leave their homeland for America between 1500 and 1870.

Further refinements of estimates of the magnitude of the Atlantic slave trade will doubtless occur. But an important by-product of these efforts to quantify the trade has been the discovery of new records in Europe and America relating to the shipping and sale of African slaves. Such records have generally been regarded as the most reliable sources for gauging the dimensions of the trade in slaves. The discovery and analysis of such records has, therefore, been a major feature of debates since 1969 over the volume of the slave trade.

A review of the shipping records unearthed since Curtin produced his census is outside the scope of this paper, but it is important to note that the discovery of such records has resulted in the publication of several compilations of voyage histories as well as the creation of various unpublished data sets of voyages. Some of the latter have been lodged in archives in Britain and the United States. Among the larger published collections are Johannes Postma's study of the Dutch slave trade; Jean Mettas's two-volume compilation of eighteenth-century French slaving voyages; Serge Daget's compilation of illegal French voyages after 1813; Jay Coughtry's study of Rhode Island slavers; and David Richardson's four-volume examination of the eighteenth-century Bristol slave trade.[6] In addition, there are now available unpublished data sets relating to slave voyages to colonial Virginia; voyages by Liverpool ships in 1744–86; Portuguese, British, and other ships in 1790–1815; and ships of various flags (or, in many cases, no known flag) in 1815–67. Other data sets have been created for the British slave trade before 1714 and again from 1780 to 1807 as well as for the eighteenth-century slave trade of London and smaller British ports such as Lancaster and Whitehaven.[7] Much work still remains to be done to trace voyages undertaken before 1660 and to fill gaps in our knowledge of voyages in later years. But, compared with the time that Curtin's census appeared, there is now a wealth of information about transatlantic slaving voyages in the period from 1660 to 1867.

It is sometimes suggested that recent quantitative approaches tend to sanitize the slave trade and need to be balanced by placing a greater emphasis on the personal experiences of the slaves themselves.[8] There are, of course, autobiographies of African slaves, such as that of Olaudah Equiano (or Gustavus Vassa) to whom one of the contributors to this volume refers.[9] Moreover, some historians have sought to draw individual and collective portraits of the lives of slaves, whether during the course of their enslavement or on American plantations.[10] This will be greatly augmented by the work of Paul Lovejoy.[11] We welcome such research. But we also believe that it is difficult to assess the significance or representativeness of personal narratives or collective biographies, however detailed, without an understanding of the overall movement of slaves of which these individuals' lives were a part. The reconstruction of slaving voyages and, even more importantly, the creation of a single, consolidated data base of voyages offers the best means available for charting the routes to slavery of Africans forced into exile from their homelands. In other words, voyage histories, when combined, represent a powerful tool for understanding the African diaspora and the contribution of Africans to the creation and development of the transatlantic world between 1500 and 1850.

Since 1992 several scholars have collaborated in seeking to build an integrated and consolidated data set of transatlantic slaving voyages. Hosted by the W.E.B. Du Bois Institute of Harvard University, the project has brought together a number of published and unpublished data sets and, through consultation of previously unused records, has also enhanced existing sets and created additional ones. Details of the various data sets included in the consolidated Du Bois Institute set are provided in Table 1.

TABLE 1
STRUCTURE AND SOURCES OF DATA INTEGRATED INTO THE W.E.B DU BOIS INSTITUTE'S
TRANSATLANTIC SLAVE SHIP DATABASE

Source by Nation	No. of Voyages	Years Covered	Collected by
Portuguese (Arrivals in Spanish America)	571	1595–1640	Enriqueta Vila Vilar
British	1,626	1644–1714	David Eltis
British/US (British American ports)	c.870	1644–1808	David Richardson Stephen Behrendt Eltis
Dutch	1,211	1675–1792	Johannes Postma
Danish	169	1683–1792	S.Green-Pedersen W. Westergaard
British (Liverpool)	2,337	1698–1779	Richardson M.M. Schofield Katherine Beedham Behrendt
British (Bristol)	2,200	1698–1807	Richardson
British (London)	c.1,600	1700–1779	James A. Rawley Behrendt Richardson
French	3,298	1707–1792	Jean Mettas Serge Daget Robert L. Stein
Various (Arrivals in Spanish America)	c.650	1707–1807	Elena de Studer Colin Palmer
British/US (Rhode Island American ports)	945	1709–1808	Jay Coughtry Behrendt
British (English outports)	c.450	1714–1777	Schofield Richardson
Portuguese (Angola)	550	1723–1772	Herbert S.Klein
British	3,132	1780–1807	Behrendt
Various (Arrivals in Havana)	c.800	1790–1820	Klein
Portuguese (Arrivals in Rio de Janeiro)	374	1795–1811	Klein
Various (traffic to Brazil, Cuba)	5,378	1806–1867	Philip D. Curtin Eltis Klein Joseph C. Miller
French	640	1814–1845	Daget

The table shows that, with the exception of some 571 voyages which were undertaken between 1595 and 1640, almost all the voyages included in the Du Bois Institute set were undertaken between the mid-seventeenth century and 1870. As yet, therefore, this data set contains little information about the Atlantic slave trade during its first century, but it does cover the years when the transatlantic traffic in slaves was at its peak. Overall, the set currently includes records of over 26,000 slaving voyages or probably more than two-thirds of those undertaken after 1650. This represents the largest data set for any area of transatlantic migration or trade currently available or, indeed, of any pre-nineteenth century migration anywhere. It is not overstating its significance, therefore, to suggest that, when more widely accessible, it will be relevant to the work of all scholars interested in the African diaspora and the African-American heritage. It will, moreover, help to illuminate the human experience of the victims of this tragic chapter in modern history.

The Du Bois Institute data set comprises over 160 fields of information about slaving voyages. These cover the geography of voyages, including ports of provenance of ships, trading places in Africa and the Americas, and ports of return; dates of departure of ships and their time schedules for different stages of their voyage; details of the construction, registration, owners, size, rig, crew and armaments of ships; and the number, age and gender of slaves loaded in Africa, of those lost during the voyage, and of those delivered or sold in the Americas. In most cases, the range of data available for individual voyages remains incomplete, with information on ships, their ports of provenance and trading places tending to be rather more abundant than that on the numbers of slaves carried and lost. Even so, the data set currently contains information about slaves shipped in over 17,000 voyages and slave mortality in some 6,100 voyages. These are very substantial foundations upon which to project long-run trends in the movement and mortality of slaves in the transatlantic traffic.

Several studies of the slave trade using data from the Du Bois Institute set have already appeared. One is an analysis of shipping productivity between 1673 and the mid-nineteenth century which reveals that long swings occurred in the productivity of shipping in the trade and argues that 'these can only be explained by African forces operating through loading times'.[12] It also suggests that there was no significant improvement in shipping productivity before the last quarter of the eighteenth century but that 'efficiency gains' in the nineteenth century 'were very strong';[13] this was presumably reflected in a relative decline of the transoceanic costs of transporting slaves. The impact of these productivity trends on trading patterns remains to be fully explored, but as children tended to fetch lower prices than adult slaves in the Americas, any significant and sustained decline in shipping costs must have encouraged carriers to ship more children. This finding is consistent with the increase in proportions of children entering the transatlantic traffic after 1800.[14]

A second and, in the context of this volume, even more important paper that uses the Du Bois Institute set explored the geography of transatlantic slaving between 1662 and 1867.[15] This provides breakdowns of ports of provenance of ships and distributions of slaving activity in Africa and the Americas. Drawing on evidence of African departure points for over 12,500 voyages, of American destinations for over 15,000 voyages, and of combined African and American data for over 11,500 voyages, the paper suggested regional patterns of slave embarkations in Africa and arrivals in the Americas that are not radically different from those of Curtin, although he confined his analysis of patterns of slaves departures to the period after 1700.

From the Du Bois Institute data, it appears that between 1662 and 1867 over four out of five slaves left Africa from just four regions – the Gold Coast, the Bights of Benin and Biafra, and West-Central Africa. The data also permit even more disaggregated analysis of departures by providing details of shipments by ports. This shows that, just as slave ship departures from Europe and the Americas were concentrated at relatively few ports, so large proportions of the slaves exported were shipped at a small number of outlets in Africa. Prominent among these were Cape Coast Castle and Anomabu on the Gold Coast; Whydah in the Bight of Benin; Bonny and Calabar in the Bight of Biafra; and Cabinda, Benguela, and Luanda in West-Central Africa. The history of those ports in this period was clearly dominated by slave trafficking. On the American side, arrivals of slaves were more dispersed geographically; nevertheless, some 40 per cent of slaves landed in Brazil, over 20 per cent in the British Caribbean, about 17 per cent in the French West Indies, and over 10 per cent in the Spanish islands. Overall, this preliminary analysis suggested that over 90 per cent of the slaves arriving in the Americas between 1662 and 1867 disembarked at places in the Caribbean islands and Brazil. Even though the United States had a substantial slave population by 1810, arrivals in mainland North America constituted probably no more than 7 per cent of the total. The main findings of this paper related, however, not to Africa and America separately, but rather to the intensity of the links between particular regions in the two continents.

Some attempt to trace connections between regions of departure and arrival of slaves was made by Curtin,[16] but the Du Bois Institute data allow one to trace in detail the principal routes to New World slavery followed by Africans. Some further refinement of the findings reported in the 1995 paper is inevitable as more data are added to the Du Bois Institute set.

Nevertheless, important links between Africa and the Americas were uncovered by the information then available. For instance, with the exception of Bahia, which largely drew on slaves from the Bight of Benin, slaves from West-Central Africa dominated arrivals in South America. In the West Indies, St Domingue also depended heavily on slaves from south of the equator, but elsewhere in the Caribbean slaves from West Africa dominated arrivals. Moreover, within the Caribbean, the proportions of slaves entering particular colonies or groups of colonies from individual sub-regions of West Africa were uneven. Thus, the Gold Coast seems to have supplied a disproportionate share of slaves arriving at Barbados, Surinam, and the Guyanas, while the Bight of Benin played a similar role in the case of the French islands outside St Domingue. In the other major Caribbean islands – Jamaica and the British Leeward Islands – the Bight of Biafra was easily the largest source of supply of slaves. Significantly, it appears that slaves from Senegambia and Sierra Leone represented a relatively small share of arrivals at the major American destinations. As the middle passage from these regions to the West Indies was shorter than that from the four regions to the south,[17] this is striking and, together with the Bight of Benin's dominance of slave arrivals at Bahia, should caution one against assuming that geography and transport costs were of overwhelming importance in shaping the patterns of transatlantic slave routes.

Like the papers just outlined, the essays in this volume rely in varying degrees on recent research on slave ship records and quantitative analyses of the slave trade. Four of the essays, directly or indirectly, use data from the Du Bois Institute set. Of the other two, one examines evidence on French slaving voyages collected by Mettas which is included in the Du Bois Institute set, while the other uses recently published quantitative studies of the British slave trade to estimate the number of Igbo forced into the transatlantic traffic after 1700. The essays here build, therefore, on modern quantitative approaches to the study of the transatlantic slave trade, though they also seek to relate more qualitative evidence to quantitative findings. More specifically, they underline the potential of the Du Bois Institute data set for investigating trends and fluctuations in slave shipments and the patterns of connections between Africa and the Americas in the two centuries after 1660. They also highlight the human costs of sustaining the slave traffic and expose some problems in tracing the ethnicity of slaves and evaluating its role in the creation of slave identities and communities in the Americas.

The essay by Eltis and Richardson extends the analysis of regional breakdowns and intercontinental links in slave labour flows which, together with Behrendt, they first developed in 1995.[18] Their paper concentrates on the Gold Coast, Bight of Benin, and Bight of Biafra, which dominated the

West African trade, and explores long-run trends in slave shipments by regions, variations in influence over regional trade by national carriers, and patterns of slave arrivals in the Americas. The evidence suggests that before 1830 slave shipments from the Bight of Benin were closely linked to demand for labour in Bahia and invariably exceeded those from the Gold Coast, while shipments from the Bight of Biafra rose in tandem with increasing British involvement in the trade and, at the height of the British trade in 1780–1807, outstripped shipments from its neighbour. As British traders also dominated the Gold Coast, it is perhaps not surprising to find that, while most slaves from the Bight of Benin travelled in Luso-Brazilian ships to Bahia, the route to slavery for those leaving the Gold Coast and Bight of Biafra more often than not led to the British Caribbean before British abolition in 1807. Thereafter, shipments of slaves from the Gold Coast collapsed, but Biafran slaves began to be shipped in greater numbers to the French islands and Cuba. In the latter case, they were joined by slaves from the Bight of Benin after 1830. Even though links between West African regions and American markets for slaves varied through time, Eltis and Richardson conclude that the distribution of peoples from West Africa in the Americas was far from random. Given the mercantilist framework within which Atlantic trade developed before 1815, it was, in fact, largely shaped by patterns of European colonial control in the Americas and by the influence of national carriers over slave shipments from regions in West Africa. What determined the latter remains an issue for further investigation.

The Du Bois Institute data set not only allows us to begin to identify the principal transatlantic slave routes, but also offers closer investigation of the experiences of slaves in the Atlantic crossing or so-called 'middle passage'. This aspect of the slave trade has, quite rightly, consistently attracted attention since the late eighteenth century when the British Parliament first debated the appalling conditions endured by enslaved Africans in the Atlantic crossing. For many, the term middle passage has become synonymous with the cruelty and inhumanity of the traffic.[19] Modern quantitative study of the middle passage was initiated by Curtin who relied heavily on data for eighteenth-century Nantes ships and figures generated by the British Foreign Office for 1817–43 in order to explore trends in shipboard mortality of slaves.[20] Since Curtin's initial work, large amounts of new data have been unearthed, with the result that the Du Bois Institute data set now contains vastly more evidence on slave mortality than was available to Curtin.[21]

The Du Bois Institute data underpin the essay on slave mortality trends by Herbert Klein and Stanley Engerman in this volume. The authors are, quite appropriately, cautious about trying to quantify overall mortality in the transatlantic slave trade. In part, this reflects the continuing incompleteness of data on shipboard slave mortality as a result of gaps in the records and inadequate knowledge of ships lost at sea, but it also reflects problems in defining the middle passage and in uncovering data on those parts of the enslavement experience of Africans that might legitimately be embraced by the concept. In particular, as Klein and Engerman remind us, we know very little about mortality at the point of enslavement or in transit to the African coast, but there are suggestions that those who boarded ship may have been only half of those originally enslaved. This broader interpretation of the middle passage and associated slave mortality has implications for comparisons that are sometimes made between slave and crew mortality in the slave trade. Even if we ignore this, however, and simply focus on slave mortality on board ship, it appears that over the three and a half centuries of the transatlantic slave trade, perhaps 15 per cent (or over 1.5 million) of those who embarked at the African coast died during the Atlantic crossing. At the peak of the trade in 1760–1810 losses of slaves on the Atlantic voyage perhaps averaged 6,000–8,000 a year.[22] Clearly, for a large number of those bound for sale in the Americas – the great majority, it should be noted, aged under twenty-five – the route to slavery ended either before leaving the African coast or in mid-ocean.

As far as trends in slave mortality on board ship are concerned, Klein and Engerman emphasize that, regardless of trading places, voyage lengths and other factors, the dominant feature of the middle passage was a wide distribution of mortality rates per voyage as measured by the number of slaves who died in the crossing as a proportion of those loaded at the African coast. Mortality rates on slave ships were highly unpredictable between one voyage and the next and added to the uncertainties surrounded to the trade. They also observe, however, that slave mortality rates tended to decline in the long run, that mortality varied by region of trade in Africa – ships from the Bight of Biafra having the worst record – and that, in the late eighteenth century, the British appear to have been the most efficient in keeping slaves alive. The last finding may partly be ascribed to Parliamentary measures after 1788 to regulate slave-carrying and improve conditions on board ship. But the general trend in mortality seems to have reflected, in part at least, a more widespread capacity among carriers to shift the overall distribution of mortality rates by reducing the incidence of shipboard epidemics through technical and other changes. A similar picture emerges from Stephen Behrendt's study in this volume of the pattern of crew mortality on board eighteenth-century British slave ships, though, as he observes, losses of crew on these ships tended to be higher than those on their French counterparts. At this stage of his research, Behrendt is unable to offer a considered explanation of this, but it is possible that it was connected with higher concentrations of British trade at the Bight of Biafra. Despite the general tendency of mortality to fall, comparisons with other contemporary oceanic migrations suggest that mortality rates on board slave ships – both for slaves and, as Behrendt so graphically shows, for crews – remained very high indeed throughout the history of the transatlantic slave trade. In this respect, the journey to the Americas was always a perilous one, whether for the African-born victims of the trade or the European and American crews who manned the ships that carried them. The contribution that increased contemporary knowledge of the extraordinary waste of life associated with the slave trade made to its eventual abolition in Britain in 1807 remains a source of debate.

Another issue that excites controversy is how the slaves who survived the middle passage and their subsequent 'seasoning' in the Americas managed to rebuild their lives. It is widely recognized that, under plantation regimes, the obstacles that slaves faced in seeking to establish their own identity or to shape the communities in which they worked were formidable. Some have noted that within most plantation systems opportunities existed for slaves to develop independent economic activities,[23] while others, including John Thornton and Gwendolyn Hall, have argued that slaves drew on the language and culture of their homelands in seeking to adjust to and influence their new social environments.[24] In the latter case, it is argued, ethnicity was especially important as slave populations in many New World societies seem to have been drawn disproportionately from a few regions or ethnic groups in Africa. In this scenario, therefore, the middle passage was more than a route to slavery that separated Africans from their past; it was a series of cultural highways that linked the history of transatlantic slave societies to the history of specific peoples of West and West-Central Africa.

Some evidence on the ethnicity of slaves has been published.[25] But we have, as yet, no overall picture of the movements of ethnic groups from Africa to the Americas. However, the patterns of transatlantic links between African and American regions revealed by Eltis and Richardson appear to be consistent with claims that there may have been concentrations of people of particular African ethnic groups in the Americas. Despite such evidence, the essays in this volume by Douglas Chambers, Peter Caron and Philip Morgan, all of which are concerned with issues relating to slave ethnicity, offer, on balance, no more than qualified support, at best, to the claims made by Thornton and others.

On the surface, Chambers appears to provide strong support for the case that ethnicity had an important influence on the life of enslaved Africans in the Americas. Concentrating on the Bight of Biafra, Chambers argues that most of the slaves shipped from the region were Igbo-speaking and, because they were largely taken by the British, they tended to be landed in British

American colonies. Within the British Americas, he suggests, particularly large numbers of Igbo-speaking slaves were to be found in Jamaica, the Leeward Islands and Virginia, though he also notes that, especially in the late eighteenth century, Igbo arrived in significant numbers in the French island of St Domingue. Seeking to investigate Igbo influences on the cultural life of slave societies, Chambers then examines evidence of 'Igboisms', including customs, diet, language and masquerades, on which, he argues, Biafran slaves 'drew in order to adapt to slavery'. In the course of his analysis, he challenges claims that slaves from the Gold Coast, notably Akan groups, had a dominant influence on Jamaican slave communities, arguing that important local institutions and practices such as *jonkonu* and *obeah*, which are sometimes attributed to Akan connections, were probably of Igbo origin. Although his argument seems broadly in sympathy with recent claims about the influence of ethnicity and ancestral traditions on slave life in the Americas, Chambers acknowledges that evidence of Igboisms is widely dispersed throughout British America and is to be found in places where, under slavery, concentrations of Igbo-speakers were probably low. This lack of symmetry between the intensity of flows of slaves between regions in Africa and the Americas and cultural carryovers is also highlighted by Morgan. Perhaps even more significantly, Chambers argues that ethno-genesis or the creation of ethnic identities, Igbo or otherwise, may have been largely a product of the trade in slaves itself, as confinement on board ship and the harshness of life on plantations encouraged slaves to group together to confront the problems arising from their enslavement. If this was so – and, as Morgan reminds us, recent work suggests that in Africa ethnic affiliations may have had only marginal significance – it appears that the concept of 'ethnicity' was rather more pliable than has sometimes been assumed.

The last point is addressed more fully by Caron in his essay on slaves in Louisiana in the first half of the eighteenth century. Caron focuses on slaves from Senegambia who, it seems, constituted about a half of all arrivals in the colony in 1718–31 and on the use by Louisiana officials of the term 'Bambara' to describe slaves from the region. Some scholars have assumed that such official labels were accurate and that the slaves so described were 'true' Bambara in the sense of being people from the Niger bend.[26] Caron reminds us, however, that European concepts of ethnicity or nationality did not correspond with those of Africans. Moreover, building on the work of Curtin,[27] he notes that, in addition to describing the ethnic-linguistic group of that name, 'Bambara' was a term used in Senegambia to describe, among other things, captives from east of the River Senegal, slave soldiers, and pagans or non-Muslims. It appears, then, that apparently precise ethnic labels were, in Senegambia at least, highly flexible. At the same time, a

close study of the origins of slaves shipped from the region by the French
in the 1720s strongly suggests that the great majority probably came from
near the coast rather than from the deep interior or Niger bend. While some
of the slaves in Louisiana may indeed have been ethnic Bambara, it appears
that many of those described as Bambara were almost certainly not.
According to Caron, this does not mean that all evidence relating to slave
ethnicities should be disregarded but, rather, that historians should be more
fully aware than they sometimes have been of the context in which labels
are used or applied.

Caron's reservations about the way evidence on ethnicity has been used
are endorsed by Morgan in the final essay in this volume. But whereas
Caron and Chambers focus tightly on particular segments of the
transatlantic slave trade, Morgan adopts a wide-angled lens and ranges
across the whole Atlantic basin, from Angola to Senegambia and from Rio
de Janeiro to Virginia. The picture he creates involves sharp contrasts. For
instance, he applauds Thornton for his vision of Atlantic history and follows
him in adopting a similar approach to the slave trade, but challenges his
depiction of ethnic identities in Africa and dismisses his use of concepts of
nation and national loyalty as anachronistic. Similarly, he draws on the work
of Eltis and Richardson on transatlantic movements of slaves and accepts
that a majority of slaves from most regions were 'funnelled ... to one region
in the Americas', but goes on to contest their suggestion that the picture of
a confusing mix of African cultures with all the attendant barriers to
establishing African carryovers in the New World needs revising. He argues
that in Africa there was a mixing of slaves as the hinterlands of the leading
ports and the trading networks that served them expanded. Further mixing
is said to have occurred in the Americas as slaves were often moved on from
their original landing places. Despite continuities in flows of slaves between
specific African departure and American arrival points, therefore, Morgan
questions the view that the slave trade was non-random and rejects the
image of 'homogeneous peoples being swept up on one side of the ocean
and set down *en masse* on the other'. As depicted by Morgan, the journey
to slavery for most Africans assumes a very different image, more
reminiscent in some respects of the 'melting pot' imagery of white
nineteenth-century migration to the United States, only in this case it was
heterogeneous groups of African peoples being thrown together in the
Americas and drawing on and modifying often very diverse individual and
collective experiences and skills in order to build new identities and
communities. In this process, African ethnicity is seen to have been, at best,
no more than one variable among many that helped to shape slave
communities, while the cultures that underpinned them are depicted as
having been fluid, permeable, pluralistic and syncretic. In the final analysis,

therefore, we are left by Morgan with the impression that the African heritage of slaves cannot be ignored but that the cultures of slave-based communities were essentially new and owed more to the conditions that Africans encountered in America than to their upbringing in Africa.

The essays in this volume do not provide an agreed set of answers to questions relating to the movement of enslaved Africans to the Americas. What they do suggest, however, is that the Du Bois Institute data set promises to be a vital source for historians seeking to investigate the structure, direction, and regional and temporal distributions of transatlantic movements of enslaved Africans. The papers offer some preliminary discussion of some of the patterns that are beginning to emerge from the reconstruction of slaving voyages. The capacity to document trading links between specific African and American regions in far more detail than hitherto represents one of the more important contributions of the Du Bois Institute data to historical research on transatlantic slaving. But as several papers in this volume attest, interpreting the impact of these linkages on the evolution of the social history of the Atlantic world remains a matter for debate. Resolving issues arising from patterns of slave movements will, of course, inevitably generate new data and raise new questions relating to transatlantic slavery.

Although we now know far more about the Atlantic slave trade than was imaginable less than thirty years ago, it is important to remind ourselves that routes to slavery for Africans led to places other than the Americas. Knowledge of the flows of slaves across the Sahara, the Red Sea and Indian Ocean has grown in tandem with that across the Atlantic.[28] But it is unlikely that we shall ever be able to document these slave trades – much less the doubtless large-scale movements of slaves within Africa – as fully as their Atlantic counterpart. In this respect, understanding of the African diaspora is bound to remain very incomplete. Nevertheless, the studies contained in this volume indicate that, by co-ordinating and integrating the data on slave movements that are available, it is possible to shed new light on important elements of the African diaspora and, more specifically, on the contribution of Africans to the making of modern Atlantic history.

NOTES

1. Philip D. Curtin, *The Atlantic Slave Trade: A Census* (Madison, Wisconsin, 1969).
2. For a review of earlier estimates, see ibid., ch.1.
3. For reviews of the debates see Paul E. Lovejoy, 'The Volume of the Atlantic Slave Trade: A Synthesis', *Journal of African History*, 23 (1982), pp.473–501; idem, 'The Impact of the Atlantic Slave Trade on Africa: A Review of the Literature', ibid., 30 (1989), pp.365–94.
4. The volume of the British slave trade between 1655 and 1807 remains the source of much debate; see Joseph E. Inikori, 'The Volume of the British Slave Trade, 1655–1807', *Cahiers*

d'Etudes africaines, XXXII (4), 128 (1992), pp.643–88; David Richardson and Stephen D. Behrendt, 'Inikori's Odyssey: Measuring the British Slave Trade', ibid., XXXV (2–3), 138–9 (1995), pp.599–615; David Eltis, 'The Volume and African Origins of the British Slave Trade before 1714', ibid., XXXV (2–3), 138–9 (1995), pp.616–27.

5. David Richardson, 'The Volume of the Slave Trade', in Seymour Drescher and Stanley L. Engerman (eds.), *Encyclopedia of Slavery* (New York, forthcoming).

6. Johannes M. Postma, *The Dutch in the Atlantic Slave Trade 1600–1815* (Cambridge, 1990); Jean Mettas, *Répertoire des Expéditions Négrières Françaises au XVIII Siècle*, eds. Serge and Michele Daget (Paris, 1978–84); Serge Daget, *Répertoire des Expéditions Négrières Françaises à la Traite Illégale (1814–1850)* (Nantes, 1988); Jay Coughtry, *The Notorious Triangle: Rhode Island and the African Slave Trade, 1700–1807* (Philadelphia, 1981); David Richardson (ed.), *Bristol, Africa and the Eighteenth-Century Slave Trade to America*, 4 vols., Bristol Record Society Publications, 1986–96.

7. Details of these data sets are given in Table 1 below.

8. James Walvin, *Black Ivory: a History of British Slavery* (London, 1992), pp.57–8, 317.

9. Olaudah Equiano, *The Interesting Narrative of the Life of Olaudah Equiano, Written by Himself*, ed. Robert J. Allison (1995 edition).

10. See, for example, Paul E. Lovejoy, 'Background to Rebellion: The Origins of Muslim Slaves in Bahia', in Paul E. Lovejoy and Nicholas Rogers (eds.), *Unfree Labour in the Development of the Atlantic World*, special issue of *Slavery and Abolition*, 15, no.2 (1994), pp.151–80; Richard S. Dunn, 'Sugar Production and Slave Women in Jamaica', in Ira Berlin and Philip D. Morgan (eds.), *Cultivation and Culture: Labor and the Shaping of Slave Life in the Americas* (Charlottesville, Virginia, 1993), pp.49–72.

11. Lovejoy is currently seeking to create a biographical dictionary of slaves shipped from Africa, as part of the UNESCO-sponsored Slave Route project, 'The Development of an African Diaspora: the Slave Trade of the "Nigerian" Hinterland, 1650–1900', which Lovejoy co-directs with Robin Law (University of Stirling) and Elisée Soumoni (National University of Benin).

12. David Eltis and David Richardson, 'Productivity in the Transatlantic Slave Trade', *Explorations in Economic History*, 32 (1995), pp.465–84 (quotation, p.480).

13. Ibid., p.480.

14. For a recent review of trends in the age and sex structure of the Atlantic slave trade see David Eltis and Stanley L. Engerman, 'Fluctuations in Sex and Age Ratios in the Transatlantic Slave Trade, 1663–1864', *Economic History Review*, 46 (1993), pp.308–23.

15. David Eltis, David Richardson and Stephen D. Behrendt, 'The Structure of the Transatlantic Slave Trade, 1595–1867', in Henry Louis Gates Jr., Carl Pederson and Maria Diedrich (eds.), *Transatlantic Passages* (forthcoming).

16. Curtin, *Atlantic Slave Trade*, pp.205–10.

17. Herbert S. Klein and Stanley L. Engerman, 'Slave Mortality on British Ships 1791–1797', in Roger Anstey and P.E.H. Hair (eds.), *Liverpool, the African Slave Trade, and Abolition* (Liverpool, 1976), p.116.

18. Eltis, Richardson and Behrendt, 'Structure'.

19. The term was, of course, used by Klein as the title for one of his books on the slave trade; Herbert S. Klein, *The Middle Passage: Comparative Studies in the Atlantic Slave Trade* (Princeton, 1978).

20. Curtin, *Atlantic Slave Trade*, pp.275–82. Curtin used data for Nantes carriers published by Gaston Martin, *Nantes au XVIII Siècle: L'Ere des Négriers (1714–1774)* (Paris, 1931) and Dieudonne Rinchon, *Le Trafic Négrier, d'après les Livres de Commerce du Capitaine Gantois Pierre-Ignace-Lievin van Alstein* (Paris, 1938).

21. It should be noted that major gaps still exist in the evidence on slave mortality, especially for pre-1790 Portuguese ships.

22. The figure of over 1.5 million deaths assumes that about 11 million left Africa, as noted earlier. The figure of 6,000–8,000 deaths a year in 1760–1810 assumes annual average shipments of 60,000–80,000 of slaves and losses of 10 per cent during the crossing. For estimates of shipments in this period, see David Richardson, 'Slave Exports from West and West-Central Africa, 1700–1810', *Journal of African History*, 30 (1989), p.10.

23. Ira Berlin and Philip D. Morgan (eds.), *The Slaves' Economy: Independent Production by Slaves in the Americas* (London, 1991).

24. John Thornton, *Africa and Africans in the Making of the Atlantic World, 1400–1680* (Cambridge, 1992); Gwendolyn Midlo Hall, *Africans in Colonial Louisiana: the Development of Afro-Creole Culture in the Eighteenth Century* (Baton Rouge, Louisiana, 1992).

25. See, for example, Curtin, *Atlantic Slave Trade*, pp.184–99; David Geggus, 'Sex Ratio, Age and Ethnicity in the Atlantic Slave Trade: Data from French Shipping and Plantation Records', *Journal of African History*, 30 (1989), pp.23–44.

26. Hall, *Africans in Colonial Louisiana*, p.43.

27. Philip D. Curtin, *Economic Change in Precolonial Africa: Senegambia in the Era of the Slave Trade* (Madison, Wisconsin, 1975), pp.178–79.

28. See, for example, Ralph A. Austen, 'The Trans-Saharan Slave Trade: A Tentative Census', in Henry A. Gemery and Jan S. Hogendorn (eds.), *The Uncommon Market: Essays in the Economic History of the Atlantic Slave Trade* (New York, 1979), pp.23–76; William Gervase Clarence-Smith (ed.), *The Economics of the Indian Ocean Slave Trade in the Nineteenth Century* (London, 1989); Elizabeth Savage (ed.), *The Human Commodity: Perspectives on the Trans-Saharan Slave Trade* (London, 1992).

West Africa and the Transatlantic Slave Trade: New Evidence of Long-Run Trends

DAVID ELTIS and DAVID RICHARDSON

The transatlantic slave trade was the largest long-distance coerced migration in history. On the African side, three regions – the Gold Coast, the Bight of Benin and Bight of Biafra – dominate the historiography. These areas tend to be seen as the centre of gravity of the traffic not just from West Africa but from the whole of sub-Saharan Africa, a situation captured by the description of a section of the Bight of Benin as 'the Slave Coast' on most maps printed before 1820. With the possible exception of Senegambia, the history of these regions is better known than the rest of sub-Saharan Africa. These regions also contained the largest population densities on the sub-continent, and, consistent with this, contained the greatest urban development and, in the cases of the Gold Coast and Bight of Benin, the most sophisticated state structures. All three regions tended to draw on largely exclusive provenance zones, and indeed there is a reasonably exclusive ethno-linguistic homogeneity within their hinterlands. Yet it is still useful to treat these areas together. African slave traders were always likely to view embarkation points in the east of the Bight of Benin and the west of the Bight of Biafra as alternate routes – particularly after Lagos began its rise to major outlet status in the late eighteenth century – and European traders often ensured that ties existed between ports in the eastern Gold Coast and western Slave Coast.[1]

In both the popular and scholarly worlds these heartland regions of West Africa – defined here as the west coast of Africa from Cape Apollonia to Cape Lopez inclusive – have a higher profile than do other regions. They are seen as the major source of slaves entering the Americas; they contain most of the sites and monuments to the slave trade on the western African littoral; and at the same time they are the subject of the majority of the monographs on the trade. The Du Bois Institute's transatlantic slave trade database permits the reassessment of the role of this region in the slave trade and uncovers many new detailed patterns in the movement of its peoples into the Atlantic trade. No long-run overview of slaving activity in any of these regions has been undertaken since the late 1970s.[2] It should be noted that the data currently available are still incomplete as far as distinguishing actual places of trade in Africa and America are concerned. Where such data are not available, we have used intended ports of embarkation and disembarkation of slaves instead. Further, for about 15 per cent of the voyages, we lack data on numbers of slaves carried. In these cases we have estimated the numbers of slaves on board from means computed from very large numbers of observations.

The database suggests that, overall, West Africa probably played a larger role in the transatlantic traffic than non-specialists have appreciated. Curtin's work and the research that his 1969 book triggered suggested that about two out of five slaves entering the transatlantic traffic did so in one of the two Bights between 1700 and 1867 (no breakdown of African origins before 1700 existing in the current literature). The new data set suggests a somewhat higher ratio – perhaps 48 per cent of all slaves – for the period 1595–1867, though much of the higher ratio comes at the expense of Senegambia, rather than regions south of the equator. West-Central Africa – in other words sites near the mouth of the Zaire river and from Luanda, Benguela and the adjacent regions – is still the dominant regional supplier of slaves in the eighteenth and nineteenth centuries as a result of this reassessment. This large region south of the equator supplied 40 per cent of the slaves entering the Atlantic slave trade. However, while West-Central Africa was far more important than any of the three individual West African regions examined here, the size of the three regions together is comparable to the West-Central African slave provenance zone as a whole. A West African/West-Central African comparison may thus be more appropriate than a strictly regional comparison.

Within West Africa as defined here, the new data suggest an increased importance for the Gold Coast and the Bight of Benin relative to other West African regions. Whereas earlier estimates gave the Gold Coast six per cent of the total trade and the Bight of Benin about 17 per cent, the distribution made possible by the new data set almost doubles the importance of the Gold Coast and increases the Bight of Benin share to 22 per cent. The Bight of Biafra's share, by contrast, falls slightly to 15 per cent.[3] In sum, the data set currently contains records of 7,085 voyages to these three regions and implies that just under 2.5 million left Africa for the Americas from points between Cape Apollonia and Cape Lopez. All but one of these voyages began between 1662 and 1863. There is no way of estimating with any precision the proportion of all voyages to these regions that the current set represents, but given the range of sources and the coverage of the major national traders, we would be surprised if the current estimates comprised less than half the Africans entering the traffic after the mid-seventeenth century from the area between Cape Apollonia and Cape Lopez. With few signs that gaps in the present data are 'clumped' by region or period, the trends suggested here are likely to be reliable, whatever opinions might be on the volume of the traffic – and therefore the share of the total represented by the present data.

FIGURE 1
SLAVES LEAVING WEST AFRICA, 1595–1866

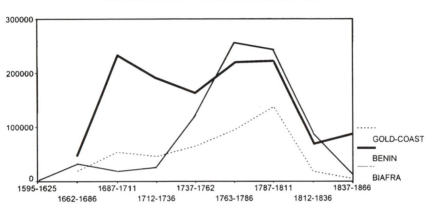

Source: All diagrams and tables in this study have been compiled from information in the Du Bois Institute slave ship data set.

The temporal distribution of these departures is shown in Figure 1, which presents estimates of slave departures grouped in broad 25-year bands. Keeping in mind that the Du Bois Institute data set is a sample only, and not a population, it is likely that departures from the Bight of Benin exceeded 10,000 per year over a period of 125 years from 1687 to 1811. Indeed, if we allow for bias in the declarations of Bahian slave ship captains in the period after the British took suppressive action against the trade after 1815, this high volume era probably extended over a century and a half to 1830. The two peaks in the traffic from this region came at the very beginning – 1687–1711 – and near the end – 1787–1811 – of these 125 years, with a rather lower, but still high and steady volume of departures in between. More refined analysis, not shown here, does little to change this picture of a large and sustained trade in people in the sense that annual fluctuations in the volume of departures were relatively small. European wars and conflicts within the African supply networks might interrupt business at particular ports and for short periods, but not until the 1830s were these disruptions anything more than temporary.

A quite different pattern emerges from the Bight of Biafra, the second most important West African region for slave departures. Here, ships and numbers carried per ship were somewhat smaller than in the Bight of Benin, 313 slaves per ship compared to 387, and ship size averaging some 122 tons in the Bight of Biafra and 192 in the Bight of Benin.[4] While slave trading began early in the Niger delta, the traffic approached Slave Coast levels only toward the mid-eighteenth century. Moreover, for a time in the late seventeenth century, slave departures from the Bight of Biafra appear to have lagged behind those from the Gold Coast. For fifty years after the 1760s, however, slave departures from the Bight of Biafra exceeded those from both the Gold Coast and the Bight of Benin, though they also subsequently fell off far more rapidly than in the Bight of Benin in the era of suppression after 1815. This rapid decline of slave shipments from Niger delta ports is well documented, with most of the few thousand leaving after the early 1840s passing through points closer to Cape Lopez.[5] As the British were always by far the most important slave traders in Biafran ports, and as British records are particularly well-represented in the data, it seems unlikely that further improvements in the data set will change the shape of the time profile for the region shown in Figure 1.

The Gold Coast was the least important of the three West African regions examined here, with total departures running at half or less of those in the other two regions. This finding is entirely consistent with recent estimates of regional departures from Africa.[6] However, the temporal distribution of this Gold Coast total is at odds with some recent estimates. Figure 1 shows departures gradually doubling in the course of the eighteenth century, as opposed to the currently accepted profile of a strong increase into 1730s followed by a gradual decrease through to the 1780s. Further contributions to the data set may yet clarify this discrepancy.

Slave traders from all parts of the Atlantic world traded in West Africa. Yet there is little doubt that the trading community was much more cosmopolitan on the Slave Coast than on the Gold Coast or the Bight of Biafra. In brief, Portuguese based in Brazil dominated trade in the Bight of Benin, with 55 per cent of all voyages recorded there setting out from Bahia. On the Gold Coast and in the Bight of Biafra, however, the British were even more dominant, sending out 81 per cent of the voyages recorded as trading (or intending to trade) on the Gold Coast and 78 per cent of those trading or intending to trade between the main outlets of the Niger River and Cape Lopez. It might be noted that one quarter of the British voyages to the Gold Coast is accounted for by voyages from the British Americas, the Gold Coast being the African mecca for the small rum-carrying ships from New England and the Caribbean. Within these British-dominated regions, an interesting specialization by port emerges, with the vast majority of slavers in the Bight of Biafra at the peak of the region's slave trade being from Liverpool, while ships from Bristol and London dominated trade with the Gold Coast. After the British, Dutch ports were responsible for the second largest number of voyages to the Gold Coast, accounting for 10 per cent of voyages to the region, while French ports played a similar role in the Bight of Biafra, accounting for 12 per cent of voyages there. After Liverpool merchants switched from slaves to palm oil in 1808, Cuban-based Spanish slave traders became the largest group in the Bight of Biafra. On the Slave Coast, French ships from a wide range of French ports were the second largest group of traders after the Portuguese, accounting for 20 per cent of voyages, but Dutch, English, and, later, Spanish (mainly Cuban) ships were also well represented.

Where did the slaves carried on these ships go after leaving West Africa? The first point to note is that many did not reach the Americas. Mortality data exist for 2,317 of the slaving voyages leaving West Africas. Of those leaving the Gold Coast (n=1,008), 14.3 per cent died on board. The equivalent figure for Slave Coast ships (n=760) was 14.6 per cent and for Bight of Biafra ships (n=496) 19.2 per cent. Mortality on ships leaving all three regions was above the average for all regions in the data set and was well above the 8.4 per cent observed for the 1,916 voyages recorded as leaving West-Central Africa. However, as always with slave ship mortality, the high variances observed – typically approaching the size of the mean itself – makes firm conclusions on interregional mortality variations difficult.[7]

The pattern of West African arrivals in the Americas was far from random. The major single destination of Gold Coast slaves was Jamaica which accounted for 36 per cent of arrivals, but as many again went to other parts of the British Americas. Thus, well over two-thirds of all slaves leaving the Gold Coast went to the English-speaking New World, Barbados being the major seventeenth-century destination and Jamaica dominating the eighteenth century. Akan cultural prominence in Jamaica (including Ahanta, Fanti, Akim and Asante peoples among others) is well rooted in the slave trade according to this data set. Spanish America, the second most important destination for Gold Coast slaves after Jamaica, accounted for 15 per cent of departures.

By comparison with the British American dominance of slave shipments from the Gold Coast, six out of every ten slaves leaving the Bight of Benin went to Bahia in Brazil, two out of ten went to the French Americas, notably St Domingue, and one out of ten went to the British Caribbean. This broad breakdown disguises, however, major shifts in time in the pattern of destinations in the Americas of slaves shipped from the Bight of Benin. In the late seventeenth century, the English Americas took the majority of slaves leaving the Slave Coast. After 1700 the Reconcavo of Bahia in Brazil and the French Caribbean replaced the English, with the former predominating until the quarter century before 1791 when the French share came closer to matching that of Bahia. From 1791 to 1830, however, Bahia took 75 per cent of deportees from the Bight of Benin. Thereafter, Cuba became more important as a market for slaves from the region, and for fifteen years after 1851 was, indeed, the only market available to shippers of slaves from the Bight of Benin. Compared to Bahia, Cuba's links with the Bight of Benin were relatively short-lived. (It is, nevertheless, striking that the strong Yoruba presence in Cuba noted by some historians should be based on such limited exposure to the region – at least compared to Cuban ties to other African regions.)

In the Bight of Biafra, a much simpler pattern emerges. In the Niger delta ports, which supplied over 90 per cent of the slaves leaving the Bight of Biafra, the first English ship is recorded as shipping slaves from Calabar in 1662 and from this point to 1807, the British took perhaps 80 per cent of all slaves from the region. Igbo and Ibibio peoples, who dominated slave shipments from the region, went to all parts of the British Americas, with Jamaica and the Leewards taking no less than three out of every five, and Barbados and the British American mainlands playing a smaller role. This region also supplied those non-British regions with which the British traded, notably the Spanish Americas. The French Americas received about 10 per cent of Biafran slaves. After the British ended their direct involvement in the traffic, the Spanish Americas, particularly Cuba, continued to draw on the Niger delta. For a decade and a half between 1814 and 1830 the revived and largely illicit French slave trade also drew on these outlets, delivering the slaves mostly to Martinique and Guadeloupe. The absence of Portuguese traders and the slight presence of the Dutch and the pre-1800 French in this area is striking.[8]

The major contribution of the Du Bois Institute data set, however, is to provide more refined geographic and temporal analyses of the slave trade. At this point in the project it is possible to identify the specific points of embarkation (as opposed to regions of departure) of 28 per cent of those leaving the Gold Coast, 37 per cent of those leaving the Bight of Benin, and 69 per cent of those leaving the Bight of Biafra. The relatively low identification rate for the Gold Coast is accounted for by the limited range of the coastline that comprises the region, or at least from which slaves could be expected. The same phenomenon in the Bight of Benin has a different origin. A large part of this region's data is drawn from passes for ships leaving Bahia de Todos os Santos for Africa. These are held at the Arquivo Publico da Bahia. Most of these ships simply declared their destinations to be the 'Mina Coast', which, following an agreement with the Dutch – the effective controllers of Portuguese access to this part of Africa – meant the four ports of Grand Popo, Whydah, Jaquin and Apa. Unhappily, the Brazilian passes do not allow breakdowns among these ports, although Whydah was certainly the most important of the four ports to the Portuguese from the 1680s, when the records begin, until the second quarter of the nineteenth century, when Lagos emerged as a serious rival. From the last third of the eighteenth century, the designation 'Mina' came to include additional ports, all east of Whydah – namely, Porto Novo, Badagry and Lagos (also commonly known as Onim).[9] After 1810, British records of the Portuguese slave trade allow a more precise identification of African embarkation points. A crude assumption that 75 per cent of those ships designated for Mina in fact took in their slaves at Whydah would perhaps not do too much violence to the historical reality, although it should be noted that in some years departures from Whydah were very low.

Table 1 presents a breakdown of departures from individual sites as far as these can be identified in the Du Bois Institute set. Most of these are shown on the accompanying map which dates from the last years of the transatlantic traffic. The concentration of departures from a handful of sites is particularly marked in the two Bight regions, but even on the Gold Coast two embarkation points – Cape Coast Castle and Anomabu – account for 76 per cent of departures.[10] On the Slave Coast, if we allow that at least 75 per cent of slaves leaving from 'Costa da Mina' were taken from Whydah, then the latter port by itself accounts for no less 695,000 slaves, or a little over two-thirds of recorded departures from the Bight of Benin. Indeed, as the current data set is clearly less than the total trade, probably well over one million slaves left from Whydah, making it perhaps the single most important oceanic outlet for slaves in sub-Saharan Africa. Lagos, the second most important Slave Coast port, lagged far behind, though in the closing years of the trade it was probably the most important embarkation point in either of the Bights, a fact accounting for the intense attention it was by then receiving from the British – at this time seeking to end the traffic rather than encourage it.[11]

In the Bight of Biafra, the concentration of departures was almost as severe, with almost 80 per cent of all slaves leaving from just two outlets, Bonny and Calabar, and a further 8 per cent leaving from a third port, New Calabar. The Cameroons and, further south, Gabon, were by comparison of only minor importance, accounting together for only one in ten of departures from the region. There is no doubt that Whydah, Bonny and Calabar were key trading sites not only in Africa, but in the whole Atlantic slave trading system. By this we mean that overall each perhaps imported more goods to be exchanged for slaves than, with the possible exception of Liverpool, any single port in Europe exported into the traffic, and Whydah may have sent more slaves into the trade than any single port in the Americas attracted in the way of arrivals.

TABLE 1
SLAVE DEPARTURES (THOUSANDS) FROM OUTLETS IN THE GOLD COAST, BIGHT OF BENIN
AND BIGHT OF BIAFRA, 1662–1863 (LISTED FROM WEST TO EAST)

	Slaves	*Ships*
Gold Coast		
Assinie	0.3	1
Axim	0.1	1
Quaqua	6.7	17
Kormantine	3.0	11
Elmina	2.4	9
Cape Coast Castle	38.9	191
Anomabu	53.9	196
Apam	1.2	5
Tantumquerry	0.4	1
Wiamba	0.2	1
Accra	7.1	24
Christiansborg	4.7	14
Alampo	2.0	6
Total identified	120.9	477
Bight of Benin		
Keta	4.0	14
Little Popo	6.1	18
Grand Popo	0.4	1
Popo (Unspecified)	11.3	36
Whydah	260.2	696
Jaquin (Offra) (Ardrah)	38.8	106
Apa (Epe)	9.3	25
Porto Novo	31.8	77
Badagry	21.0	57
Lagos	63.5	162
Costa da Mina	579.5	1,497
Benin	29.5	84
Total identified	1,055.5	2,773
Bight of Biafra		
Rio Nun	2.2	9
Formosa	0.2	1
Rio Brass	5.0	16
New Calabar	46.3	150
Bonny	240.4	678
Andony	0.8	3
Calabar (or Old Calabar)	196.5	633
Bimbia	1.1	4
Cameroons	22.7	63
Cameroons River	4.8	16
Corisco	0.3	2
Gabon	25.3	84
Cape Lopez	6.6	26
Total identified	552.2	1,686

MAP 1
PORTS OF EMBARKATION OF SLAVES AT THE GOLD COAST, BIGHT OF BENIN
AND BIGHT OF BIAFRA, 1662–1863

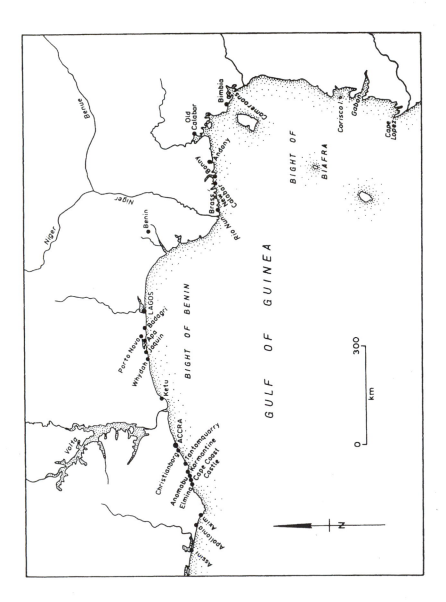

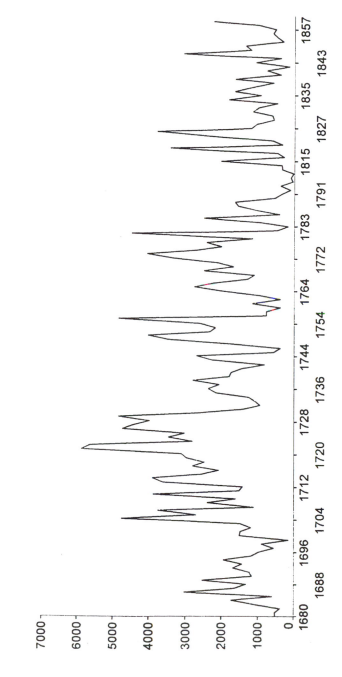

FIGURE 2
ANNUAL SLAVE DEPARTURES, WHYDAH, 1680–1863

TABLE 2
SLAVE DEPARTURES (THOUSANDS) FROM THE BIGHTS OF BENIN AND BIAFRA: MAJOR
OUTLETS FOR SLAVES BY TWENTY-FIVE YEAR INTERVALS, 1662–1863

	Slaves (thousands)	Ships
Whydah		
1662–1686	7.9	23
1687–1711	44.2	102
1712–1736	75.6	223
1737–1761	40.8	108
1762–1786	41.7	107
1787–1811	5.8	21
1812–1836	24.2	70
1837–1866	19.9	42
Eastern Bight of Benin[a]		
1712–1736	0.4	1
1737–1761	5.3	14
1762–1786	28.8	65
1787–1811	16.5	39
1812–1836	26.7	83
1837–1866	39.3	94
Bonny		
1712–1736	7.3	27
1737–1761	63.6	176
1762–1786	96.8	253
1787–1811	22.4	66
1812–1836	47.8	149
1837–1866	2.5	7
Calabar		
1662–1686	14.0	55
1687–1711	12.3	47
1712–1736	15.3	66
1737–1761	34.2	98
1762–1786	77.2	218
1787–1811	21.9	74
1812–1836	20.4	71
1837–1866	1.1	3
South-East Bight of Biafra[b]		
1712–1736	0.5	1
1737–1762	6.5	18
1762–1786	30.9	90
1787–1811	4.7	24
1812–1836	11.6	42
1837–1863	6.6	20

a. includes Porto Novo, Badagry and Lagos combined.
b. includes Gabon, Bimbia, Cameroons, Corisco, Cape Lopez.

An examination of the temporal distribution of departures at these major ports is presented in Table 2. Gold Coast ports are excluded because none of them rivalled the Bights ports listed in this table. Whydah's greatest relative importance came in the quarter century from 1712 to 1736. As a result, peak departures from Whydah fall outside the periods for peak departures from the Bight of Benin as a whole shown in Figure 1. Given the attention Dahomey has received in the historiography, Figure 2 provides annual totals for Whydah as well. Interestingly, the peak of departures corresponds with the era of internal instability in Whydah and its conquest by Dahomey in 1727. It also includes most of the 1730s. Conquest by Dahomey did bring about an immediate decline in departures, but this was very short-lived, and while departures in the 1730s were below those of earlier decades, they were still running at over 1,000 per year – higher than the 1740s and much higher than, say, the twenty years from 1791 to 1810. Cumulatively, more slaves left Whydah after the conquest than before, and close inspection suggests that the decline in the 1730s may have been due more to weakness in the Brazilian markets than to supply constraints. One possible explanation for the quarter-century peak in the Whydah trade was the fact that the period from 1712 to 1736 saw the least disruption from European wars of any of the quarter centuries listed. The troughs in departures in 1756–62, 1779–84 and 1790–1814 are clearly associated with European conflict. Moreover, the decline of the slave trade of Dahomey in the 1760s and 1770s suggested by Akinjogbin turns out scarcely to have existed – except in comparison with the pre-1727 era.[12]

Apart from European wars, fluctuations in departures from Whydah at the end of the eighteenth century and thereafter are best explained by increased competition from other outlets in the Bight of Benin. The shift eastwards in the main flow of departures is very marked in the annual breakdowns of departures. Badagry was most important in the late 1770s, and Porto Novo in the following decade. Lagos became of major importance at the end of the Napoleonic Wars and, as already noted, from 1837 down to the British take-over, sent more slaves each year into the Atlantic trade than did Whydah. It is important to note here that the key to understanding this situation lies in Africa rather than Europe. The collapse of the Oyo Empire and the flow of slaves associated with this event was probably the major impulse behind the emergence of these eastern outlets.[13] Table 2 shows departures from the three ports grouped together. Yet the most easterly of all, Benin, appears to have followed a path independent of these events. It is at least clear that with nearly 30,000 departures in the seventy years after 1721, Benin was not sealed off from the slave trade to quite the extent that earlier interpretations would have us believe.[14] Outlets between Whydah and Porto Novo – Jaquin and Apa – supplied slaves only in the middle quarters of the eighteenth century, according to these data, which capture nothing of slaving activity there before 1700. Likewise, the western ports are underrepresented here. These were clearly more important before 1750 than after, but so far the DuBois Institute set has provided a disappointingly small amount of detail on Keta, the Popos and Awey.

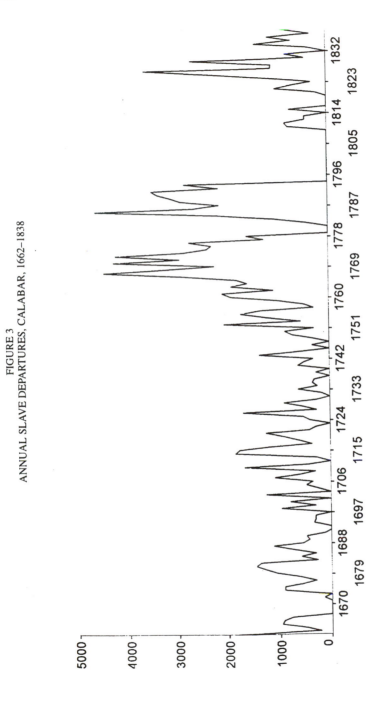

FIGURE 3
ANNUAL SLAVE DEPARTURES, CALABAR, 1662–1838

In the Bight of Biafra, it was the ports due east of the Niger delta which entered the trade first. The first record of a departure at Calabar in the present data set is for 1625, and from the early 1660s down to the late 1830s (with the exception of the 1690s) departures were rarely far short of a thousand a year. Figure 3 gives the annual trend line for this embarkation point. By the 1780s and 1790s shipments from Calabar were three or four times earlier levels, yet they still lagged behind the flow of slaves from the River Bonny at this time. Bonny entered the trade as early as the 1660s, one of the Efik chiefs being named after an English slave captain of the period. However, Bonny does not show up in the present data set until 1712, but by the 1770s and 1780s was sending more people into the trade than Whydah at its peak. This time profile also holds for the other major Niger delta outlet of New Calabar as well as the less important outlets of Bimbia and Cameroon to the east of Calabar and Gabon to the south. The most southerly outlets, Corisco and Cape Lopez were significant only in the nineteenth century. Unlike the Slave Coast ports which tended to take turns in stepping up trading volumes, swings in departures at Biafran ports north of Corisco tended to coincide with each other. During the years from the 1760s to the 1790s, all these ports contributed to the record stream of departures from the Bight of Biafra. It is much more difficult to link these trends with African political and economic developments than it is in the Bight of Benin. But perhaps there is a significant point here. The massive number of departures through the eastern rivers of the Niger delta and the Cross River was neither the product nor the cause of the rise and fall of major new political structures. The Kings of Bonny and Dukes of Calabar remained rulers of what were essentially still trading enclaves at the end of the eighteenth century and continued to be enclaves throughout, first, the slave trading and palm oil era, and then after 1839, the palm oil era proper. Indeed, beyond the growth of Duke Town at the expense of Old Town in the Cross River, the rise of *Ekpe*, and the consolidation of the Aro trading network, it is difficult to see how political structures and the distribution of power at Bonny and Calabar differed in 1830 from what they had been in the 1660s when slave trade volumes were very low or non-existent.[15]

Some additional insights are possible if we take into account the age and sex characteristics of the coerced migrants. It is now clear that over the last two centuries of the slave trade the proportion of males and especially the proportion of children in the traffic both increased. In addition, it is also now clear that substantial variations existed in the sex and age profiles of slaves from the different African coastal regions supplying the trade. Generally, the Gold Coast, the Bight of Benin, and the Bight of Biafra shared in the general increase in male and child ratios over two centuries, but all three regions typically sent fewer males and fewer children into the traffic than did other areas at any given period. Indeed, a larger proportion of women was always to be observed among those leaving the Bight of Biafra than from any other major embarkation zone in sub-Saharan Africa.[16] Table 3 provides additional detail to this broad picture by presenting age and sex ratios among those leaving the major ports within the Bights broken down by century – the data not yet being sufficiently abundant to allow working with the quarter-century intervals used earlier. The table focuses once more on the three leading outlets in the regions – Whydah, Bonny, and Calabar – and two composite categories comprising the three most important embarkation points in eastern Bight of Benin – Badagry, Porto Novo and Lagos – and the outlets south of Calabar – Gabon, Bimbia, Cameroon, Corisco and Cape Lopez. Data for the Gold Coast as a whole are added for comparative purposes. Recorded observations are rather small for the grouped ports, but we expect to be able to increase these in the near future.

Generally the extra detail provided by these more localised breakdowns simply confirms the larger picture. All outlets shared in the trend toward more males, fewer women, and more children through time. These broad similarities across embarkation points should not be allowed to obscure significant differences, however. In the Bight of Benin, a smaller proportion of deportees from the eastern ports than from Whydah were boys and girls, although the gap did narrow in the nineteenth century and for boys, at least, becomes statistically insignificant. In addition, while shares of women leaving Whydah on the one hand, and ports further east on the other, do not seem markedly different after controlling for time, the 40 per cent fall in the proportion of women leaving the eastern Slave Coast between the eighteenth and nineteenth centuries is rather larger than the 27 per cent fall among those leaving Whydah. The more than threefold increase in the share of children among slave departures from Whydah, albeit over two centuries, is also worthy of note. The major political and military event in the hinterland of the Bight of Benin outlets in the late eighteenth and early nineteenth centuries was the collapse of Oyo. The resulting disturbances can plausibly explain why relatively more slaves left the eastern ports over time, but it is harder to make a link between the collapse of the Oyo empire and a surge in the number of children entering the slave trade. Interestingly, the pattern on the Gold Coast is closer to that displayed at Whydah – the point on the Slave Coast in Table 3 most adjacent to the Gold Coast – than to that at any other West African port. Nevertheless, the high ratio of women in the seventeenth century, the subject of frequent comment by contemporaries, is reminiscent of the Bight of Biafra.[17]

In the Bight of Biafra, the minor ports south and east of Calabar had smaller shares of women and more children among their deportees than did either of the major ports, though the differences are less marked in the nineteenth century than earlier. The principal points of note in the Bight of Biafra, however, relate to changes at the major ports through time.\At Bonny, the decline in the proportion of women entering the trade – from 40 to 14 per cent – is the largest observed for any outlet. The fourfold increase in the ratio of children at both Calabar and Bonny,\apparently confined to the period from the eighteenth to the nineteenth century, is also dramatic. Both the decline in the share of women and the rise in proportion of children carried from east and south of the Bight of Biafra were much less than among the slaves leaving the main ports of Bonny and Calabar, though we should take note of what is at present a relatively small number of observations here.

TABLE 3

MEAN PERCENTAGES OF AFRICAN MALES, WOMEN, MEN, GIRLS AND BOYS CARRIED TO THE AMERICAS FROM MAJOR OUTLETS IN THE BIGHTS, 1662–1863 (NUMBER OF OBSERVATIONS IN THOUSANDS IN PARENTHESES)

	Males	Women	Men	Girls	Boys	
Gold Coast						
1662–1700	56.0	41.0	49.4	3.0	6.5	(12.8)
1701–1809	66.6	28.3	54.6	5.5	11.7	(57.3)
1810–1863	–	–	–	–	–	
Whydah						
1662–1700	58.1	37.1	49.3	4.8	8.8	(11.5)
1701–1809	62.0	30.0	48.6	7.9	13.5	(42.6)
1810–1863	63.2	21.3	37.5	16.2	25.0	(7.4)
Eastern B. of Benin[a]						
1662–1700	–	–	–	–	–	
1701–1809	63.4	33.8	57.5	2.6	6.0	(6.6)
1810–1863	67.4	20.2	44.0	12.4	23.3	(13.6)
Bonny						
1662–1700	–	–	–	–	–	
1701–1809	56.2	40.3	52.7	3.5	3.4	(20.0)
1810–1863	68.2	14.3	51.3	17.1	17.3	(12.2)
Calabar						
1662–1700	49.5	47.3	39.0	3.4	10.3	(5.5)
1701–1809	57.4	38.6	50.9	5.9	4.6	(12.2)
1810–1863	64.7	16.6	42.8	18.8	21.9	(7.3)
South-East Bight of Biafra[b]						
1662–1700	–	–	–	–	–	
1701–1809	62.0	29.8	48.6	8.7	12.4	(2.0)
1810–1863	62.5	18.3	38.3	18.9	24.5	(4.9)

a. includes Porto Novo, Badagry and Lagos combined.
b. includes Gabon, Bimbia, Cameroons, Corisco, Cape Lopez.

To what extent can the regional trends be explained by shifts in the flow of slaves from outlets located *within* the regions themselves – in other words by shifts in the relative importance of individual embarkation points? The short answer supplied by Table 3 is very little. In the Bight of Benin, the minor ports increased significantly in importance so that a major impact on the overall ratios is possible. However, some elementary interactive analysis suggests that this was not the case. This involves two steps. First, we recalculate Table 2 so that the time periods correspond with those in Table 3 (century-long instead of quarter-century), and in addition compute the proportion of the total departures from the region accounted for by each outlet (or grouping of outlets) in each century. We then select the age/sex ratios for which change over time appears to be greatest – the proportion of women and the proportion of children – and ask the question how would the ratios in the nineteenth century have been different from what they were if the distribution of departures among ports had changed, but the demographic profile from each outlet had remained constant between the eighteenth and nineteenth centuries. For the Bight of Benin, the women ratio would have increased slightly rather than declined, and the child ratio would have fallen by 17 per cent rather than increased. The same question posed in the Bight of Biafra results in about 10 per cent of the observed rise in child ratios being explained by shifts in the distribution of departures between ports, but the women's ratio stays constant. It is thus clear that the key factor influencing trends in the demographic structure of the slave trade was not shifts between one strongly differentiated African region and another. Differences between ports certainly existed, but these do not explain the major changes through time – shared by all ports – that emerge from the historical record.

It is obviously easier to highlight these large changes than account for them – whether we look within or without Africa. Why, over time, would fewer women, more men, and more children of both sexes leave *all* ports? These trends were as strong when the trade was expanding between the seventeenth and eighteenth centuries as they were between the eighteenth and nineteenth centuries, when the volume of departures declined. European wars, indeed events in the Atlantic World generally, might have had temporary effects, but it is difficult to pinpoint any developments in Europe or the Americas that could account for these secular trends. Plantation crop type, for example – a factor that might be construed, potentially, as a major influence on the demographic profile of peoples entering the slave trade – remained largely constant throughout most of the two centuries of the trade covered here. From the seventeenth century to the 1820s, it was sugar production, and sugar production alone, that absorbed 90 per cent of those carried across the Atlantic. Thereafter, coffee became important, but the pattern of more children, fewer women, and more men held for all branches of the traffic – the one that led to Cuban and Bahian sugar plantations as well as the one that fed their coffee counterparts in southern Brazil. In effect, the demographic characteristics of the coerced migrant flow from Africa changed from one of rough balance between males and females and the presence of some children in the seventeenth century, to one in which males and children predominated by the nineteenth century. Such a pattern, observed across a wide range of African cultures, political and social structures, and economic activities, should pose something of a challenge for specialists in African history.

❴To the extent that the age and sex of the forced migrants reflect African patterns of slave supply as well as the requirements of European planters in the Americas (and behind them European consumers of plantation produce), the three West African regions examined here exhibit interesting similarities. They provide evidence which, taken together with other cultural traits as diverse as language structure, religion, and even musical instruments, provides grounds for treating the three regions as a unit when pursuing the topic of cross-Atlantic influences – at least for some purposes.[18] For example, in parts of Jamaica today, 'Igbo' is a term for a nation or sub-group within a religion that is called 'Akan' by all adherents and has clear Akan origins. We are on the threshold of acquiring much more precise knowledge of the direction and composition of the slave trade from West Africa to the Americas. Full recognition of the traits shared by West African peoples will permit more effective use of the new Du Bois Institute data set in nailing down what it was Africans carried with them and what it was that they developed after their arrival. Clearly, the forced migration from West Africa to the Americas was no more random and chaotic than was its free European counterpart.❵

NOTES

Research for this paper was supported by funding from the National Endowment of the Humanities. For comments on an earlier draft of this study, we wish to thank Stanley L. Engerman and participants at the York University (Canada) conference, 'The African Diaspora and the Nigerian Hinterland', held in February 1996.

1.   Aboh, a major slave market at the head of Niger delta supplied slaves to both Bight of Benin and Bight of Biafra outlets. Also see the comments in 'Extracts from Mr Lyall's Journal', in Macgregor Laird to Malmesbury, 14 March 1859, Public Record Office FO 84/1095, on slaves destined for the Atlantic slave trade being carried down the Niger River. These slaves could only have been embarked via the lagoons of the Slave Coast. More generally see Mahdi Adamu, 'The Delivery of Slaves from the Central Sudan to the Bight of Benin in the Eighteenth and Nineteenth Centuries', in Henry A. Gemery and Jan S. Hogendorn (eds.), *The Uncommon Market: Essays in the Economic History of the Atlantic Slave Trade* (New York, 1979), pp.172–8.

2. Apart from the syntheses on the Atlantic slave trade published by Paul Lovejoy ('The Volume of the Atlantic Slave Trade: A Synthesis', *Journal of African History*, 23 [1982], pp.473–501 and 'The Impact of the Atlantic Slave Trade on Africa: A Review of the Literature', ibid., 30 [1989], pp.365–94), which evaluate the relative importance of African regions, the last full assessment of either region was Patrick Manning, 'The Slave Trade in the Bight of Benin, 1640–1890', in Gemery and Hogendorn (eds.), *The Uncommon Market*, pp.107–40. For studies on parts of the period covered here see Robin Law, *The Slave Coast of West Africa, 1550–1750: The Impact of the Atlantic Slave Trade on an African Society* (Oxford, 1991), and David Northrup, *Trade Without Rulers: Pre-Colonial Economic Development in South-Eastern Nigeria* (Oxford, 1978).

3. For assessments of earlier quantitative work on the slave trade and comparisons between this and findings based on the Du Bois Institute set, see David Eltis, David Richardson and Stephen D. Behrendt, 'The Structure of the Transatlantic Slave Trade, 1595–1867', in Henry Louis Gates Jr., Carl Pedersen and Maria Diedrich (eds.), *Transatlantic Passages* (forthcoming). For the modern starting point of this work see Philip D. Curtin, *The Atlantic Slave Trade: A Census* (Madison, Wisconsin, 1969).

4. For tonnage, numbers are 181 ships with a standard deviation of 59.5 in the Bight of Biafra, and for the Bight of Benin 332 ships were used to calculate the mean, the standard deviation being 91.3. Definitions of tonnage varied over time and between countries. These data were calculated after attempts to standardize the data; see the appendix to David Eltis and David Richardson, 'Productivity in the Transatlantic Slave Trade', *Explorations in Economic History*, 32 (1995), pp.465–84 for the procedures used.

5. For the ending of the traffic in the Bights see David Eltis, *Economic Growth and the Ending of the Transatlantic Slave Trade* (New York, 1987), pp.168–73, and more recently, Robin Law, 'An African Response to Abolition: Anglo-Dahomian Negotiations on the Ending of the Slave Trade', *Slavery and Abolition*, 16 (1995), pp.281–311.

6. David Richardson, 'Slave Exports from West and West-Central Africa, 1700–1810: New Estimates of Volume and Distribution', *Journal of African History*, 30 (1989), pp.1–22.

7. For a fuller discussion of the inter-regional differentials see the article by Herbert S. Klein and Stanley L Engerman in this volume.

8. See Eltis, Richardson and Behrendt, 'The Structure of the Transatlantic Slave Trade, 1595–1867', Table 7 for a more precise breakdown of destinations in the Americas within the major African regions of provenance.

9. Much of this is based on Pierre Verger, *Flux et Réflux de la Traite des Nègres entre Le Golfe de Benin et Bahia de Todos os Santos du XVIIe au XIXe siècle* (Paris, 1968), pp.3–5. For the relative importance of Whydah see Law, *Slave Coast of West Africa*, pp.118–48.

10. Before 1740, Dutch slave ships from the Gold Coast obtained almost all their slaves at the Dutch castle of Elmina, even though they enter the Postma data set with designation 'Gold Coast'. A recoding of this embarkation point yields the result that these three ports supplied 82 per cent of Gold Coast slaves from known destinations (36 per cent from Anomabu, 26 per cent from Cape Coast Castle, and 21 per cent from Elmina).

11. Lagos, of course, was also far more accessible to the mid-nineteenth century British navy than was Whydah. The town of Whydah was located beyond the range of British guns and the Admiralty recognized that it could not be taken without a massive commitment of resources. See Admiralty to Malmesbury, 9 February 1858, enclosure, Commander Wise, 21 December 1857, Public Record Office FO 84/1068.

12. I.A. Akinjogbin, *Dahomey and its Neighbours, 1708–1818* (Cambridge, 1967), pp.76–7, 141–51; cf. Law, *Slave Coast of West Africa*, pp.103–4, 284–6.

13. Akinjogbin, *Dahomey and its Neighbours*, pp.169–71; Robin Law, *The Oyo Empire c. 1600–c. 1836: A West African Imperialism in the Era of the Atlantic Slave Trade* (Oxford, 1977); idem, 'Dahomey and the Slave Trade: Reflections on the Historiography of the Rise of Dahomey', *Journal of African History*, 27 (1986), pp.237–67.

14. Ryder's account of slaving activity in Benin is broadly consistent with the pattern displayed by the data set. Alan Ryder, *Benin and the Europeans, 1485–1897* (New York, 1969), pp.196–238.

15. For a convenient description of the 'ritual trading' networks supplying Bonny, the Cross

River and Cameroon (the Aro, Ekpe and Bilaba), see Ralph Austen, *African Economic History* (London, 1987), pp.94–5. For Gabon and its slave supply networks, see Henry Bucher, 'The Atlantic Slave Trade and the Gabon Estuary', in Paul E. Lovejoy (ed.), *Africans in Bondage: Studies in Slavery and the Slave Trade* (Madison, Wisconsin, 1986), pp.136–54.

16. Eltis, Richardson and Behrendt, 'Structure of the Transatlantic Slave Trade'; David Eltis and Stanley L. Engerman, 'Fluctuations in Sex and Age Ratios in the Transatlantic Slave Trade, 1663–1864', *Economic History Review*, 46 (1993), pp.308–23.

17. See, for example, Stede & Gascoigne, Barbados, 4 April 1683, Public Record Office, T 70/16, f.50; Stede & Skutt, Barbados, to Royal African Company, 22 August 1688, T 70/12, p.31; Royal African Company to Petley Wyborne and Henry Stronghill, 8 August 1688, T 70/50, f.70; Royal African Company to Browne, Peck, and Hicks at Cape Coast Castle, 23 July 1702, T 70/51, f.131.

18. See John Thornton, *Africa and Africans in the Making of the Atlantic World, 1400–1680* (Cambridge, 1992), pp.184–92, 235–71 for a discussion of the language and religious commonalities.

Long-Term Trends in African Mortality in the Transatlantic Slave Trade

HERBERT S. KLEIN and STANLEY L. ENGERMAN

The transatlantic slave trade from Africa to the European settlements in the New World has been only one of many large-scale international movements of free and enslaved peoples in recorded history, but it has clearly been one of the most frequently studied and discussed. The slave trade was entered into by merchants and vessels from all the western European powers; it involved trade with most areas of the West African coast as well as some of the East African coast, and it led to sales of slaves throughout the regions of the western hemisphere. The overall slave trade persisted for more than three centuries, was quite large, involving at least 10–12 million slaves, and since the carrying capacities of slave-trading vessels was small – averaging about 300 slaves per vessel[1] the trade entailed a large number of ships and consisted of many voyages from several different nations. Because of the role of slavery in New World settlement, and given the general range of mercantilist policies by European nations, the trade and its vessels were often regulated by government policies. These policies included the granting of monopolies to slave trading companies, controls regarding provisioning of ships, and also regulations affecting the numbers of slaves to be carried on ships of different sizes and tonnages.

Debates among contemporaries and, subsequently, among scholars, cover many issues. Particularly noteworthy have been those debates concerning the consequences of the granting of monopoly privileges to favoured companies, such as the English Royal African Company,[2] and those estimating the extent to which mortality on the 'middle passage' could be reduced from high levels by the introduction of appropriate government regulations, as well as the effects of changes in mortality rates on profit rates. The death rates on slave ships, of slaves and also of the crews, had attracted attention as one part of the attack on the slave trade (if not directly on slavery itself), and both the high overall mortality rates as well as some particularly bad cases of mortality on individual ships provided the argument that the system as practised was inhumane and inefficient, and should be either regulated (at a minimum) or abolished. In Britain, Dolben's Act of 1788 was the first major legislated attack by the British on slave ship mortality, following Parliamentary debate and discussion as to the expected effects of such regulation on mortality and profits.[3] The Act linked the maximum number of slaves to be carried to the tonnage of ships. Such a relation had also been presented in a Portuguese act of 1684, which also regulated the food and water to be carried on board, and the intent to improve slave accommodations in transit led to similar Dutch regulations in 1789. Dolben's Act also provided bonuses to those ship captains and surgeons achieving relatively low death rates. The British regulations did change over the next decade, the number of slaves carried being based upon the dimensions of the vessel not tonnage, but this concern with mortality continued through 1808, as long as the British slave trade remained legal.[4]

About one century after the transatlantic slave trade ended, the analysis of mortality in the slave trade again became an issue, this time among scholars who have concentrated more on explaining patterns and rates of mortality and the determinants of mortality, including the examination of the nature of the specific diseases that caused the deaths of slaves and the crew.[5] Of particular interest was the trend in mortality over time, of obvious importance in itself, but also to permit better calculations of the numbers of slaves transported and the numbers arriving from the available but incomplete data. Variables used to explain these trends have included the number of slaves carried per vessel, the ship's tonnage, the number of slaves carried per ton (or other ship dimensions), and the number of days at sea between Africa and the Americas, as well as various other aspects of the slave-trading process within and on the coast of Africa. As the studies have become more systematic, distinctions have been recognized between the mortality rates for departures from different parts of Africa, differences by the nationality of the ships carrying slaves, and also mortality differences based on New World ports of arrival, differences not easily explained by ship dimensions, sailing times, or other variables.

The new data set prepared by the Du Bois Institute represents a major step forward in the attempt to deal with the many issues and problems of analysing the slave trade, including the study of shipboard mortality. It is drawing together many different data sets of slave trade data, for several different flag carriers, and in making them as consistent as is possible, permitting examination for comparative purposes. This is, of course, a most difficult task to undertake, given that few of these sources were based on a systematic and standardized form, for any country, let alone across countries. Some of the data sets have been collected by other scholars, and used by them in published works, before being made available to the

Institute. Others are newly processed and have not been previously examined. The expansion in available information has increased the number of voyages for which we now have information, and will therefore permit more comparisons across time and place than has heretofore been possible. It is obvious that use of these sources, based on listings prepared by contemporaries for several different countries over several different centuries, is not problem free, since recording methods differed, and the presence (or absence) of certain key pieces of information varied over time. There are also problems of interpretation arising from the fact that the distribution of surviving records which form the data set is no doubt different from that which would have occurred if we had all the data from the entire slave trade. This might be due either to systematic factors influencing data collection and presentation, or to the accidents of data survival and retrieval. Nevertheless, the care in preparation of what is made available should make this a better data set to use to study the slave trade than if such a systematic presentation was not undertaken or if the analysis were limited to only one body of data, for one nation or region.

⟨Before seeing where the analysis of this data set takes us in the study of slave trade mortality, it will be useful to see what questions the data set does not permit us to answer. A most general piece of information on the slave trade, available on only a limited number of records, concerns the length of time between the departure from Africa and the date of arrival in the Americas – the sailing time or voyage length. This is for those ships that have completed the voyage. If, however, the voyage was not complete and the vessel lost at sea, due to wartime destruction, a wreckage, or rebellion, then the losses of slaves are more difficult to determine.[6] There is also some information on time on the coast spent loading, but this is so for only a limited number of voyages.⟩

For several reasons we cannot answer questions about the overall mortality in the transatlantic slave trade.[7] We most frequently know what were the deaths from the time of leaving the coast to the time of arrival in the Americas – the so-called middle passage. We do not know, however, after the number of deaths, the original enslavement in Africa – including the losses of life in the capture of slaves, the deaths during the march to the coast, and the mortality during the time spent on the coast before sailing, either when held by African traders or European shippers. Nor can we estimate those deaths after arrival in the Americas that may have been attributable to prior conditions, including both the voyage and the delayed effects attributable to African enslavement. Further losses occurred after arrival in the New World, both during the time awaiting sale, as well by the increased rates during the initial period of adjusting to the local environment and working conditions.

⟨This allocation of the losses of African lives between capture within Africa and settled location within the New World was examined by Thomas Fowell Buxton in 1840.\Buxton described the mortality losses at five different stages of the enslavement process: 'The original seizure of the slaves; the march to the coast, and detention there; the Middle Passage; the sufferings after capture [of slave vessels by the anti-slave trade fleet] and after landing; and the initiation into slavery, or the "seasoning", as it is termed by the planters.' Buxton argues that the total loss of life in this process is about 70 per cent of the 'victims of the slave trade'. He estimates that the losses within Africa between enslavement activities and departure from the coast were 50 per cent; mortality in the middle passage accounted for 25 per cent of the slaves embarked; and of those landed, 20 per cent died in seasoning. By his estimates, the middle passage accounted for 17.9 per cent of deaths in the slave trade, with 71.4 per cent of deaths occurring within Africa. There have been several recent attempts to update Buxton's estimates of mortality prior to the middle passage. These are for different periods and regions, and also for varying time in transit, but while the range is wide, and the estimates varied, they generally exceed the mortality rates on the transatlantic crossing, with works by Hogendorn and by Miller placing the mortality rate from point of captivity to the coast at about 50 per cent.[8]⟩

The issues can pose a problem in the attribution of deaths to specific stages of the shipment of slaves. Diseases that were initially generated in Africa will be mixed in with the diseases caused by conditions on the slave ship, while those diseases that originated on board ship might have led to deaths not at sea but only after arrival in the Americas. These factors will influence any attempt to explain mortality at sea based upon ship-specific or region-specific variables. But there is no major difference in the use of these ship data to study slave trade mortality from the data used in the study of other historical problems, which also work from limited documentation and the use of supplementary data to answer historical questions.

Why is the middle passage such a widely studied event? First, it is the part of the slave trade system that provides the best recording of information dealing with the numbers of slaves involved and their mortality in transit. Second, there is the importance of the European involvement in the middle passage, and, unlike the internal movement of slaves within Africa, the European practice of detailed record-keeping and of government regulation of the transatlantic traffic in slaves. Thus shipboard mortality became the focus of many of the debates in western Europe regarding the slave trade, and there was concern both with the mortality of slaves during the transatlantic passage and the deaths of the crew in the slave trade. While the shipboard mortality of slaves was used to demonstrate the harshness of the trade, it was the high mortality among the crew that was used by the British abolitionist, Thomas Clarkson, in his arguments to end the slave trade. To those who supported the slave trade as a 'nursery for seamen', Clarkson argued that, to the contrary, the rates of mortality of the crew on slave ships were considerably higher than for crews on other routes, including the commodity trade with Africa.[9]

Our discussion of results here will be somewhat tentative, since we have utilized only a sub-sample of the data set, which is itself a sub-sample of the slave trade, with, in both cases, the precise shares of different trades not certain. For the present analysis we have utilized only those ships for which relatively complete data are available, and for which the patterns of slaves loaded and landed, and mortality, appear consistent.[10] This does leave enough observations, however, to reach conclusions on certain major issues and to raise some questions for further analysis.

The basic findings in regard to long-term trends in slave ship mortality, are somewhat familiar from the many earlier studies.[11] The basic measure of interest, reflecting the concerns of contemporaries, is the mortality rate per voyage – the number of slaves who were recorded as died in the middle passage (or else the difference between slaves loaded and slaves landed) divided by the number of slaves loaded on the African coast.[12] The most significant pattern for understanding mortality in the middle passage is the very wide distribution of mortality rates by voyage. This is found even when holding constant other features, including sailing times, ship sizes, African embarkation areas, and the age–sex composition of slaves carried. There was a broad range of outcomes, with very many quite different experiences, even for the same captains or the same nationality of shippers. Very high mortality rates tend to be associated with unexpectedly long voyages, or with unusual outbreaks of disease, but, in general, it is the very broad range of outcomes rather than any bunching at specific mortality rates that has been the main characteristic of the transatlantic slave trade.

While we are concerned with factors that influence the mortality in the transatlantic slave trade, it has been demonstrated that the mortality per voyage on slave ships exceeds those of other transoceanic voyages at the same time, although those voyages also have a wide range of outcomes. Studies of other voyages and their comparisons with the slave trade indicate lower mortality rates for ships carrying convicts, contract labourers, military troops, and free immigrants.[13] As with the slave ships, these voyages experienced declines in their mortality rates over time, with, in some cases, the magnitude of the decline exceeding that of the slave ships.

From the initial period, 1590–1700, slave shipboard mortality declined to less than half its initial level in the late eighteenth century. While the decline was relatively monotonic over time, there was a large decline in the

FIGURE 1
RELATIVE DISTRIBUTION OF SLAVE LOSSES DURING THE MIDDLE PASSAGE (TWO TIME PERIODS)

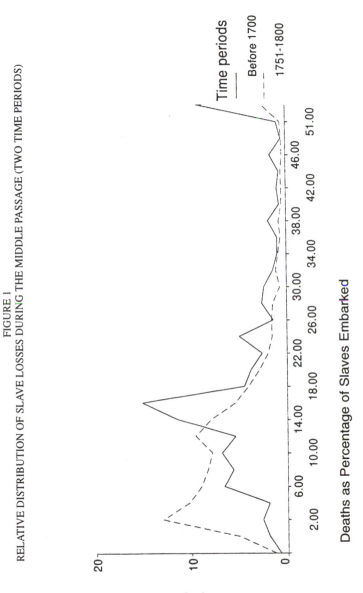

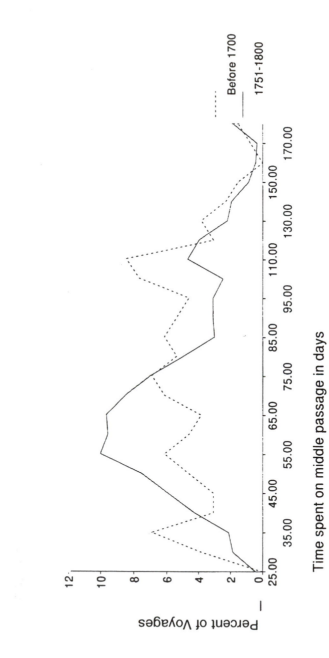

FIGURE 2
RELATIVE DISTRIBUTION OF MIDDLE PASSAGE VOYAGE TIME (TWO TIME PERIODS)

last quarter of the eighteenth century, a period in which British ships achieved an unusually low slave mortality. As sharp as was the decline in the mean of slave mortality rates, the median of slave ship mortality declined even more rapidly, with the entire distribution of mortality rates shifting down (see Figure 1). In the last forty years of the slave trade, when it was restricted to mainly Spanish and Portuguese vessels, mortality rates rose again, but they did not reach pre-1800 levels. Although there were declines in time spent in the middle passage, particularly in the late eighteenth and early nineteenth century, it is doubtful that speedier voyages alone were sufficient to explain the observed declines in mortality (see Figure 2).

TABLE 1
MORTALITY BY FLAG CARRIERS (%)

	(n)	Portugal	(n)	Spain	(n)	Dutch	(n)	French	(n)	British	(n)	All
1590–1700			(67)	29.8[a]	(139)	14.3			(195)	21.3	(401)	20.3
1701–1750					(427)	15.8	(488)	15.6	(176)	15.4	(1091)	15.6
1751–1800	(93)	8.6			(607)	14.0	(698)	12.5	(846)	10.6	(2287)	11.8
1801–1820	(657)	8.2	(12)	4.2	(6)	9.5	(8)	6.3	(112)	15.0	(807)	9.1
1821–1867	(962)	9.1	(136)	11.8			(16)	15.0	(124)	9.4[b]	(1380)	10.4
Total	(1712)	8.7	(215)	17.2	(1180)	14.7	(1210)	13.8	(1453)	12.9	(5966)	12.4

a. Portuguese vessels carrying slaves for Spain.
b. Not British Flag.

This decline over time was seen for each of the major slave trading nations in the eighteenth century, but none was as steep as was that of the British (see Table 1).[14] The ratio of mortality rates, 1751–1800 to 1701–50, was 0.80 for the French, 0.89 for the Dutch, and 0.69 for the British. This indication of relative British efficiency is consistent with the growing importance of the British in the international slave trade, and of the expanding British economy internationally.[15] To some extent the decline was influenced by the legislation regarding the numbers of slaves to be carried, which also included provisions for shipboard surgeons, and bonuses paid to captains and surgeons on ships with low mortality. While there were regulations on numbers of slaves carried for other nations, none required surgeons or paid bonuses for holding down the rate of mortality. In the nineteenth century the mortality rates of the relatively new and important Spanish-American and Brazilian flag carriers were at levels above those that the British had achieved in the last decades of its slave trade, but below those of French and Dutch shippers.[16] From his studies of numerous migrations in the nineteenth century, Ralph Shlomowitz has pointed to the important role played in the absence of correct medical knowledge by administrative reforms and various empirical approaches in lowering the rates of mortality over time.[17] Thus whatever forces of institutional, technical, and organizational change influenced mortality in the slave trade, they apparently became widely diffused among all trading nations. Some of the key changes in ship construction may have reflected technological developments, but there were also changes in vessel design and organization that permitted a change to more optimal speed or size for the shipowners, and there were also some organizational and medical changes without any new technology. The rising prices of slaves would have meant that there would have been an increased return to improved care of slaves in the middle passage. It is probable that the overall reductions in mortality rates reflected some combination of these various types of change.

An important factor explaining the pattern of declining mortality rates is that, given the large number of ships involved in the trade, and the shifting overall distribution of mortality rates, some widespread changes had occurred. These changes affected not just a limited number of shippers but a great majority of them. There was a large increase in the share of voyages coming in at relatively low mortalities (however low is defined). Correspondingly, the percentage of ships with mortality rates above a selected threshold fell, meaning that over time there were relatively fewer ships with very high mortality rates. While the explanations for the changes at these two ends of the distribution may differ, it is clear that the process of diffusion of information and techniques among shipowners and captains played a crucial role in this measured mortality decline.

TABLE 2
MORTALITY BY AFRICAN REGION OF DEPARTURE (%)

	(n)	All	(n)	1590–1700	(n)	1701–1750	(n)	1751–1800	(n)	1801–1820	(n)	1821–1867
Senegambia	(247)	12.8	(33)	13.6	(94)	10.6	(105)	15.6	(8)	9.0	(7)	6.4
Sierra Leone	(286)	8.6	(12)	11.0	(17)	12.0	(174)	9.4	(28)	6.7	(55)	6.4
Gold Coast	(1,041)	13.2	(69)	21.6	(243)	15.5	(636)	12.4	(83)	5.9	(10)	7.7
Benin	(758)	13.8	(83)	17.5	(301)	17.1	(185)	13.6	(34)	5.1	(155)	7.4
Biafra	(480)	17.4	(30)	29.5	(24)	43.2	(280)	15.1	(18)	9.5	(128)	15.6
West-Central Africa	(2,117)	9.2	(103)	22.9	(169)	12.1	(634)	9.4	(503)	7.7	(708)	7.1
South-East	(248)	18.3			(1)	29.5	(8)	19.3	(46)	19.9	(193)	17.6
Misc.	(673)	15.5	(71)	19.2	(242)	15.7	(249)	13.9	(79)	16.7	(36)	15.9
Total	(5,854)	12.5	(401)	20.3	(1,091)	15.6	(2,271)	12.1	(799)	9.0	(1,292)	9.8

Tables 1 and 2 show significant differences in mortality rates, among European flag carriers, and also persisting differences in mortality from various African ports of departure. Table 2 indicates that the mortality rate differences by African region of departure remain rather systematic during the period studied, with a general persistence in the nature of the differentials over time.[18] A rough measure of this pattern can be seen by examining the seven regions for five time periods – three regions are either always above or always below the average mortality rate for that time period, and two differ in direction in only one period. While there are those persistent differences by port of departure, Table 2 also indicates that all regions had mortality rate declines over time and generally had their lowest rates in the nineteenth century. While the lowest rate among the major regions classified, for West-Central Africa, is for the region with the shortest average sailing time, in general the times at sea cannot alone explain the magnitude of differences in mortality rates by African port. It might be expected that, in general, these persistent differences in the transatlantic mortality rates based on African port of departure reflect as much the conditions in Africa as the characteristics of the ships and the voyages. They were influenced by changes in catchment areas within Africa, shifts that occurred with political and economic changes, and that influenced the age–sex composition of the slaves sent as well their overall physical condition. Therefore, more attention should be given to the slave losses inland, to the costs of transporting slaves to the coast, and to the time spent on the coast prior to transatlantic sailing. In regards to length of voyage, there was some increase in mortality with numbers of days at sea, particularly for those unexpectedly long voyages on which water and provisions ran short, and accelerated the spread of disease. For the great number of voyages, however, there was little variation in mortality that could be directly explained by differences in the number of days at sea.

There was some decline in mortality rates with tonnage of ship, except for a limited number of very large vessels. This probably reflected the nature of ship construction and measurement, with the area used for slaves increasing more rapidly than did overall measured tonnage. There is a small positive correlation of mortality with slaves carried per ton, but there is no indication of a sharp distinction between so-called 'tight packers' and 'loose packers'. The number of slaves per ton was always high on slave ships, higher than on other voyages. This means that while the numbers carried per ton might help explain why slave ships had higher mortality than did other transport vessels, within the general range of slaves per ton carried there was no additional effect, despite the arguments made in the 'packing' debate.

As we have indicated, there remain a number of puzzling aspects regarding the transatlantic slave trade. The large dispersion of mortality experiences, even within specific national carriers and for departures from specific

African ports, demonstrates the role of the particular factors influencing individual voyages. Similarly the higher mortality rates on slave vessels, for crew as well as slaves, compared with all other transoceanic carrying trades, further suggests the unusual conditions determining the supply of slaves and influencing the middle passage experience on slave-carrying voyages. The persistent differentials in mortality rates by African port of departure points to the importance of further studies of the initial process of enslavement within Africa and in the march to the coast. Since the middle passage accounts for a relatively limited number of all deaths in the overall transatlantic slave trade, it would obviously be useful to extend the analysis to these other steps within the enslavement process.

NOTES

1. The average number of slaves per vessel was computed from the Du Bois Institute data set. See also Herbert S. Klein, *The Middle Passage: Comparative Studies in the Atlantic Slave Trade* (Princeton, 1978). There was some upward trend over time, offset by the onset of regulation beginning in the late eighteenth century. These estimates imply that there were over 30,000 separate voyages in the transatlantic slave trade.
2. On the slave trade of the Royal African Company, see, in particular, K.G. Davies, *The Royal African Company* (London, 1957); David W. Galenson, *Traders, Planters, and Slaves: Market Behavior in early English America* (Cambridge, 1986).
3. See Klein, *Middle Passage*, pp.141–75, and Herbert S. Klein and Stanley L Engerman, 'Slave Mortality on British Ships, 1791–1797', in Roger Anstey and P.E.H. Hair (eds.), *Liverpool, the African Slave Trade, and Abolition* (Liverpool, 1976), pp.113–25, for a discussion of the impact of Dolben's Act on the number of slaves carried.
4. See Charles Garland and Herbert S. Klein, 'The Allotment of Space for African Slaves aboard Eighteenth-Century British Slave Ships', *William and Mary Quarterly*, 3rd series, 42 (1985), pp.238–48, for an examination of ship design and the relation between various physical dimensions, tonnage, and carrying capacity. For the Portuguese decree, see Klein, *Middle Passage*, pp.29–30. The Dutch regulation is noted in Johannes Menne Postma, *The Dutch in the Atlantic Slave Trade, 1600–1815* (Cambridge, 1990), pp.287–8.
5. For recent studies of the mortality rates on slave vessels and their causes, see, for example, Richard H. Steckel and Richard A. Jensen, 'New Evidence on the Causes of Slave and Crew Mortality in the Atlantic Slave Trade', *Journal of Economic History*, 46 (1986), pp.57–77; Raymond L. Cohn, 'Deaths of Slaves in the Middle Passage', *Journal of Economic History*, 45 (1985), pp.685–92; David Eltis, 'Mortality and Voyage Length in the Middle Passage: New Evidence from the Nineteenth Century', *Journal of Economic History*, 44 (1984), pp.301–18; Raymond L. Cohn and Richard A. Jensen, 'The Determinants of Slave Mortality Rates on the Middle Passage', *Explorations in Economic History*, 19 (1982), pp.269–82; Galenson, *Traders, Planters, and Slaves*, pp.29–52; Joseph C. Miller, 'Mortality in the Atlantic Slave Trade: Statistical Evidence on Causality', *Journal of Interdisciplinary History*, 11 (1981), pp.385–423; David Northrup, 'African Mortality in the Suppression of the Slave Trade: The Case of the Bight of Benin', *Journal of Interdisciplinary History*, 9 (1978), pp.47–64; and David Richardson, 'The Costs of Survival: The Transport of Slaves in the Middle Passage and the Profitability of the 18th-Century British Slave Trade', *Explorations in Economic History*, 24 (1987), pp.178–96.
6. See, however, the studies reconstructing such lost vessels by Stephen D. Behrendt, 'The British Slave Trade, 1785–1807: Volume, Profitability and Mortality' (unpublished Ph.D. thesis, University of Wisconsin, 1993) and by Joseph E. Inikori, 'Measuring the Unmeasured Hazards of the Atlantic Slave Trade: Documents Relating to the British Trade', *Revue*

française d'histoire d'outre-mer, 83 (1996), pp.53–92. Inikori places estimated losses at about 10 per cent of all voyages, but notes that the effect was to add altogether no more than one or two percentage points to the overall mortality rate.

7. See Thomas Fowell Buxton, *The African Slave Trade and its Remedy* (London, 1840; 1967 edition), Ch.2. For a participant's description of the stages of the enslavement experience within Africa, the middle passage, and New World arrival, as well as his experiences as a slave and in the antislavery movement, see *The Interesting Narrative of the Life of Olaudah Equiano, Written by Himself* (1791). Clearly the debates on mortality due to enslavement and mortality in the middle passage refer to two quite different sets of issues.

8. See, for example, Jan S. Hogendorn, 'Economic Modelling of Price Differences in the Slave Trade between the Central Sudan and the Coast', *Slavery and Abolition*, 17 (1996), pp.209–22; Joseph C. Miller, *Way of Death: Merchant Capitalism and the Angolan Slave Trade, 1730–1830* (Madison, Wisconsin, 1988), pp.153, 441. For other discussions of this problem, see Patrick Manning, *Slavery and African Life: Occidental, Oriental, and African Slave Trades* (Cambridge, 1990), p.58 and Paul E. Lovejoy, *Transformations in Slavery: A History of Slavery in Africa* (Cambridge, 1983), pp.60–3.

9. See Thomas Clarkson in Sheila Lambert (ed.), *House of Commons, Sessional Papers of the Eighteenth Century* (Wilmington, Delaware, 1975), vol.69, and his subsequent publications of these data. Clarkson used the muster rolls and related records of slave vessels from Liverpool, London, and Bristol to estimate the overall loss of crew, of about 20 per cent. He then compared crew losses with that for other trades, including Newfoundland, Greenland, the East Indies, Petersburg, and also the trade with Africa which did not involve slaves, and made allowance for differences in sailing times. The losses in the African commodity trading vessels were only one half of those on slavers, in part because of less time spent loading on the coast. For a study of crew mortality at various stages of the slaving voyage, see Stephen D. Behrendt's essay in this volume.

10. Thus some of the patterns shown in Tables 1 and 2 may not accurately reflect the mortality experiences of different national flag carriers or of slaves of different African origins. For the discussion in this paper, particularly noteworthy is the absence of Portuguese data on mortality prior to the 1790s.

11. See, for example, the sources cited in note 5 above. Since the Du Bois Institute data set includes most of the materials used in earlier studies of individual nations, some similarity of results is to be anticipated. The ability to make comparisons among nations represents a major contribution of this data set.

12. The reason for our using this measure (mortality rates per voyage) is to allow separate discussion of the effects of length of voyage on mortality and to highlight the impact of unusually long voyages on slave deaths in transit. Since earlier studies indicate that the correlation between mortality rates and sailing times was low, except for the very long voyages, division of mortality rates by sailing times gives an artificial pattern regarding the timing of deaths during the voyage. See Steckel and Jensen, 'New Evidence'; Klein, *Middle Passage*; Galenson, *Traders, Planters, and Slaves*, pp.48–51.

13. See the summary studies by Raymond L. Cohn, 'Maritime Mortality in the Eighteenth and Nineteenth Centuries: a Survey', *International Journal of Maritime History*, 1 (1989), pp.159–91; Robin Haines, Ralph Shlomowitz and Lance Brennan, 'Maritime Mortality Revisited', *International Journal of Maritime History*, 13 (1996), pp.133–72; Ralph Shlomowitz (with co-authors Lance Brennan and John McDonald), *Mortality and Migration in the Modern World* (Aldershot, 1996).

14. The British mortality decline was highly concentrated in the last two decades of its slave trade, falling to less than one-half the 1776–89 level in the years 1790–1807. In no year after 1790 was the mortality rate above 8 per cent, and in no year after 1794 was it above 4 per cent. To indicate the uniqueness of the British mortality experience, the decline in mortality between the 1776–89 average and 1790–1807 for other carriers was only about 16 per cent. And while these other nations had, in the post-1790 period, frequent rates below 10 per cent, the lowest annual mortality rate was above 6 per cent, higher than the British average for the eighteen years between 1790 and 1807. The British mortality rate per day at sea declined sharply after 1790, meaning that the pattern cannot be explained by changing time in the

middle passage. The non-British ships, however, had a relatively constant mortality per day at sea after 1776. For a detailed breakdown of slave mortality on British vessels before 1780 and 1799, pointing to a very strong post-1792 decline, see Stephen D. Behrendt, 'The Annual Volume and Regional Distribution of the British Slave Trade 1780–1807', *Journal of African History* (forthcoming).

15. For more direct examination of total factor productivity in the slave trade, see David Eltis and David Richardson, 'Productivity in the Transatlantic Slave Trade', *Explorations in Economic History*, 32 (1995), pp.465–84.

16. There were numerous Portuguese slave ships in the seventeenth and eighteenth centuries, but the information did not contain mortality data. The Portuguese (and Brazilian) data in Table 1 start with 1795, so we cannot determine the overall trend in Portuguese mortality.

17. Shlomowitz, *Mortality and Migration*, pp.10–11, and also the various case studies presented.

18. The same systematic differences by African regions are seen in the mortality rates per day at sea, and their declines over time, indicating the importance of factors other than days at sea in explaining these mortality differentials.

Crew Mortality in the Transatlantic Slave Trade in the Eighteenth Century

STEPHEN D. BEHRENDT

During the past ten years historians have written several new studies on the mortality of non-slave shipboard populations in the eighteenth and nineteenth centuries. The passenger groups examined include European emigrants to colonies and to the United States, British convicts to North America and Australia, and African, Indian, Chinese, and Pacific islander indentured labour to the Americas, South Africa, Mauritius, Australia, and Fiji.[1] By comparison, there have been only two recent studies which present new information on crew mortality in the transatlantic slave trade. Using voyage details from surgeons' logs, Steckel and Jensen analysed crew mortality rates on the African coast and middle passage for 92 British slave voyages in 1792–96.[2] From examination of muster rolls, Behrendt calculated the mortality losses of captains in the Bristol and Liverpool slave trades between 1785 and 1807.[3] Several earlier studies of crew mortality on slave ships relied on Rinchon's pioneering research of the major French slaving port of Nantes more than fifty years ago[4] and Unger's examination of selected slave voyages organized by the Dutch Middelburg Commercial Company.[5] Other works include Mettas' examination of crew mortality on 24 slave voyages from Honfleur in 1763–88 and 452 French slave voyages to the Angolan coast in 1714–91 and Stein's analysis of crew mortality on 130 slave voyages from Nantes in 1715–78.[6]

As mentioned in the introductory paper by Eltis and Richardson in this volume, in the 1970s Jean Mettas collected and organized slave voyage data for Nantes and other French ports; in 1978 and 1984 the Dagets published the data in the *Répertoire des Expéditions Négrières Françaises au XVIIIe Siècle*. These French slave voyage data, which have been scanned into the Du Bois Institute data set, contain information on the number of crew at the outset of the voyage and the deaths of sailors on each of the five stages of slaving voyages – namely, the outward passage, the stay at the African coast, the middle passage, the time in the Americas, and the homeward passage.[7] There is crew mortality information for 1,792 of the 3,343 French slave voyages between 1691 and 1793 contained in the Mettas–Daget catalogue. In this large sample, there are also dates of departure and arrival on select voyage legs which permit analysis of crew mortality by time and place.

Detailed information on crew mortality in the British slave trade is contained in ledgers of Liverpool and Bristol muster rolls.[8] During the period of the British slave trade, there are musters which record information on the crew sailing on four out of five Liverpool slave voyages between 1770 and 1807.[9] Bristol muster rolls survive from voyages which sailed from 1748 to 1794.[10] The musters report the names of the crew and the dates of their discharge, desertion, impressment, or death. Some musters list crew rank or cause of death. Departure and return dates are given, and other departures and arrivals throughout the voyage can be inferred from dates of crew discharge or desertion.[11] We have presently integrated into the Du Bois Institute data set slave voyage information from 2,120 Liverpool muster rolls in 1780–1807. Of this total, musters report reliable data on crew deaths for 1,963 voyages, of which 1,709 successfully completed the triangular voyage and returned to Liverpool.[12]

By examining this large run of Liverpool musters, one can determine the number of crew on the outward passage to Africa and the number of 'original' crew deaths during the triangular voyage.[13] These data are contained in the Du Bois Institute set in two of the twelve variables concerning crew mortality. These twelve variables are:

1. Crew at the outset of the voyage
2. Crew deaths prior to the African coast (voyage leg one)
3. Crew deaths on the African coast (voyage leg two)
4. Crew who sailed from the African coast (crew at outset of middle passage)
5. Crew deaths in the middle passage (voyage leg three)
6. Crew who arrived in the Americas
7. Crew deaths in the Americas (voyage leg four)
8. Crew who sailed from the Americas
9. Crew deaths on the homeward passage (voyage leg five)
10. Crew who arrived at the port of return
11. Crew deaths prior to Americas (inferred from 2, 3, 5 above)
12. Crew deaths on the voyage

In selecting these variables, it was decided to include the basic crew mortality information which would be reported in most maritime history sources.[14] Sub-sets of data which report additional crew mortality information, however, may be linked easily to the Du Bois Institute data set.

This paper will analyse the new crew mortality data for the French and British slave trades contained in the Du Bois Institute set. It will also examine two sub-sets of data compiled from a selection of Liverpool slave voyages in the periods 1770–75 and 1801–7. It will analyse aggregate crew mortality on the triangular voyage, crew mortality by region of trade, crew mortality by voyage leg, and crew mortality by rank. Mortality on the maritime legs of the voyage (legs one, three and five) will be compared to the mortality experience of other non-slave shipboard populations. French and British crew mortality data on the African coast and in the Americas (legs two and four) will be compared to that of other European migrant groups. The essay will conclude with some brief comments about the relationship between crew and slave mortality.

Previous studies have shown that between 1748 and 1792 about 17 per cent of the outward bound crew of slave ships from Nantes died during the voyage and that most deaths occurred on the African coast and middle passage. Based on a sample of 598 voyages, these Nantes data suggest that crew mortality declined from 18.7 per cent in 1748–72 to 14.7 per cent in 1773–92.[15] The mortality data from our larger sample of 1,570 completed voyages from all French slaving ports corroborate these findings. As Table 1 shows, about 17 per cent of the outward bound crew died in the eighteenth-century French slave trade.[16]

TABLE 1
VOYAGE CREW MORTALITY IN THE FRENCH SLAVE TRADE, 1711–95 (by five-year periods)

Five-year period	Voyage sample[a]	Mortality loss (%)	Voyage duration (days)	Mortality rate[b]
1711–1715	38	23.1	498.5	13.9
1716–1720	61	21.0	475.1	13.3
1721–1725	64	22.8	512.2	13.4
1726–1730	68	16.5	525.3	9.4
1731–1735	54	20.8	537.2	11.6
1736–1740	94	19.8	549.9	10.8
1741–1745	97	18.7	539.9	10.4
1746–1750	46	21.1	555.4	11.9
1751–1755	138	17.3	518.9	10.0
1761–1765	70	20.9	517.5	12.1
1766–1770	172	20.0	540.7	11.1
1771–1775	145	12.2	488.8	7.5
1776–1780	88	12.4	496.3	7.5
1781–1785	91	17.7	488.3	10.9
1786–1790	263	14.1	472.9	8.9
1791–1793	81	12.3	440.1	8.4
Totals	1,570	17.2	506.3	10.2

Source: Atlantic slave trade database, Du Bois Institute, Harvard University (see introduction). Data for Tables 1–8 are computed from this consolidated slave voyage set.

Note: Table 1 excludes data from the five-year periods, 1706–10, and 1756–60 because of small sample sizes (less than ten voyages). The eighteenth century French slave trade ended in 1793.

a. Sample includes data from French slave voyages which completed the triangular journey.
b. Crew deaths per 1,000 crew per 30-day period.

Most crew deaths were on the African coast and middle passage, though about one in four deaths were in the Americas.[17] The data show a reduction in crew mortality loss over the course of the century, from 20 per cent in 1711–70 to 14 per cent in 1771–93. This reduction was not associated with faster triangular voyages: crew mortality rates declined from 11.3 to 8.6 crew deaths per thousand crew per month (of 30 days)[18] during the same two periods.

For comparative purposes, we can evaluate French crew mortality by African region based on triangular voyage data. The relevant data are presented in Table 2.

TABLE 2
VOYAGE CREW MORTALITY IN THE FRENCH SLAVE TRADE
(by African region of trade)

African region	Crew mortality loss		Crew mortality rate	
	Voyage sample[a]	Mortality loss (%)	Voyage sample[a]	Mortality rate[b]
Senegambia	150	14.8	149	9.6
Sierra Leone- Windward Coast	123	15.3	122	9.1
Gold Coast	116	15.9	115	8.7
Bight of Benin	404	18.3	401	10.6
Bight of Biafra	107	17.1	106	11.0
West-Central Africa	628	16.0	628	9.3
South-East Africa	11	8.3	11	5.0
Totals	1,539	16.5	1,532	9.7

a. Sample includes data from French slave voyages which completed the triangular journey.
b. Crew deaths per 1,000 crew per 30-day period.

Note: African regions arranged from north to south.

Though this is a crude measurement, because of varying coastal slave-loading rates and different voyage lengths on the outward and middle passages, the breakdowns suggest that crew mortality rates were highest on French slave voyages to the Bight of Benin and Bight of Biafra and lowest on voyages to South-East Africa (Madagascar and Mozambique) and the Gold Coast. On the middle passage alone, from a sample of 1,535 French slave voyages we find that crew died at a rate of 15.1 per thousand crew per month.[19] The highest mortality rates occurred in the middle passage on voyages which had slaved at West-Central Africa (19.4 per thousand per month) and the Bight of Biafra (17.3 per thousand per month). For European shipboard populations in the eighteenth century, greater mortality rates of about 50–60 crew deaths per thousand crew per month have been calculated from small samples of British convict voyages to North America in 1719–36 and British and German troop shipments to the West Indies and North America during the American Revolution. German adult male emigrants to Pennsylvania on 14 voyages between 1727 and 1805 died at mortality rates of 15.8 per thousand per month, a rate very similar to that of French crew in the middle passage.[20] On ships sailing from the two principal regions of French slaving activity in the eighteenth century – the Bight of Benin and West-Central Africa – the highest crew mortality rates in the middle passage occurred, as Table 3 shows, when vessels sailed to the Americas during months of comparatively high levels of rainfall in these regions. The lowest crew mortality in the Atlantic crossing occurred on ships sailing during the dry season.[21] This finding is consistent with other studies which found evidence of increased European mortality during African rainy seasons.[22] Greater amounts of stagnant water (in pools or in open casks) fostered larger populations of *Aedes aegypti*, *Anopheles gambiae*, and *Anopheles melas*, the principal mosquito vectors of the yellow fever virus and malarial parasites on the West African coast.[23]

TABLE 3
MIDDLE PASSAGE CREW MORTALITY IN THE FRENCH SLAVE TRADE
(by African region and month)

	Bight of Benin			West-Central Africa	
Month of sail from Benin	Voyage sample	Mortality rate[b]	Month of sail from Angola	Voyage sample	Mortality rate[b]
January	28	18.7	January[a]	59	22.2
February	18	10.0	February[a]	55	22.9
March	39	15.1	March[a]	55	19.6
April	34	19.0	April[a]	37	11.7
May[a]	25	18.8	May	43	18.8
June[a]	35	15.9	June	45	19.6
July[a]	25	29.5	July	38	9.9
August[a]	18	17.9	August	37	20.0
September[a]	26	14.4	September	44	14.4
October	36	13.3	October	42	10.5
November	28	12.0	November[a]	45	15.5
December	40	18.0	December[a]	57	22.6
Totals	352	16.9	Totals	557	17.8

a. Months of greatest rainfall (wet season).
b. Crew deaths per 1,000 crew per 30-day period. We approximate the number of crew on the middle passage as the original crew less deaths on the outward passage and coast of Africa. We assume that no additional crew embarked on the African coast.

Turning to the British slave trade, the calculation of crew mortality data from muster rolls continues the work begun in the 1780s by the British abolitionist Thomas Clarkson. For the Liverpool trade, Clarkson calculated the crew mortality of the 'last eighty-eight vessels in this trade, that had returned to Liverpool from their respective voyages in the September of the year 1787'. Clarkson calculated that 20.5 per cent or 631 crew died out of the 3,082 crew taken on during the triangular voyages of these ships.[24] Regarding the Bristol and London slave trades, he reported that 'Every vessel from the port of Bristol loses ... almost a fourth of the whole crew', while 'Every vessel from the port of London loses ... between a fourth and a fifth of the whole complement of her men.'[25] For the year 1786 Clarkson estimated that the British slave trade employed 5,000 seamen and that 1,130 were 'upon the dead list'.[26] In Spring 1791 a House of Commons committee examined muster rolls for 350 Liverpool and Bristol slave voyages in 1784–90. The musters indicated that 2,643 'original' crew died out of 12,263 enlisted, a mortality loss of 21.6 per cent.[27] The committee report also noted the average voyage length, and one can calculate from this information mortality rates of 16.7 crew deaths per thousand crew per month for the Liverpool and Bristol slave trades.[28] Furthermore, the parliamentary abstract separated the deaths of crew who drowned, were killed or were lost. Of the 2,400 crew deaths on 298 Liverpool slave voyages from 1784 to 1790, 159 crew were reported drowned, 27 were killed, and six were lost. Of the 285 deaths on 52 Bristol slave voyages in the same period, six crew drowned, one was killed, one was lost, and one died 'falling from the mast'. Thus, on these voyages 93 per cent of the crew 'died', six per cent drowned, and one per cent were 'killed'.

Analysis of Liverpool slave voyage muster rolls confirms the accuracy of these contemporary findings and extends the period of examination to the years from 1780 to 1807. For these years there are muster rolls for 1,709 Liverpool slave voyages which completed the triangular journey. Evidence for these voyages is presented in Table 4. As the table shows, 17.8 per cent or 10,439 out of the 58,778 crew who entered pay in Liverpool died during these voyages. The average duration of these voyages was about a year; mortality rates, as shown in Table 4, were 14.7 crew deaths per thousand crew per month. In the Liverpool slave trade, crew mortality declined over the two decades prior to abolition, from 15.7 deaths per thousand per month in 1780–93 to 13.8 deaths in 1794–1807. There are additional crew mortality data for 254 Liverpool slave voyages which did not return to England. Including these with those for completed voyages, it appears that, in all, there were 12,234 deaths among the 66,323 crew reported sailing from Liverpool on 1,963 Liverpool voyages, a mortality loss of 18.4 per cent.[29] Of the total of 12,234 deaths, 10,639 crew were reported to have 'died', 1,314 to have drowned, and 281 to have been killed. A smaller sample of Bristol and Liverpool musters indicates that of the crew who 'died', about four in five deaths were from 'fevers' (mainly yellow fever or malaria), one in ten were from 'fluxes' (mainly dysentery), and a small proportion arose from a variety of respiratory, urological, or diet-deficiency diseases.[30] Also, in the period from 1780 to 1807, 20 Liverpool vessels were lost at sea with the loss of 349 crew by drowning.[31] Most other drownings occurred while vessels traded at the African coast. About half of the crew reported killed were killed by slaves. From the sample of 1,709 Liverpool slave voyages, crew mortality data for 1,651 voyages where the African location of trade could be determined were examined.[32] Shown in Table 5, the results reveal large regional variations in crew mortality rates. Crew members embarking at Liverpool, for example, were three times more likely to die on slaving voyages to the Gambia River than on voyages to the Gold Coast. As in the French trade, crew mortality levels on ships trading at the Gold Coast were comparatively low.

TABLE 4

VOYAGE CREW MORTALITY LOSS ON LIVERPOOL SLAVE VOYAGES, 1780–1807

Year	Voyage sample	Mortality loss (%)	Triangular voyage (days)	Mortality rate[a]
1780	13	23.7	442.9	16.1
1781	21	15.0	385.2	11.7
1782	21	9.9	305.8	9.7
1783	64	19.9	388.4	15.4
1784	48	21.4	350.0	18.3
1785	53	21.0	367.5	17.1
1786	59	24.1	447.1	16.2
1787	56	22.3	404.1	16.6
1788	60	19.4	386.8	15.0
1789	55	14.3	367.7	11.7
1790	80	17.4	360.2	14.5
1791	77	18.2	348.0	15.7
1792	97	22.4	388.6	17.3
1793	29	23.6	360.8	19.6
1794	46	19.4	365.9	15.9
1795	33	14.9	354.8	12.6
1796	52	14.5	357.7	12.2
1797	56	10.6	322.7	9.9
1798	104	17.1	347.4	14.8
1799	83	20.0	378.2	15.9
1800	87	18.2	371.3	14.7
1801	92	16.9	333.0	15.2
1802	98	14.0	324.8	12.9
1803	52	12.9	354.5	10.9
1804	78	17.3	353.3	14.7
1805	64	16.8	339.2	14.9
1806	83	15.1	352.3	12.9
1807	48	17.0	424.5	12.0
Totals	1,709	17.8	364.2	14.7

a. Crew deaths per 1,000 crew per 30-day period.

Sample: 10,439 deaths of 58,778 crew who sailed from Liverpool on 1,709 slave voyages, 1780–1807, which returned to Liverpool after landing slaves in the Americas.

TABLE 5

VOYAGE CREW MORTALITY RATES IN THE LIVERPOOL SLAVE TRADE, 1780–1807

(by African region)

African region	Voyage sample	Mortality loss (%)	Triangular voyage (days)	Mortality rate[a]
Gambia River	19	30.3	330.9	27.5
Sierra Leone	89	25.5	342.6	22.3
Windward Coast	193	21.3	368.3	17.3
Gold Coast	129	10.7	407.8	7.9
Bight of Benin	82	21.6	433.9	14.9
Bight of Biafra	729	18.4	349.1	15.8
West-Central Africa	410	14.9	361.4	12.4
Totals	1,651	17.7	362.7	14.6

a. Crew deaths per 1,000 crew per 30-day period.

Note: African regions arranged from north to south.

Sample: 10,109 deaths of 56,968 crew who sailed from Liverpool on 1,651 slave voyages, 1780–1807, which returned to Liverpool after landing slaves in the Americas.

To examine crew mortality during the triangular voyage with more precision, a sub-set of 158 Liverpool slave voyages was created for the period 1770–75, with five variables to record the number of crew at risk per voyage leg. A sixth variable was added, the voyage identification number, to link this sub-set of 158 records to the Du Bois Institute set which includes variables for crew deaths per voyage leg, dates of sail between legs, and locations of trade. We can thus calculate death rates throughout the voyage and by African region. On the outward, middle and homeward passages, the number of crew at risk takes into account the timing of sailor deaths. On the African coast and in the Americas, the number of crew at risk takes into account crew deaths, desertions, discharges, and the dates when 'new' crew enlisted. Most deaths occurred during the first months of trade on the African coast. In the Americas, most crew deserted ship or were discharged within a few days or weeks of arrival. New crew usually entered pay close to the dates of sail from England, Africa or the Americas. The number of crew-days per voyage leg were calculated, because deaths, desertions and discharges do not occur at regular intervals.[33]

Table 6 presents the new data on crew mortality by voyage leg from the sub-set of Liverpool voyages in 1770–75. Mortality losses and rates are calculated from the original crew on each voyage leg; death losses and rates are calculated from the crew at risk totals. Regarding the percentage distribution of crew deaths by voyage leg, this Liverpool sample is consistent with the French slave trade data presented earlier, as a majority of deaths occurred at the African coast and in the middle passage. Death rates were highest on the African coast, averaging 45.8 crew deaths per thousand crew per month and, at these levels, were three times the French coastal mortality in 1715–78 calculated by Stein and twice the British rates in 1792–96 calculated by Steckel and Jensen.[34] Middle passage death rates of 28 crew per thousand crew per month in the 1770s were also greater than these French and British samples, but less than the eighteenth-century voyage mortality of convicts and soldiers cited earlier.[35]

TABLE 6
CREW MORTALITY IN THE LIVERPOOL SLAVE TRADE, 1770–75
(by voyage leg)

Voyage leg	Beginning crew	At risk crew	Crew deaths	Mortality loss %	Death loss %	Voyage duration (days)	Mortality rate[a]	Death rate[a]
Outward passage	4,660	4,645	30	0.64	0.65	67.5	2.8	2.9
African coast	4,655	3,969	1,300	27.93	32.75	214.5	39.1	45.8
Middle passage[b]	3,205	3,139	151	4.71	4.81	51.7	27.3	27.9
Americas	3,055	2,381	91	2.98	3.82	45.4	19.7	25.2
Homeward passage	2,439	2,420	44	1.80	1.82	53.3	10.1	10.2

a. Rates per 1,000 crew per 30-day period.
b. Middle passage defined as the voyage from the last African location to the first port of arrival in the Americas.

Note: Outward passage and Middle Passage voyage duration (by African region) calculated from Liverpool and British slave voyage data, 1770–1807. Mortality losses and rates calculated from beginning crew totals; death losses and rates calculated from crew at risk totals.

Sample: Crew mortality data from 158 Liverpool slave voyages, 1770–75, which completed the triangular journey. Totals include all crew who entered pay at any point of the voyage.

The monthly crew death rates in the Americas were, at 2.5 per cent, greater than those for most other migrant groups in the late eighteenth and early nineteenth centuries. This rate is, for example, two to three times higher than that of British troops in the West Indies in 1819–36, before the 'mortality revolution' later in that century.[36] The crew mortality in the Americas in 1770–75 was not exceptional, however, when measured against the catastrophic mortality of British soldiers during the yellow fever epidemic in St. Domingue in the mid-1790s.[37] Indeed, we will probably find a sharp rise in crew mortality for all voyages trading in the Caribbean during wartime as frequent troop arrivals maintained human population densities necessary to sustain the yellow fever virus. Furthermore, the threat of impressment into the British navy increased the movement of sailors and contagious disease in West Indian harbours and on land.[38] Death rates on the homeward passage would also presumably increase during war years. In the peace years of 1770 to 1775, the monthly death rate on the homeward passage of ten crew deaths per thousand crew is comparable to the mortality level on twelve British convict voyages to North America in 1768–75 when the death rate averaged 12.5 deaths per thousand per month.[39] As can be seen in Table 6, the crew death rates on the homeward passage were three times greater than the rates on the outward passage. Most crew deaths on the final voyage leg were from yellow fever or malaria acquired in Africa, on the middle passage, or in the Americas.

In the sample of 158 British slave voyages in 1770–75, all but five voyages slaved within one African region, allowing analysis of regional variation in crew mortality.[40] Data on crew mortality by African trading region are provided in Table 7. These indicate that death rates varied along the African coast from a low of 11.8 deaths per thousand crew per month on the Gold Coast to 84–85 deaths per thousand in the Gambia River and at the Bight of Benin.[41] Though based on a small sample of 17 voyages, the death rates in the last two regions are, outside the catastrophic troop mortality during the yellow fever epidemic in St. Domingue, the highest recorded for any seagoing population or migrant group.[42]

TABLE 7
COASTAL CREW MORTALITY IN THE LIVERPOOL SLAVE TRADE, 1770–75
(by African region)

African region	Voyage sample	Beginning crew	At risk crew	Crew deaths	Mortality loss (%)	Death loss (%)	African coast voyage duration (days)	Mortality rate[a]	Death rate[a]
Gambia River	6	160	125	67	41.9	53.6	189.2	66.4	85.0
Sierra Leone	7	116	105	17	14.7	16.2	146.0	30.2	33.3
Windward Coast	28	1,071	853	477	44.5	55.9	292.5	45.6	57.3
Gold Coast	15	412	390	30	7.3	7.7	196.0	11.2	11.8
Bight of Benin	11	354	255	165	46.6	64.7	230.4	60.7	84.2
Bight of Biafra[b]	78	2,281	2,016	509	22.3	25.2	192.2	34.8	39.3
West–Central Africa	8	202	179	33	16.3	18.4	230.8	21.2	23.9

a. Mortality and death rates per 1,000 crew per 30-day period.
b. Death rates for select Biafran ports are as follows: Old Calabar, 26 voyages (47.5); Bonny, 22 voyages (33.1); Cameroons, 18 voyages (33.5).

Note: African regions arranged from north to south. Mortality losses and rates calculated from beginning crew totals; death losses and rates calculated from crew at risk totals.

Sample: Crew mortality data from 153 Liverpool slave voyages, 1770–75. Totals include all crew who entered pay at any point of the voyage.

As most crew died from yellow fever and malaria, it is reasonable to assume that large variations in regional mortality, for example, between the Gambia River and the Gold Coast, relate to the frequency of contact between non-immune sailors and *Aedes* and *Anopheles* mosquito vectors. Mosquito population densities, moreover, relate directly to precipitation levels (or flooding).[43] In the late eighteenth century the British occupied James Fort at the mouth of the Gambia River as well as a 'considerable number of establishments' on both banks. British vessels slaved along the Gambia as far as Barokunda Falls, 300 miles upriver.[44] The first 100 miles of the lower Gambia are bordered by mangrove forests, saline swamps, and alluvial flats, and the riverside lands thereafter are characterized for 200 miles by open fresh-water swamps and grassy flats. From recent surveys, average annual precipitation at the mouth of the Gambia River was 53 inches; and there are major spring tides in the lower Gambia which dictate flood levels.[45] The most important malaria vectors in the Gambia are the freshwater-breeding *Anopheles gambiae* and the salt water breeding *Anopheles melas*. Studies have shown that *A. gambiae* live during the rainy season from June to October and have a higher infection rate because they live longer and are less zoophilic. *A. melas* mosquitoes can live for a few months into the November–May dry season and are the main malaria vector in the western Gambia outside the usual summer transmission period. Comparatively few anopheline mosquitoes, however, live during the six or seven months of the dry season. In the Gambia forests live large numbers of monkeys and baboons which act as the reservoir hosts of the yellow fever virus. *Aedes aegypti* thrive during the rainy season though inter-human transmission by *A. aegypti* also has been documented in the November–May dry season. Malaria and yellow fever still pose major health problems in the Gambia today.[46] Given this disease environment, it is not surprising that in the late eighteenth century many non-immune British crew trading up the Gambia River died at epidemic rates.[47]

By contrast, the climate and physical geography of the British slave-trading regions along the Gold Coast (or modern Ghana) may have supported a less dense mosquito population. Furthermore, mariners had limited on-shore contact. At Accra precipitation levels measured about 30 inches a year on average in 1888–1960, and rain falls more evenly throughout the year than in the Gambia, allowing year-round transmission of yellow fever and malaria in Ghana.[48] The British organized the slave trade on the Gold Coast through forts and factories along a 200-mile coastline from Apollonia in the west to Accra in the east. By the late eighteenth century, trade centred around Anomabu fort. Slaves confined at these locations were sold to coastal traders, fort officials and British merchants. As the Gold Coast lacks large harbours, British and other European vessels anchored well away from the pounding surf. Forts at Dixcove and Sekondi were accessible, but only to small coastal vessels. Cape Coast Castle was the administrative centre of British trade; there resided an African Company surgeon who managed the 'hospital' and storerooms.[49] Crew on board British (and French) slavers on the Gold Coast, therefore, died at lower rates because they spent less time on shore in, probably, a comparatively less deadly disease environment. The coastal forts and factories also could supply captains with provisions and medical supplies.

We have seen that there were variations in crew mortality by year, voyage leg, season of sail from Africa, and region of trade on the African coast. A sub-set of 313 Liverpool slave voyages from the early 1800s was also created to assess whether crew mortality varied by rank. In this file, I recorded the voyage histories of each crew member in six variables: a rank variable; the date of discharge, death, or desertion; and boolean variables assessing whether there was a crew death, and whether the crew member 'died', drowned, or was killed.[50] A seventh variable was added, the voyage identification number, to link this sub-set Institute of 11,399 records to the Du Bois set, thus drawing upon the dates of departure of vessels from Liverpool to calculate voyage time per crew. The results are reported in Table 8. As the table shows, captains and first mates died at the lowest rate in the late Liverpool slave trade. Surgeons had the highest mortality; one in four died on the voyage, a mortality rate double that of first mates. These differences in mortality are probably due to the degree of immunity each mariner had to yellow and malarial fevers. Mariners who survived fevers on the African coast gained immunities to future attacks and were promoted to higher rank on subsequent slave voyages.[51]

Crew making their first voyage in the slave trade – usually surgeons, and some sailors, coopers and carpenters – had higher mortality. The fact that surgeons had the highest mortality may not be surprising. These men had the most contact with slaves and crew who were sick; they entered the slave trade without previous maritime experience; and they frequently left the vessel to examine slaves for sale on shore. First mates may have had the lowest mortality because they gained immunities on previous voyages and frequently remained offshore in command while the captain organized the purchases of slaves.

There are two important questions yet to consider in this essay: first, why did crew mortality decline in the late eighteenth century; and, second, why did crews on ships in the British slave trade die at greater rates than those in the French trade?

The decline in British crew mortality is more evident when we include mortality data from the sub-set of 158 Liverpool voyages for 1770–75 with our figures for 1780–1807. For the period 1770–75, the aggregate (original) crew data reveal that, of the 4,660 crew who enlisted, 1,493 crew died, suggesting a loss by mortality of 32 per cent. Given an average voyage duration of 434.5 days in 1770–75, this suggests a crew mortality rate of 22.1 crew deaths per thousand crew per month. These mortality levels are higher than for all five-year periods in the French slave trade or for the British trade between 1780 and 1807.

TABLE 8

VOYAGE CREW MORTALITY IN THE LIVERPOOL SLAVE TRADE

(by rank)

Rank or Station	Number	Deaths	Mortality loss (%)	Days on board (ave.)	Mortality rate[a]
Captains, supercargoes	325	47	14.5	303.2	14.3
1st mates	318	38	11.9	293.0	12.2
2nd, 3rd, 4th, 5th mates	742	114	15.4	258.1	17.9
Surgeons, surgeons' mates	333	76	22.8	279.9	24.5
Carpenters, coopers, joiners	669	114	17.0	259.6	19.7
Other crew	9,012	1,430	15.9	240.1	19.8
Totals	11,399	1,819	16.0	246.9	19.4

a. Crew deaths per 1,000 crew per 30-day period.

Sample: Crew mortality data from 313 Liverpool slave voyages, 1801–7.

The declines in aggregate crew mortality in the late eighteenth century were due mostly to shifts in the region of trade on the African coast. In both the French and British slave trades, there were shifts away from the higher-mortality Senegambia region and Bight of Benin to the lower-mortality Angolan coast over the course of the eighteenth century. Two-thirds of the French trade was to the Benin Coast in the early eighteenth century; more than half of French slavers traded on the Angolan coast in 1760–90.[52] The British trade to Angola, which comprised only 5–6 per cent of the total British trade in 1780–91, increased to about a third of the total trade in 1792–1807.[53] We also have evidence, however, that mortality rates declined through time on British ships trading at specific African markets. For example, closer analysis of the large sample of 729 Liverpool slave voyages to the Bight of Biafra reported in Table 5 reveals that monthly crew mortality rates declined from 1.70 per cent in 1780–93 to 1.48 per cent in 1794–1807. Taking only the crew who 'died' (that is, excluding crew who drowned or were killed), these monthly mortality rates are 1.63 per cent and

1.36 per cent, respectively. Muster roll information suggests that this decline in aggregate crew mortality was the result of fewer ship-board epidemics at the Bight of Biafra and all West African regions. For example, at least half the 'original' crew 'died' on 26 or 16.5 per cent of the 158 Liverpool slave voyages in 1770–75, whereas half the outbound crew died on 37 (4.6 per cent) of 809 Liverpool slave voyages in 1780–93 and on 32 (2.8 per cent) of 1,154 Liverpool slave voyages in 1794–1807.[54]

What explains the decline in crew epidemics on board British slave vessels? It is useful, first, to look at specific trading practices on the coast during the 1770s and early 1780s before addressing this question. James Stanfield, a mariner in the Liverpool slave trade, believed that crew mortality was caused primarily by the cruelty of officers, contagion on board ship because of confined air, the provisioning duties of crew on the African coast, and the cleaning of ship holds. Stanfield wrote in 1788:

> Among the many causes of destruction, which originate from the trade, and not from the climate, the bulk-heads between the decks, excluding a salutary circulation of air, have been insisted upon as producing their effects. But there is another, which has not claimed such notice, and which yet is a terrible assistant to African mortality. This is the fabricating of an house over the vessel for the security of slaves, while on the coast.
>
> This enclosure helps the stagnation of air, and is, in that point of view, dreadful: but it is more fatal in the act of its preparation. I know nothing more destructive than the business of cutting wood and bamboe, for the purpose of erecting and thatching this structure. The process is generally by the river-side. The faces and bodies of the poor seamen are exposed to the fervour of a burning sun, for a covering would be insupportable. They are immersed up to the waist in mud and slime; pestered by snakes, worms and venomous reptiles; tormented by muskitoes, and a thousand assailing insects; their feet slip from under them at every stroke, and their relentless officers do not allow a moment's intermission from the painful task. This employment, the cruelty of the officers, and the inconceivably shocking task of scraping the contagious blood and filth, at every opportunity, from the places where the slaves lie, are, in my opinion, the three greatest (though by no means the sole) causes of the destruction of seamen, which this country experiences by the prosecution of the trade in slaves.

Stanfield also attributed crew mortality to poor nourishment, a scarcity of water, crowded living conditions, and the fact that most of the crew slept upon deck.[55]

Stanfield's pamphlet, published by the abolitionist James Phillips, perhaps influenced Members of Parliament to amend the Dolben Act of 1788.[56] The Dolben Act had set limits on the number of slaves British vessels could transport from the coast, effectively reducing the number of slaves loaded per ton by 13 per cent. Consequently, the number of crew shipped per ton declined by 17 per cent. Furthermore, the Act required that surgeons certify for the slave trade. In 1789 an amendment stipulated the terms of contract between captain and crew. Among the clauses, sailors were required to receive a regular diet of daily provisions and sleeping accommodations for at least half the crew below deck.[57] The captain also agreed to 'hire and employ the Natives in their Craft, to wood and water the said Ship, during her Continuance on the Coast of *Africa*, if such Natives can be procured' and 'whenever the Officers and Seamen are employed trading in Craft up the Rivers' the captain will 'furnish the Parties so employed with a sufficient Quantity of painted Canvas, or Tarpawling, for an Awning, and Provisions for the Time'. In 1799 Parliament passed a further regulation act which increased aerial space below deck for slaves and set a maximum slave per crew ratio of ten to one as well as a maximum loading level of 400 slaves. The new space requirements reduced loading levels to about one slave per ton; this amounted to a 47 per cent reduction on pre-1799 levels. With fewer slaves to control, crew size declined by 13 per cent.[58]

Parliament passed these three acts to reduce crowding, the amount of 'contagion' generated below deck, and the cycle of disease transmission between slaves and crew. Did they improve the health and working conditions of sailors? Several studies have shown that there is no relationship between ship-board mortality and crowding.[59] The minimum diets required by the Dolben Act amendment were still nutritionally inadequate and would not have increased sailors' ability to withstand yellow fever or malaria.[60] The medical qualifications of surgeons certainly improved after the Dolben Act. Some surgeons entered the slave trade after a period of hospital study where they learned about the relationship between hygiene, sanitation and epidemic diseases. Despite this, doctors would not have been able to treat crew with yellow fever, though tonics of Peruvian, or cinchona, bark, which we know now contains quinine, may have proved effective against malaria.[61]

Perhaps the improved health of slaves, suggested by the lower slave mortality on the middle passage in the 1790s, reduced transmission of fevers and gastro-intestinal diseases between slaves and crew during and after slave loading on the African coast.[62] But why did slave mortality decline in the 1790s? The 1788 Dolben Act raised shipping costs[63] and may have prompted British slaving merchants to pay greater attention to hygiene and sanitation on board ship in an attempt to lower slave mortality. Specifically, coal tars may have been used in the last two decades of the British slave trade as disinfectants. Archibald Cochrane developed a new process of manufacturing tar from coal in 1781 and he believed that tar would protect hulls from worms that lived in warm waters.[64] In the late 1780s British manufacturers offered to supply the African Company storeships with various coal tars and varnishes. The British Coal Tar Office claimed that soaking planks in coal tars 'destroys insects and their eggs, and by empoisoning Wood to a certain depth, prevents the entrance of those worms which feed on, and lodge in wood'. They recommended that other coal tars could be used 'for Ships masts, sides, and decks which, in warm Climates, are apt to rent and open, by the heat of the sun' and to blacken yards and mast-heads.[65] Painting and fumigating vessels with coal tar may have killed bacteria and mosquitoes on board ship, thus reducing chances of an outbreak of amoebic dysentery, malaria, or yellow fever. Recent work on English voyages to Australia has suggested that improved shipboard hygiene and sanitation in the mid-nineteenth century, promoted by government agencies, helped lower passenger mortality.[66] Fifty years earlier, British merchants also may have employed new methods to disinfect slave vessels effectively. When William Young inspected the Bristol slave ship *Pilgrim*, anchored in Kingstown Bay, St. Vincent in December 1791, he found the interior of the ship 'as clean as a Dutch cabinet'.[67] Though the *Pilgrim* slaved for eighty-two days at Bonny in the Bight of Biafra during the rainy season, the vessel lost only five of 371 slaves on her sixty-four day passage to America. Moreover, only one sailor died (on the homeward passage) of the 35 crew who shipped out from Bristol.[68] By the last years of the trade, medical authorities, in fact, contrasted the cleanliness of British slavers with government transports.[69]

The clause in the Dolben Act amendment requiring captains to hire Africans to provision slave vessels on the coast would have reduced the contact of non-immune crew with African disease environments. Captain Robert Hume stated that during his voyages in the 1790s he employed sixty to eighty African sailors to trade for provisions along the Windward Coast. This practice he deemed necessary to avoid 'burying a great Number of White Men'.[70] Hume's commercial transactions with African sailors may not have been prompted by British legislation, however. Rather, the development of African coastal economies may have led to a reorganization of trading practices. As Klein has suggested in regard to the long-term decline in slave mortality,[71] epidemics may have been less frequent in the late British slave trade because of efficiencies gained in marketing slaves on the African coast. In Table 4 we see that during the years of lowest crew mortality – 1782 and 1797 – British slavers made the fastest triangular voyages. This suggests that there were minimal delays in loading slaves.[72] If African traders could increase productivity in provisioning British vessels and supplying slaves, British merchants could organize voyages to minimize shipping costs and perhaps avoid African rainy seasons.[73] Moreover, in regions such as the Gambia River and the Windward Coast, there would be less need for crew to travel up rivers to seek out slave suppliers. If African merchants increased the regularity of slave supplies from the upper to the lower Gambia, for example, fewer British vessels would have to sail along the fresh water swamplands where *A. gambiae* thrived.

Why was crew mortality in the French slave trade lower than that in the Liverpool trade in 1771–75 and 1781–93? In the first period, mortality rates in the Liverpool trade were three times greater than in the French trade, while in the later period, they were twice as great. In part, these mortality differences are explained by varying voyage leg duration. Triangular French slave voyages took, on average, 80–100 more days to complete than Liverpool voyages, primarily because French vessels remained in the West Indies for many months. On the West African coast, French captains sometimes completed trade more quickly than their Liverpool counterparts. For example, the ships involved in 143 French slave voyages in 1771–75 remained on the African coast for 170 days on average, whereas, as Table 6 shows, 158 Liverpool slavers took 215 days on average to complete their trade on the coast during more or less the same period. French slavers thus spent a greater part of their triangular voyages in less deadly disease environments. French slave ships also may have been manned by greater proportions of 'seasoned' crew who had gained immunities to yellow or malarial fevers on previous voyages to Africa or the Americas. In the British trade, captains frequently hired 'landmen' who were not apprenticed to sea and may have died at high rates.[74] There may have been comparatively few landmen on French vessels. It is also possible that French merchants paid greater attention to ship-board medical care, hygiene and sanitation during the period from 1771 to 1793.

Even though there was a reduction in crew mortality in the late eighteenth-century French and British slave trades, merchants organized slave voyages to maximize profitability regardless of potential crew loss. European vessels continued to slave in regions of Africa such as the Gambia River and Bight of Benin which were comparatively unhealthy for sailors. Merchants also organized some voyages to arrive in Africa during the rainy season. For example, they tried to send slave vessels to Bonny in June or July so that they would arrive there after the harvest when yam stocks were plentiful. By arriving at Bonny in August or September, slave vessels would be expected to reach the Americas during the December–January sugar harvest when demand for slaves was relatively high. The primary aim of merchants in the late eighteenth century was to minimize slave deaths in the middle passage to ensure a profitable voyage. Minimizing crew mortality was a secondary consideration.

NOTES

1. Raymond L. Cohn, 'Maritime Mortality in the Eighteenth and Nineteenth Centuries: A Survey', *International Journal of Maritime History*, 1 (1989), pp.159–91; Robin Haines, Ralph Shlomowitz, and ·Lance Brennan, 'Maritime Mortality Revisited', *International Journal of Maritime History* (1996), pp.133–72.
2. Richard H. Steckel and Richard A. Jensen, 'New Evidence on the Causes of Slave and Crew Mortality in the Atlantic Slave Trade', *Journal of Economic History*, 46 (1986), pp.57–77.
3. Stephen D. Behrendt, 'The Captains in the British Slave Trade from 1785 to 1807', *Transactions of the Historic Society of Lancashire and Cheshire*, 140 (1991), pp.79–140. More than one in four captains died in the trade during these years.
4. Dieudonné Rinchon, *Le Trafic Négrier, d'après les Livres de Commerce du Capitaine Gantois Pierre-Ignace-Liévin van Alstein*, 1 (Paris, 1938), pp.146, 247–96; Philip D. Curtin, *The Atlantic Slave Trade: A Census* (Madison, Wisconsin, 1969), pp.282–6; Herbert S. Klein, *The Middle Passage: Comparative Studies in the Atlantic Slave Trade* (Princeton, 1978), pp.180, 190–207; Robert L. Stein, *The French Slave Trade in the Eighteenth Century: An Old Regime Business* (Madison, Wisconsin, 1979), pp.98–100; Herbert S. Klein and Stanley L. Engerman, 'A Note on Mortality in the French Slave Trade in the Eighteenth Century', in Henry A. Gemery and Jan S. Hogendorn (eds.), *The Uncommon Market: Essays in the Economic History of the Atlantic Slave Trade* (New York, 1979), pp.266–8.
5. W.S. Unger, 'Bijdragen tot de Geschiedenis van de Nederlandse slavenhandel II', *Economisch-Historisch Jaarboek*, 28 (1958–60), pp.26–7; Johannes Postma, 'Mortality in the Dutch Slave Trade, 1675–1795', in Gemery and Hogendorn (eds.), *Uncommon Market*, p.260. Postma published slightly revised captains' mortality figures in a later work (*The Dutch in the Atlantic Slave Trade, 1600–1815* (Cambridge, 1990), pp.156–7, 377–89). As Postma notes, there are few surviving records which document crew mortality in the Dutch slave trade. Many records, such as logbooks of the Dutch West India Company, have been lost almost entirely. Sources which detail crew mortality for other transatlantic slave trades also are lacking.
6. Jean Mettas, 'Honfleur et la Traite des Noirs au XVIIIe Siècle', *Revue française d'histoire d'outre-mer*, 60 (1973), pp.20–2; idem, 'Pour une Histoire de la Traite des Noirs Française: Sources et Problèmes', *Revue française d'histoire d'outre-mer*, 62 (1975), pp.38–9; Robert Stein, 'Mortality in the Eighteenth-Century French Slave Trade', *Journal of African History*, 21 (1980), pp.35–41.
7. In his notes, Mettas recorded the dates and locations of crew deaths in the French slave trade. The Dagets, however, grouped crew deaths by voyage leg in the two-volume catalogue. Jean Mettas in Serge and Michèle Daget (eds.), *Répertoire des Expéditions Négrières Françaises au XVIIIe Siècle*, 2 vols. (Paris, 1978, 1984), I, pp.xv–xvi.
8. In 1747 Parliament ordered that customs houses record 'ship's agreement and crew lists' in 'An Act for the Relief and Support of maimed and disabled Seamen and the Widows and Children of such as shall be killed, slain or drowned in the Merchants Service' (20 Geo. II c.38, XX). For British voyages in the eighteenth century, there are also surviving muster rolls from the ports of Dartmouth, Plymouth, and Shields. Public Record Office (hereafter PRO) information leaflet no.5, p.3.
9. PRO, BT 98/33-69; Behrendt, 'Captains in the British Slave Trade', p.81.
10. Bristol musters are kept at the Society of Merchant Venturers Hall, Bristol. Kenneth Morgan, 'Shipping Patterns and the Atlantic Trade of Bristol, 1749–1770', *William & Mary Quarterly*, 46 (1989), pp.532–4; David Richardson (ed.), *Bristol, Africa and the Eighteenth-*

Century Slave Trade to America, Bristol Record Society, vol.3 (1991), p.x.

11. For example, during war years sailors frequently deserted ship upon arrival in the Americas.

12. Crew deaths were often not recorded on the Liverpool muster roll when the vessel was captured on the outward passage or middle passage. For some musters from the 1780s, it is not possible to differentiate between crew discharges or deaths.

13. I have not yet determined crew deaths by voyage leg from all Liverpool slave voyage muster rolls.

14. For example, in the British Trade, Mediterranean Passes record the number of crew at the outset of the voyage, Naval Office shipping lists report the number of crew who arrive in the Americas, and Seamen's Sixpence ledgers enumerate the crew who returned.

15. Curtin, *Atlantic Slave Trade,* p.283. See also Klein and Engerman, 'Note on Mortality', p.263.

16. I would like to thank David Eltis for calculating the crew mortality data for the eighteenth-century French slave trade.

17. Klein's analysis of the Nantes data, 1711–77, indicated that more than half the crew deaths occurred on the African coast and about a third took place on the middle passage (Klein, *Middle Passage,* p.197 n.44). From new French slave trade data on 1,730 voyages, we calculate that 3 per cent of crew deaths occurred on the outward passage; 42 per cent on the African coast; 22 per cent in the middle passage; 26 per cent in the Americas; and 7 per cent on the homeward passage.

18. Crew deaths per thousand crew per thirty-day period (approximating a month) is the standard measurement of maritime mortality. Cohn, 'Maritime Mortality', p.187. Regarding the importance of distinguishing between mortality losses and rates in the transatlantic slave trade, see Joseph C. Miller, 'Mortality in the Atlantic Slave Trade: Statistical Evidence on Causality', *Journal of Interdisciplinary History,* 11 (1981), pp.385–409.

19. This contrasts with a middle passage mortality rate of 18.5 crew deaths per thousand crew per month on 130 Nantes voyages in 1715–78. Stein, 'Mortality in the French Slave Trade', pp.37, 40.

20. Klein, *Middle Passage,* p.71; Cohn, 'Maritime Mortality', pp.188–9; Haines, Shlomowitz, and Brennan, 'Maritime Mortality Revisited', p.135.

21. Monthly rainfall data for the mid-twentieth century are found in Great Britain Meteorological Office, *Tables of Temperature, Relative Humidity and Precipitation for the World* (London, 1958), Part IV, pp.13–15, 120–5. For Benin, the sample of 352 French slave voyages yielded crew death rates on the middle passage of 16.9 and a standard deviation of 20.7. For West-Central Africa, the sample of 557 voyages yielded death rates of 17.8 and a standard deviation of 29.4. We excluded voyages which were lost on the passage. In the Bight of Benin sample, standard deviations ranged from 10.8 (in November, during the dry season) to 41.7 (in July, the height of the rainy season). In West-Central Africa, standard deviations ranged from 11.7 (in July, during the dry season) to 37.2 (in December, during the rainy season). There was thus greater variance around mean crew mortality rates during the rainy season, suggestive of epidemic mortality on some voyages.

22. Mettas, 'Honfleur et la Traite des Noirs', p.22; Mettas, 'La Traite des Noirs Française', p.38; K.G. Davies, 'The Living and the Dead: White Mortality in West Africa, 1684–1732', in Stanley L. Engerman and Eugene D. Genovese (eds.), *Race and Slavery in the Western Hemisphere: Quantitative Studies* (Princeton, 1975), pp.94–6. As Davies notes, contemporaries frequently commented on the fatal rainy seasons in Africa. Steckel and Jensen, however, suggest that rain did not influence the chances of crew deaths from fevers or gastrointestinal diseases, the two most common causes of death. Steckel and Jensen, 'Slave and Crew Mortality', p.67.

23. R. Mansell Prothero, *Migrants and Malaria in Africa* (Pittsburgh, 1965), p.100; Walther H. Wernsdorfer and Ian McGregor (eds.), *Malaria. Principles and Practice of Malariology,* 2 vols. (London, 1988), II, pp.1384–5.

24. Thomas Clarkson, *An Essay on the Impolicy of the African Slave Trade* (Freeport, New York, 1971 edition), pp.50–2. These 88 Liverpool voyages sailed to Africa from 7 December 1784 to 23 December 1786 (PRO, BT 98/46, No.8; PRO, BT 98/47, No.340). I re-examined the 88 musters and found that Clarkson made only a few errors in counting. He also mistakenly

included data from two African produce vessels in his totals.

25. Clarkson, *Impolicy of the African Slave Trade*, pp.53–5.

26. Clarkson estimated that more than 1,500 crew left their slave vessels in Africa and the West Indies (they either deserted or were discharged) and that most of these sailors died or 'were rendered unserviceable at home' through illness. In all, he stated that 1,950 out of 5,000 slave trade crew 'were lost to the service of [England] by the prosecution of the slave trade in the year 1786'. Clarkson also calculated that more than twice as many sailors died in the slave trade than in the East India, West India, Petersburg (timber), Newfoundland (fishing) or Greenland (whaling) trades combined. Ibid., pp.54–75).

27. Roger Anstey, *The Atlantic Slave Trade and British Abolition* (Atlantic Highlands, New Jersey, 1975), p.32, n.95.

28. *Journal of the House of Commons*, 46 (1790–91), pp.337, 397, 433. In the debate on the abolition of the slave trade on 18–19 April 1791, speakers in the Commons and Lords cited these aggregate crew mortality data. *Parliamentary History of England*, 29 (1791–92), p.270; The Senator; *Or, Clarendon's Parliamentary Chronicle*, 2 (1791), pp.569–70, 604–5.

29. Including mortality in the Bristol and London slave trades, I estimate that there were about 20,000 crew deaths in the British slave trade, 1780–1807.

30. Stephen D. Behrendt, 'The British Slave Trade, 1785–1807: Volume, Profitability, and Mortality' (unpublished Ph.D. thesis, University of Wisconsin-Madison, 1993), pp.330, 341. See also Steckel and Jensen, 'Slave and Crew Mortality', p.62.

31. The greatest loss of life occurred on the slave ship (and letter of marque) *Saint Ann* (249 tons). All 61 crew on board drowned when the ship was lost on the homeward passage in 1798 (PRO, BT 98/59, No.342; William Fergusson Irvine (ed.), *An Index to the Wills and Inventories now preserved in the Probate Registry at Chester, 1791–1800* (Liverpool, 1902), will of Captain Robert Jones).

32. Sources report the locations of African trade for four in five British slave voyages, 1780–1807. For most other voyages, I based my estimates on the location of slaving on reported African destinations from England and/or slave voyage histories of captains, shipowners, merchants, and vessels (see Stephen D. Behrendt, 'The Annual Volume and Regional Distribution of the British Slave Trade, 1780–1807: 'The Annual Volume and Regional Distribution of the British Slave Trade, 1780–1807', *Journal of African History* forthcoming).

33. For example, a slave vessel arrived on the African coast with fifteen crew and remained there for six months. The original crew on voyage leg 2 (African coast) is fifteen. On the Coast, four sailors deserted ship after two months and two sailors died after two months. On the day of sail from Africa, three crew were hired to sail on the middle passage. Thus, nine crew remained on the coast for six months (180 days) and six crew remained for only two months (60 days). The total number of crew-days is 1,980. As the vessel remained on the coast for 180 days, the crew at risk on the coast is eleven (1,980 crew-days/180 days). It is standard procedure to define the average shipboard population at risk as the number of passengers embarked less half the voyage deaths. This method examines the mid-voyage population, and assumes that deaths occurred at regular intervals during the voyage leg (Cohn, 'Maritime Mortality', pp.162–3; Haines, Shlomowitz, and Brennan, 'Maritime Mortality Revisited', p.136). As I calculated the number of crew-days per outward, middle, and homeward passages, my crew at risk totals do not always equal the mid-voyage population.

34. Stein, 'Mortality in the French Slave Trade', pp.37, 40; Steckel and Jensen, 'Slave and Crew Mortality', p.61.

35. See above note 20.

36. Philip D. Curtin, 'Epidemiology and the Slave Trade', *Political Science Quarterly*, 83 (1968), p.203.

37. David Geggus, 'Yellow Fever in the 1790s: The British Army in Occupied Saint Domingue', *Medical History*, 23 (1979), pp.45–6; idem, 'The Cost of Pitt's Caribbean Campaigns, 1793–1798', *Historical Journal*, 26 (1983), pp.699–706.

38. Slave trade surgeon, Elliot Arthy, listed a variety of factors which he believed contributed to high crew mortality in the Americas: 'the desertion of seamen from one merchantman to another, in order to obtain large sums of money for the run-home from the West-Indies; their

leaving their ships, and going on-shore, to avoid being impressed; their exposure to the causes of the Yellow Fever in the boating duty; their disorderly conduct when, on those several occasions, they are on-shore; the badness of their accommodations both in health and sickness; [and] their want of proper medical assistance and attendance'. Elliot Arthy, *The Seamen's Medical Advocate* (London, 1798), pp.146–9. Perhaps with these mortality concerns in mind, Parliament passed an act in 1797 to try to prohibit the desertion of seamen from British merchant vessels in the West Indies (37 Geo. III c.73). This law fined captains who employed 'deserted' sailors and regulated the wages paid to crew for the 'run home'.

39. Haines, Shlomowitz, and Brennan, 'Maritime Mortality Revisited', p.135.

40. Locations of slaving are listed in *Lloyd's List* and in the Liverpool plantation registers. An important government document reports the intended slaving location for Liverpool slave voyages, 1750–76 (PRO, BT 6/3, ff.100–29). Almost all Liverpool slave voyages slaved at their intended destinations.

41. Davies also notes that in the early eighteenth century the Royal African Company station at the Gold Coast was healthier for Europeans than bases at the Gambia, Sierra Leone, or Whydah. Davies, 'Living and the Dead', p.93.

42. Tom W. Shick, 'A Quantitative Analysis of Liberian Colonization from 1820 to 1843 with Special Reference to Mortality', *Journal of African History*, 12 (1971), pp.51–7; Davies, 'Living and the Dead', pp.83–98; Philip D. Curtin, *Death by Migration: Europe's Encounter with the Tropical World in the Nineteenth Century* (Cambridge, 1989); Antonio McDaniel, *Swing Low, Sweet Chariot: The Mortality Cost of Colonizing Liberia in the Nineteenth Century* (Chicago, 1995), pp.91–135.

43. M.W. Service, 'The Effect of Weather on Mosquito Biology', in T.E. Gibson (ed.), *Weather and Parasitic Animal Disease*, World Meteorological Organization, Technical Note No.159 (Geneva, 1978), p.153.

44. Philip D. Curtin, *Economic Change in Pre-Colonial Africa: Senegambia in the Era of the Slave Trade*, 2 vols. (Madison, Wisconsin, 1975), II, pp.84, 296–7; S.M.V. Golbery, *Travels in Africa. Performed during the years 1785, 1786, and 1787*, 2 vols. (London, 1803), II, pp.112–13. British vessels anchored near James Island and paid an anchorage fee to Nomi rulers who controlled territories there. Nomi sailors handled the river trade and they assisted in navigating vessels upstream. British merchant, William Lyttleton, owned property 450 miles up the Gambia, and may have been the only British slave merchant to live on the upper Gambia. F. William Torrington (ed.), *House of Lords Sessional Papers, 1798–99* (Rahway, New Jersey, 1975), III, pp.181–2, evidence of William Lyttleton; Robin Hallett (ed.), *Records of the African Association, 1788–1831* (London, 1964), pp.132, 146.

45. Great Britain Meteorological Office, *Tables of Temperature*, p.74; U.S. Department of Commerce, *World Weather Records, 1951–60* (Washington, D.C., 1967), V, p.174.

46. T.P. Monath *et al.*, 'Yellow Fever in the Gambia, 1978–1979: Epidemiologic Aspects with Observations on the Occurrence of Orungo Virus Infections', *American Journal of Tropical Medicine & Hygiene*, 29 (1980), pp.912–5; J.H. Bryan, '*Anopheles gambiae* and *A. melas* at Brefet, The Gambia, and their Role in Malaria Transmission', *Annals of Tropical Medicine and Parasitology*, 77 (1983), pp.1–10; B.M. Greenwood and H. Pickering, 'A Review of the Epidemiology and Control of Malaria in The Gambia, West Africa', *Transactions of the Royal Society of Tropical Medicine and Hygiene*, 87, Supplement 2 (1993), pp.3–11.

47. For example, the brig *Maria* arrived at Jamaica from the Gambia, 'with only one white Man on board, the Captain & the rest of the People having died on the Passage' (*Lloyd's List*, 30 November 1773). In 1805 the Liverpool slave ship *Mars* was captured by the Spanish: 'the *Mars* had lost 25 of her people by sickness, which is said to have been the cause of her capture. She was bound from the river Gambia with 200 slaves for Charleston'. Twenty-three of twenty-nine crew died in August–October 1805 during the rainy season. Three other sick sailors were sent on shore (*Royal Gazette and Bahama Advertiser*, 17 January 1806; PRO, BT 98/66, No.245).

48. Rainfall levels varied along the Gold Coast (Ghana). To the west, average precipitation at Axim, 1943–52, was 83 inches, with half of the rain falling in May–June. Great Britain Meteorological Office, *Tables of Temperature*, p.75; U.S. Department of Commerce, *World Weather Records*, V, p.179. Axim was the location of a Dutch fort. British slavers traded

farther east, closer to Accra. Perhaps the reddish loam soils of the Gold Coast allow greater drainage than, for example, the clay soils of the Gambia. R.C. Muirhead-Thomson, 'Recent Knowledge about Malaria Vectors in West Africa and their Control', *Transactions of the Royal Society of Tropical Medicine and Hygiene*, 40 (1947), p.512; M.E.C. Giglioli and I. Thornton, 'The Mangrove Swamps of Keneba, Lower Gambia River Basin. 1. Descriptive Notes on the Climate, the Mangrove Swamps, and the Physical Composition of their Soils', *Journal of Applied Ecology*, 2 (1965), pp.81–103. Most documented outbreaks of yellow fever in Ghana have occurred on the coast and in the region around Accra (David Scott, *Epidemic Disease in Ghana, 1901–1960* (London, 1965), p.49).

49. K.G. Davies, *The Royal African Company* (London, 1957), pp.240–52; John Adams, *Remarks on the Country Extending from Cape Palmas to the River Congo* (London, 1966), pp.7, 159.

50. For these 313 Liverpool slave voyages, which sailed from late 1801 through early 1807, the rank (or station) of each crew member is recorded in the muster rolls. Ranks are listed infrequently in the Liverpool musters before the year 1801. As shown in Table 8, for convenience various ranks are grouped into six categories.

51. For example, in the 1790s mariner Hugh Crow survived several fevers and was promoted to mate of larger Liverpool slave vessels and then to captain in 1798. *Memoirs of the Late Captain Hugh Crow of Liverpool* (London, 1970 edition), pp.34, 64–6.

52. David Richardson, 'Slave Exports from West and West-Central Africa, 1700–1810: New Estimates of Volume and Distribution', *Journal of African History*, 30 (1989), pp.12, 14.

53. Behrendt, 'Annual Volume'.

54. Studies on both slave and non-slave ship-board populations have shown that small numbers of voyages usually experienced epidemic mortality rates and thus mortality on most voyages was below average. Cohn, 'Maritime Mortality', p.175; Klein and Engerman, 'Note on Mortality', pp.263–5.

55. James Field Stanfield, *Observations on a Guinea Voyage. In a Series of Letters Addressed to the Rev. Thomas Clarkson* (London, 1788), pp.14–16. On a Liverpool slave voyage in 1786, another sailor recalled how captains re-allocated provisions to healthy crew and slaves: 'No sooner was a wretched sailor's name entered on the sick list, than the pitiful allowance of a quarter of a pound of beef, and the small glass of brandy, were denied him, without any thing being given in lieu thereof. A little bad bread, with a proportionate quantity of water, was nearly the whole of what the patients had to subsist on'. William Butterworth, *Three Years Adventures, of a Minor, in England, Africa, the West Indies, South-Carolina and Georgia* (Leeds, 1822), p.41.

56. For a sympathetic appraisal of Stanfield's tract, see the London *Monthly Review*, 79 (July–December 1788), pp.70–1.

57. The articles of agreement stipulated that crew were to receive 'a quarter of a pint of spirits, or half a pint of wine' per day. Daily water allowances also were legislated, but the amount was not specified.

58. Behrendt, 'British Slave Trade', pp.161–3, 342; 28 Geo. III c.54; 29 Geo. III c.66; 39 Geo. III c.80.

59. Charles Garland and Herbert S. Klein, 'The Allotment of Space for Slaves aboard Eighteenth-Century British Slave Ships', *William & Mary Quarterly*, 42 (1985), pp.238–48; David Eltis, *Economic Growth and the Ending of the Transatlantic Slave Trade* (New York, 1987), p.137.

60. J. Watt, J. Freeman and W.F. Bynum (eds.), *Starving Sailors. The Influence of Nutrition upon Naval and Maritime History* (Greenwich, 1981). Undernourished sailors would have a lowered antibody response to yellow fever. G. Thomas Strickland (ed.), *Hunter's Tropical Medicine* (Philadelphia, 1991), p.948. Nutrition levels do not play a role in malaria infection. Wernsdorfer and McGregor (eds.), *Malaria*, I, pp.759–63.

61. Behrendt, 'British Slave Trade', pp.177–87.

62. On the African coast and middle passage, slaves were at greater risk of dying from gastrointestinal diseases; crew were at greater risk of dying from fevers. Steckel and Jensen, 'Slave and Crew Mortality', pp.60–2. Stein argues that slave and crew mortality levels in the Nantes trade rose and fell together. Stein, 'Mortality in the French Slave Trade', pp.38–41.

63. David Eltis and Stanley L. Engerman, 'Fluctuations in Sex and Age Ratios in the Transatlantic Slave Trade, 1663–1864', *Economic History Review*, 46 (1993), p.314.

64. Research suggests that coal tar derivatives (phenols) are superior wood disinfectants. Susan C. Morgan-Jones, 'Cleansing and Disinfection of Farm Buildings', in C.H. Collins *et al.* (eds.), *Disinfectants: Their Use and Evaluation of Effectiveness* (London, 1981), pp.205–9.

65. PRO, T 70/1556, George Glenny to African Committee, British Coal Tar Office, 7 July 1788; *Description of, and Directions for using the Different Kinds of Coal Tar and Varnish, prepared by the British Tar Company, at their Works, in Shropshire, Staffordshire, and in Scotland* (undated pamphlet, c.1780s), pp.1–15.

66. Haines, Shlomowitz, and Brennan, 'Maritime Mortality Revisited', pp.142–63.

67. Cited by Richard B. Sheridan, 'Sir William Young (1749–1815): Planter and Politician, with Special Reference to Slavery in the British West Indies' (unpublished paper, 1996). I am grateful to Professor Sheridan for providing a copy of this paper.

68. House of Lords Record Office, Main Papers, House of Lords, 28 July 1800, f.2; Society of Merchant Venturers, Bristol Muster Rolls, 1791–92, No.111.

69. James Veitch, *A Letter to the Commissioners for Transports, and Sick and Wounded Seamen, on the Non-Contagious Nature of the Yellow Fever; and Containing Hints to Officers, for the Prevention of this Disease Among Seamen* (London, 1818), pp.59–64.

70. Torrington (ed.), *Lords Sessional Papers, 1798–99*, III, p.102, evidence of Robert Hume.

71. Klein, *Middle Passage*, p.160.

72. I estimated a crude voyage efficiency index based on triangular voyage duration and the approximate number of slaves that Liverpool vessels loaded in 1780–1807. Based on the sample of Liverpool voyages in Table 4, the years of greatest 'efficiency' were 1782, 1781, and 1797, with ratios of 0.64, 0.85, and 0.88 voyage days/slaves loaded, respectively.

73. In a sample of British slave voyages sailing to the Gambia, only 22 of 103 voyages sailed from England in May–September, suggesting that captains tried to avoid arriving at the Gambia during the June–October rainy season. Efficiencies in slave marketing would determine whether the vessels could sail from the Gambia before the next seasonal rainfall.

74. Sheffield noted that the crew of a slave vessel set out to carry 500 slaves 'generally consists of 20 real seamen, and 30 or 40 landsmen, the very dregs and outcasts of the community; the real sailors are necessary for the navigation of the ship, the others are employed to attend the negroes on the coast and middle passage'. Lord John (Holroyd) Sheffield, *Observations on the Project for Abolishing the Slave Trade* (London, 1791), p.18.

'My own nation': Igbo Exiles in the Diaspora

DOUGLAS B. CHAMBERS

When Olaudah Equiano (c.1745–97) was taken on board the slave ship that carried him out of the Bight of Biafra he feared for his life. Everything he saw that day seemed to confirm these initial fears that the whites (whom he suspected were evil spirits) had acquired him in order to eat him or perhaps to sacrifice him to their gods. Equiano also saw, however, other people 'of my own nation' on board which, as he later remembered, 'in a small degree gave ease to my mind'. These people, whom he recognized as fellow 'natives of Eboe', or 'Eboan Africans', or simply 'my countrymen', told the young boy what little they knew: that 'we were to be carried to these white people's country to work for them'; that this country was a far distant one; that they had their own women there; and that the whites used 'some spell or magic they put in the water when they liked, in order to stop the vessel'.[1]

At the end of his Atlantic crossing, at Barbados in 1756, Equiano and his fellow slaves again feared that the whites were planning to eat them. These fears, Equiano reported, caused 'much dread and trembling among us, and nothing but bitter cries to be heard all the night'. Finally, the whites brought some 'old slaves from the land to pacify us'; these 'old slaves' had presumably not forgotten their natal language. Equiano wrote: 'They told us we were not to be eaten, but to work, and were soon to go on land, where we should see many of our country people. This report eased us much. And sure enough, soon after we landed, there came to us Africans of all languages.'[2]

Years later, in 1772, when he was a grown man, Equiano went to Kingston, Jamaica, where he was impressed by the numerous Africans he saw there, and especially how those people grouped themselves by their particular ethnicities during their free time. On Sundays, he noted, African slaves gathered in large numbers at a general meeting place outside of town. 'Here', wrote Equiano, 'each different nation of Africa meet and dance after the manner of their own country. They still retain most of their native customs; they bury their dead, and put victuals, pipes, and tobacco, and other things, in the grave with the corpse, in the same manner as in Africa.'[3]

Although Equiano did not mention seeing other Igbo among 'each different nation of Africa' in Jamaica, other near contemporaries did. In 1788 Captain Hugh Crow, who became a major trader at Bonny in 1791–1810, witnessed the public execution of an Igbo man in Jamaica. He reported that the man's 'Eboe friends continued to cheer him with the hope that he would return to his own country [after his death] until he was turned off the scaffold.'[4] Over twenty-five years later, Matthew Lewis, who kept a journal of his time in western Jamaica in 1815–17, observed how his slaves grouped themselves according to their ethnicity; he noted, for example, that one day he 'went down to the negro-houses to hear the whole body of Eboes lodge a complaint against one of the book-keepers'.[5] Even recent arrivals such as Lewis quickly learned to identify individual slaves by their African ethnicities. In one passage Lewis described a conflict between two of his adult male slaves named Pickle and Edward, both of whom were said to be 'Eboes'. Pickle, Lewis reported, had accused Edward of breaking into his house and stealing some of his goods. Upon being asked by Pickle to use 'obeah' to find where the stolen goods were, Edward was said to have gone out at midnight and to have collected the requisite herb and prepared it the proper way, but then, according to Pickle, to have used obeah to poison him rather than using it to find the stolen property as promised. As proof of being 'obeahed' by his fellow Igbo slave, Pickle claimed that 'he had a pain in his side, and, therefore, Edward must have given it to him'.[6]

The Argument

The Igbo peoples were a distinct ethno-historical group who shared a distinctive set of ancestral traditions and drew on the same or very similar material, social and ideological resources in order to adapt to the situations in which they commonly found themselves as slaves. They were a people whom modern scholars can study as a separate 'nation' in the transatlantic diaspora. The Igbo diaspora originated in the Nigerian hinterland of the Calabar coast and was immense, amounting to perhaps some 1.4 million people in the era of the Atlantic slave trade. About half, or some 750,000, of those forcibly shipped to the Americas left in the period from 1750 to 1807. For the most part, Igbo were shipped by the British and were taken to British America. The movement of Igbo had, therefore, important consequences for the historical development of a number of British American slave societies.

Although fiercely localistic in their home areas, Igbo-speaking peoples, once thrown into the diaspora, embraced a collective identity derived from being a member of 'my own nation'. As the English explorer, W.B. Baikie, put it in the 1850s, 'In I'gbo each person hails ... from the particular district where he was born, but when away from home all are I'gbos.'[7] When S.W. Koelle solicited information around 1850 from Igbo-speakers who had been 'recaptured' and sent by the British to Sierra Leone in the 1820s and 1830s, they told him that 'certain natives who have come from the Bight are called 'Ibos'. Koelle went on to note, however, that, in 'speaking to some of them respecting this name, I learned that they never had heard it till they came to Sierra Leone'. Before being thrown into the slave trade, he wrote, such people knew 'only the names of their respective districts or countries'.[8] Like Olaudah Equiano, once taken from their homeland, they came to see each other as fellow 'natives of Eboe' and members of 'my own nation'.

These various Igbo-speaking peoples in the Calabar backcountry were the main sources for the transatlantic slave trade from the Bight of Biafra. It is likely, or at least possible, that they comprised 80 per cent or more of the Africans loaded on European slave ships there.[9] The structure of the export trade in slaves from Calabar, in which Igboized coastal bigmen brokered exchanges between newly arrived European captains and a series of Igbo-speaking headmen in the interior villages, combined with certain other social and political changes to make Igbo-speaking peoples the region's principal source population for slaves.

The rise of a new meritocratic elite in the densely populated interior regions of Nri-Awka and Isuama, whose wealth was fuelled by the importation of commodity-currencies like iron bars and copper rods brought by new traders such as the Aro, encouraged the export of people as slaves.[10] The community-culture of Eboan society, with its mix of gerontocracy and meritocracy, of fatalism and localism, of *obia* (or 'doctoring') and *aja* ('sacrifice'), lent ideological support to a system of exchange that transferred large numbers of people as slaves to entrepôts on the coast.

Until recently, anthropologists and historians tended to emphasize the heterogeneity of social, cultural, and economic patterns of life in Igboland. The basic ethnographic sources, produced as adjuncts to the administration of twentieth-century British colonialism, stressed the multiplicity of sub-ethnic groups among the Igbo-speaking peoples. The most comprehensive ethnographer counted some 29 'sub-tribes' and 59 'clans'; another estimated that 'there must be at least 2,000 [distinctive] Ibo clans'.[11] The classic summary ethnological report of Forde and Jones documented five basic Igbo groups, with a total of 13 separate sub-groups.[12]

Earlier generations of historians tended to focus on the various mercantile city-states or village-groups that ringed Igboland, from the Niger mini-monarchies of Onitsha and Aboh, to the Delta polities (Brass-Nembe, New Kalabar, Bonny, Okrika, and later Opobo), and the trading towns of the Calabar (Cross) River, especially the group of settlements that made up Old Calabar.[13] More recently, however, and perhaps in response to a revival of 'traditional' Igbo culture in the wake of the 1967–1970 Nigerian Civil War, there has been a tendency to argue in favour of the homogeneous nature of a loosely definable pan-Igbo culture, and of placing the evolution of regional socio-cultural and political forms within the context of a broader Igbo history.[14]

The Numbers

In the whole era of the transatlantic slave trade, about one in seven Africans transported to the New World originated from the Bight of Biafra.[15] A review of recent secondary literature and classic primary sources suggests that, of the 11.6 million people estimated to have been shipped from Africa between 1470 and 1860, some 1.7 million were transported from the Bight of Biafra. Of these 1.7 million, about 1.2 million, or some 70 per cent, were taken during the period from 1700 to 1809. Taking the rather longer period from 1700 to 1840, it appears that 1.5 million people were loaded as slaves onto European ships at the Calabar coast. Assuming that only 50 per cent of those originally enslaved were actually shipped to America, this suggests that around 3 million people were enslaved and uprooted in the hinterland of the Bight of Biafra in the century and a half after 1700.[16] The contribution of the Bight of Biafra to the transatlantic slave trade rose sharply in this period, from approximately one-tenth of the traffic before 1750 to one-fifth of it in the following quarter century and one-fourth in the years from 1780 to 1809. The data upon which these calculations are made are presented in Tables 1 and 2.

TABLE 1
ESTIMATES OF THE NUMBER OF SLAVES EXPORTED, 1470–1867[17]
(FIGURES ROUNDED)

Years	Bight of Biafra	Africa
1470–1600	20,000	367,000
1601–1699	125,000	1,868,000
1700–1809	1,212,800	6,672,000
1811–1867	353,100	2,738,000
Total	1,710,900	11,645,000

Overall, I estimate that about 80 per cent of the people shipped from the Bight of Biafra as slaves were Igbo-speaking. Many of the others may well have been Igboized through long-term contact. The first slaves shipped from the region before 1650 were mostly Ijo and coastal non-Ijo such as Delta Edo, Ogoni, Andony, and Ibibio.[18] In the sixteenth and early seventeenth centuries when the Biafran export slave trade was very limited and largely based on the plundering of near delta villages by local warlords, non-Igbo were captured and sold in relatively high proportions. Pereira in 1508 identified the peoples of the rivers along the coast as 'Jos' (Ijos) without mentioning Igbo, and of the 17 communities of 'caravalies particulares' that in the early seventeenth century Sandoval mentioned by name, at least 11 can be identified as non-Igbo.[19] During the major period of slave exportation between the 1680s and 1830s, however, when the source of captives shifted steadily inland, the proportion of Igbo rose dramatically, perhaps reaching four out of five of the people shipped overseas as slaves. This suggests, as Table 3 reveals, that in total up to 1.4 million Igbo were put on European ships as slaves during the whole slave trade era.

TABLE 2

ESTIMATES OF SLAVES EXPORTED, BY PERIOD, 1470–1870

(ALL CARRIERS; FIGURES ROUNDED)

Years	Bight of Biafra	Average per Year	Africa	Percentage from Biafra
1470s–1600	20,000	200	367,000	5.5
1600–1650s	25,000	500	631,000	4.0
1660s–1699	100,000	2,500	1,237,000	8.0
1700–1749	273,600	5,500	2,430,000	11.3
1750–1779	409,100	13,600	2,083,000	19.6
1780–1809	530,100	17,700	2,159,000	24.6
1811–1840	333,700	11,100	1,962,000	17.0
1841–1870	19,400	970	776,000	2.5
Total	1,711,000		11,645,000	15.0

TABLE 3

IGBO EXPORTED IN CALABAR TRADE, 1470–1867[20]

Years	%	Number of Igbo
1470–1600	33	6,660
1600–1650s	50	12,500
1660s–1699	75	75,000
1700–1809	80	970,240
1811–1867	80	282,480
Total		1,346,880

As Table 4 shows, the vast majority of these Igbo were loaded on British ships and were thus bound for the British Americas. Of the estimated 1.2 million people exported from the Bight of Biafra in the period from 1700 to 1809, about 95 per cent were probably carried away on British ships. Put another way, it appears that during the eighteenth century the Bight of Biafra supplied over one-third of the Africans carried in British ships and that during the peak years of the Bight trade in 1750–1807, the region supplied over 40 per cent of the slaves of British ships (see Table 5). Assuming that Igbo constituted 80 per cent of those shipped, and that 20 per cent died in the Atlantic crossing, then it would seem, on the basis of the figures given in Table 4, that nearly 750,000 Igbo-speaking people reached the Americas in British ships between 1700 and 1807. The vast majority of these probably disembarked in the British Caribbean and North American mainland, thus accounting for perhaps a third of all slave arrivals in these colonies in this period. Such concentrations of Igbo arrivals had important consequences for the development of slavery and society in the era of revolution in British America.[21]

TABLE 4
BRITISH SLAVE TRADE FROM CALABAR 1700–1807

Years	Biafra	Igbo
1700–9	19,350	15,480
1710–19	44,820	35,856
1720–29	59,990	47,992
1730–39	61,330	49,064
1740–49	75,880	60,704
1750–59	104,050	83,240
1760–69	134,980	107,984
1770–79	151,120	120,896
1780–89	211,000	168,800
1790–99	170,070	136,056
1800–07	123,000	98,400
Total	1,155,590	924,472

Source: Richardson, 'Slave Exports', p.13.

TABLE 5
REGIONAL EXPORTS OF ENSLAVED ATLANTIC AFRICANS, 1700–1807

	Sene-gambia	Sierra Leone	Gold Coast	Bight of Benin	Bight of Biafra	West Central
1700–1749	144,860	60,470	201,190	110,210	261,370	311,460
1750–1779	43,210	276,420	88,610	88,250	390,150	94,200
1780–1807	5,520	146,920	118,660	34,840	504,070	233,860
Total	193,590	483,810	408,460	233,300	1,155,590	639,520
1750–1807	48,730	423,340	207,270	123,090	894,220	328,060

Source: Richardson, 'Slave Exports'.

Slaving in the Hinterland

The export slave trade of the Bight of Biafra reached further inland over the course of two centuries. In the sixteenth century, individual Kalabari and associated villages raided each other, with one village group, Agbaniye Ejika (Bile), remembered as the most disruptive and warlike. According to one historical anthropologist, 'Bile got its slaves by sacking neighbouring Delta villages, rather than by trade with the hinterland'.[22] The oral traditions mark the disruption of this early predatory period, and they contrast with the later expansion of New Calabar under King Amakiri I. Whereas the early Bile attacks had scattered villages, perhaps creating refugee settlements, in the seventeenth century New Calabar colonized other village groups and offered protection from the ravages of slave-raiding in return for acknowledgement of Elem Kalabari's suzerainty.[23] This small regional shift in power is remembered in the following extract from a twentieth-century popular song: 'Agbaniye Ejika ama fama te /Amachree ama paka mam' ['Agbaniye Ejika destroyed towns/Amachree founded towns'].[24]

The rise of Bonny in the late seventeenth and early eighteenth centuries was based on creating ties with interior Igbo peoples and cornering the market on trade with Europeans. Ibani principal men, who headed their own 'canoe-houses' under the paramountcy of one (or often two) local kings, apparently built their trade on their connections with Ndoki and Ngwa Igbo of eastern Isuama on the headwaters of the Imo River, initially for yams, later for slaves, and finally for palm-oil. The early Bonny king-lists emphasize that the immediate descendants of the culture-hero king, Asimini, who gained office by persuading the Europeans to trade at the town, were Ngwa Igbo. The oral histories relate that Asimini gave his daughter in marriage to one 'Opoli of Azuogu in the Ndoki country', and that she returned to rule Bonny as Queen Kambasa. Her son, Kumalu, whose name later was one commonly given to children in Ngwa-Igboland, succeeded her as king. The name 'Kumalo' suggests a ruthless, perhaps 'evil' ruler, and seems to evoke slave trading. All of this must have taken place in the seventeenth century, as these changes predated the Pepple (or Perekule) dynasties of the pre-colonial era. In the mid-nineteenth century, the Ibani still referred to the Ndoki as 'brothers'.[25]

Before it could benefit from the ties with Ngwa-Igboland, however, Bonny and its allies had to fight a series of wars to defeat the Kalabari, Okrika, Ogoni, and Andony peoples who occupied land between the sea and Isuama.[26] These conflicts are remembered in Bonny oral histories, which explain the rise of the littoral village-group in mythic terms. In order to 'widen the river' at Bonny point, the culture-hero Asimini was made to sacrifice a daughter, and thus started the rite of sacrificing a virgin woman every seven years in order to propitiate the god of the sea wind. The new cult of the war-god Ikuba, whose totem was the monitor lizard or *iguana* (as well as the 'house of skulls') which so fascinated European visitors in the eighteenth and nineteenth centuries, was also a function of Bonny's new reach into the interior.[27] Elem Kalabari traditions state that Bonny stole the European trade from them, and describe the process in terms of a conflict in spiritland between the tutelary gods, that is, Ikuba of Bonny and Owoamekaso of New Calabar:

> After Oruyingi (Mother of the gods) had given birth to all the gods of all *ibe* [named peoples] in the delta, she asked them to make requests for the benefit of their people. Owoamekaso asked for a book that would attract European ships to Elem Kalabari. After they left the presence of Oruyingi, Ikuba became jealous and tried to seize the book. In the ensuing struggle, Ikuba was able to make off with the larger fragment of the book, and so got the bigger ships calling at the port of Bonny, only smaller ships being able to go upstream to Elem Kalabari.[28]

As Map 1 illustrates, pre-colonial Igboland had three overlapping trade systems, each of which served to link people in the densely populated central plateaux with sources of outside goods that were controlled by various other peoples on the peripheries of the region. In the Niger system of cowrie-based canoe-trading, the mini-monarchies of Aboh, Asaba, and Ossomari rose out of trading villages and incorporated the cultural influences of Benin, Nri-Awka, and the non-Igbo Igalla, respectively.[29] In central and eastern Igboland, African brokers demanded payment in a distinctive assortment of trade-goods based on manillas (iron and/or copper ingots), iron bars and guns.[30] The early leading market-towns in central Igboland included Azumini, Obegu, and Ohuhu, all on the middle or upper reaches of the Imo River, whence merchants brokered trade with Igboized rulers at Kalabari, Bonny, and, by the 1820s, Opobo. To the east, the fierce itinerant Aro merchants, who were protected in their travels by the divine sanction of Chukwu (hence calling themselves *umuchukwu* or 'god boys'),[31] conducted slaves to the group of towns on the lower Cross River known collectively as 'Old Calabar'. Hailing from the oracle of Arochukwu, and relying on the muscle of their armed porters (and their relations) as much as on their reputation for retribution, the Aro ran major and minor fairs at villages all across Igboland in the eighteenth and nineteenth centuries.

The largest fairs, such as that at Bende in the mid-nineteenth century, lasted four days every twenty-fourth day (that is, one *izu* every three *izu ukwu*), and were scheduled so that traders making rounds could attend several of them in succession. Bende was said to be 'two to four days' journey north from Bonny', and in the mid-nineteenth century was,

MAP 1
EXTENT OF IGBO CULTURE

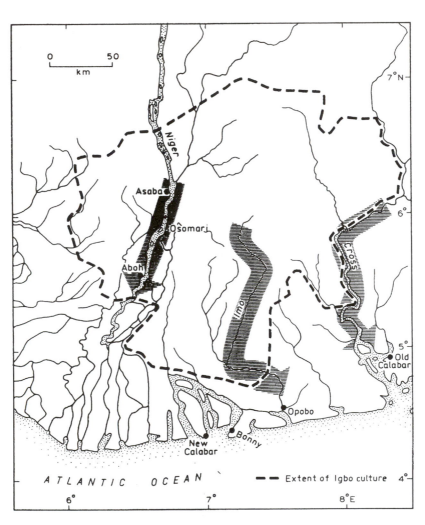

according to Baikie, 'a grand depot for slaves, as well as for palm-oil and provisions, and supplies with the former New Kalabar, Bonny, and Andony, as well as other neighbouring countries'. Baikie also noted that when the 'foreign slave trade was being actively carried on, this town was in the zenith of its wealth and importance, and even since has declined but little, as it still remains the centre of the home slave mart for the coast, and the south of I'gbo'.[32]

This Eboan world was one in which nothing happened by chance; leaving anything to chance was, therefore, dangerous.[33] Sacrifice was the principal way that people in historical Igboland attempted to create order out of the events of their individual and collective lives. Sacrifice, the ritual killing of consecrated victims, structured much of Eboan African ritual life. Igbo people understood that they sacrificed living things because the deities demanded it. The sacrifice was a prerequisite for gaining the benefits that came with 'feeding' a particular spirit; or it could be the means of placating a powerful spiritual being, a prerequisite for avoiding the wrath of capricious deities who constantly demanded attention. The more powerful the deity, or the more powerful the need for 'asking' (*a-juju*), the more valuable must be the sacrificial victim. Some sacrifices, called *ichu aja* (or 'joyless' sacrifice), were of worthless, disfigured or ugly things, such as rotten eggs, sick chickens, aborted lambs, or lizards. Such sacrifices were made specifically to distract otherwise malevolent spirits, 'much as a dangerous dog is given a bone to keep it busy'.[34] The most specialized sacrifices were to remove the 'abomination' of having violated a taboo (*nso*), usually thought of as a transgression against *Ani* (the ground or Earth Deity), and therefore requiring the services of an Nri-man, because the *ndi Nri* were the only people with the power to remove such pollution. More generally, Igbo sacrificed regularly to the ancestors (*ndi ichie*) and the spirits (*ndi muo*), offering not just libations at every meal but at periodic personal and collective rites, at times of misfortune, or at funerals, festivals, harvests, and other calendrical events. At Bonny in the 1820s, for example, the people performed sacrifices 'at different periods, which are governed by the Moon'. At such events they would 'offer up Goats & Fowls as a sacrifice to their departed Progenitors, & the more especially if they had performed any signal achievements'. At one large festival at Bonny in 1826, when the king distributed rum, cloth, beads and brass manillas to the general population, 'Goats, Dogs & Fowls were sacrificed in immense numbers – long poles on which were suspended dead carcuses [*sic*] of the canine race met the eye at every turn.'[35]

In his narrative, Equiano recounted that sacrifices were made all the time. He remembered that they marked special events, especially for thanksgiving and were most often were done by the lineage heads (*okpala*) and other leading men:

They have many offerings, particularly at full moons; generally two at harvest before the fruits are taken out of the ground: and when any young animals are killed, sometimes they offer up part of them as a sacrifice. These offerings, when made by one of the heads of a family, serve for the whole. I remember we often had them at my father's and my uncle's, and their families have been present. Some of our offerings are eaten with bitter herbs. We had a saying among us to any one of a cross temper, 'That if they were to be eaten, they should be eaten with bitter herbs'.[36]

The *dibia*'s control over 'medicine' (*ogwu*) and his ability to communicate with the spirits to find out what to 'feed' them may have made them increasingly important in Igbo life as contact with Aro traders intensified in the eighteenth and nineteenth centuries. In fact, *dibia* may have played a major role in the increasing use of oracles and petitions to *Chukwu* and in relations with the Arochukwu, and therefore in the displacement of the older Nri hegemony with a new one based on petitioning (*a-juju*) and sacrifice (*aja*). This is evident especially in the contrast between the pacifist role of the Nri, one of whose main functions was to remove the abomination caused by the shedding of human blood, and a secondary function of *dibia* which was to provide the special *ogwu* that facilitated warfare.

The rise of *dibia* to great power throughout Igboland in the era of the slave trade, however, may have come in part from arrogating the ability to 'sacrifice' humans, and then having them sent away instead of having them killed (and thus avoiding the required intervention by an Nri-man). Just as a successful sacrifice to the spirits was signalled by the appearance of vultures who carried the sacrifice to the *muo* world, so may have the appearance of Aro and other interior traders demanding people in order to please and placate them seem like the vultures sent by the spirits for a sacrifice.[37]

It should be noted, moreover, that *dibia* and *juju* were closely connected with the secret-societies and masquerades, whose members generally were the most powerful in the village and village-group. The only other figure that would have had the kind of authority to send people away would have been each compound's headman or the *okpara*, or the *ndi Nri*, but it is likely that the secret-societies and *Mmuo* (or masquerades) were instrumental in such seizures. Not only could the powerful local men act with impunity and anonymity in *Mmuo*, and with the sanction of the local *dibia*, but they were precisely the ones who had the personal connections with outside long-distance traders.

Walter Rodney may have been right, therefore, to argue that the export of slaves tended to increase social exploitation within source areas, but, as far as historical Igboland is concerned, he would be surprised to find that the form such exploitation took was 'traditional'.[38] The question arises, however, did the people who were seized or sent away see themselves as outcasts or exiles? Did they turn their collective backs on things and ways Eboan, or did they strive to re-create as much of their Eboan African world as they could in the new worlds that they entered after the Atlantic crossing? But first, where did these diasporic Igbo go?

Destinations

Up to 20 per cent of the slaves embarked in the Bight of Biafra, as the paper by Klein and Engerman in this volume shows, died before reaching America. Moreover, in the nineteenth century, significant numbers of Igbo, amounting to at least 30,000 between 1821 and 1839 alone, were landed at Sierra Leone. Retaken by anti-slave trade patrols, these 'recaptured' Igbo have been little studied even though European explorers and Christian missionaries of the 1840s and 1850s relied on Sierra Leonean Igbo as guides and translators during their initial ventures up the Niger and Cross rivers.[39]

As noted earlier, however, probably about 750,000 Igbo reached the Americas between 1700 and 1809. As the British dominated slave shipments from the Bight of Biafra in this period, it seems reasonable to assume that most landed in the Anglophone Caribbean. Since Igbo were widely regarded as unsatisfactory slaves by their European masters, it is possible that disproportionate numbers of them were sold in the more marginal regions of plantation agriculture in the New World. This seems to have been the case in the French colonies, where, according to David Geggus, 'Igbo slaves, in large measure females, show up disproportionately in Guadeloupe and the least-developed parts of Saint Domingue.'[40] By contrast, slaves from the Slave Coast (Ewe, Fon and others), who were usually regarded with greater favour by planters, tended to be shipped to the prime areas of French Caribbean sugar-production. Whether this pattern was replicated in the British colonies is uncertain, but, if it was, then one might anticipate that, in the first half of the eighteenth century, relatively few Igbo went to Jamaica, Antigua, and St Kitts, where sugar production was expanding vigorously, and relatively large numbers went to Barbados, where sugar production was stagnating, the Bahamas, and the mainland North America, especially the Chesapeake. After 1760, when the tide of Igbo exiles was at its height, it is likely that Igbo were shipped in relatively large numbers to the islands of the Lesser Antilles and to areas around Montego Bay and Savannah la Mar in western Jamaica.[41]

While the precise pattern of Igbo arrivals in the Americas has yet to be determined, scholars are beginning to identify those parts of Anglophone and Francophone America where one might anticipate discovering a major Igbo presence in the diaspora. It is believed that in the eighteenth century, the Chesapeake, the Bahamas and Leeward Islands, and Jamaica were probably the most common destinations of diasporic Igbo. Scholars have noted the striking similarities in Atlantic creole languages, especially in the Anglophone Americas, as well as the wide distribution of certain elements of slave culture, including *obeah, jonkonu* (especially the so-called root version with its associated cow-horn and ragman maskers, and 'gambys' or box-drums), and the term *buckra*. Given that in 1750–1807 British planters received probably twice as many Igbo as any other African ethno-historical group (and perhaps four times the number of people from Gold Coast),[42] it is important to investigate how the Igbo ethnicity of those arriving from the Bight of Biafra contributed to the 'bricolage' and historical development of the various Afro-Caribbean slave societies in the British Americas.

Igboization

In some colonies such as the Chesapeake piedmont in the second quarter of the eighteenth century Igbo forced migrants were 'first-comers'. In such cases, they set the basic patterns of material, social and ideological culture of enslaved communities to which succeeding waves of saltwater (for example, Western Bantu and Mande) and creole (or tidewater) slaves acculturated. In other colonies such as post-1750 Jamaica Igbo were 'second-comers' who 'Igboized' existing institutions and cultural patterns as people drew on ancestral material, social and ideological resources in order to adapt both to slavery and to the culture of slaves already there. In both cases, Igbo made use of what they had at hand to fashion what they needed in order to sustain themselves, to forge connections amongst and between each other, and to make sense of their new worlds. This African-derived process of *bricolage* was one of mixing and matching, of adapting and adopting a combination of new and old ways of doing and of being, and often resulted in Igboesque regional 'common traditions'.[43]

Examples of Igboisms

We can see evidence of Igboization in the food ways, power ways, and magic ways of slaves in Anglophone American slave societies.[44] These various Igboesque artifacts suggest the range of material, social and ideological resources on which enslaved Eboan Africans drew in order to adapt to slavery.

Masters generally provided their slaves with only the barest essentials needed to shelter, feed and clothe the people. Many slaves, therefore, had their own provisioning grounds, whether kitchen gardens, house-yards or outlying plots, where they grew their own fruits and vegetables. One of the most common slave-grown vegetables was *Hibiscus esculentus*, whose podlike fruit was a staple of slaves' 'one-pot' cooking practices. Slaves used okra to thicken stews and soups, and the mucilaginous vegetable practically represented slave (and, in the United States, southern) food ways.[45]

'Okra' was an Igbo word (*okro*).[46] People in other parts of western Africa knew and grew the vegetable, called 'nkru-ma' in Twi and variations of '–ngombo' in Western Bantu languages. But it was Igbo people who brought the most common name of 'okra' into English. The word appeared in English dictionaries in the eighteenth century, notably the Oxford English Dictionary (1707, 1756 editions), although the plant remained largely unknown to whites until the nineteenth century. Thomas Jefferson, for example, did not have okra grown in his garden until 1809.[47]

The vegetal part of the basket of African-American 'soul food' indicates a strong Igbo presence in Anglophone slave food ways. Most notable were 'yams' (both *Dioscorea* and *Ipomoea batatas*); black-eyed peas (or cowpeas) *Vigna unguicuilata*); 'greens' (*Brassica sp.*); watermelon (*Citrullus vulgaris*); and eggplant (*Solanum melongena*). The last was also known as 'Guinea squash' in Virginia around 1800, but whites did not eat it.[48] In the nineteenth and early twentieth centuries in Igboland, the basic kitchen crops were yams, black-eyed peas, greens, squashes, pumpkins, and okra and watermelons, as well as gourds and groundnuts and Guinea squash, and coco-yams, plantains and bananas (but not cassava).[49] In the diaspora, Igbo continued to grow yams and maintained nearly all the secondary subsistence crops of their ancestral village agriculture except for coco-yam, plantains, bananas, and papaws (or papayas). The loss of plantains and bananas seems to have been made up with maize and meal, while butter and lard replaced palm-oil and cayenne replaced melegueta pepper. Okra, associated with fertility as well as with proverbial knowledge in some parts of pre-colonial Igboland, black-eyed peas (which in the south of the United States are still reputed to bring good luck if eaten on New Year's Day), and squashes, watermelons, gourds, 'greens', and other forms of material culture quickly reappeared and remained as staples of African-American slave food ways.[50]

There is also clear evidence of Igboization in slave power ways. Fischer has defined power ways as 'attitudes toward authority and power' and 'patterns of political participation'.[51] Slaves in Anglophone America drew on similar social resources to order their individual and collective lives. Although the influence of Akan on the Maroons of eighteenth-century Jamaica has attracted much attention from historians, there is evidence of a clear Igbo influence on those who stayed on the local plantations. The world of the plantation was essentially divided into two largely separate spheres; that of the whites and that of the slaves.[52] In the British Atlantic, whites learned to call blacks 'niggers' and slaves learned to call their masters (and other whites) 'buckra'. The widespread use of the latter term reflected the ubiquity of Igbo peoples in the diaspora or, for slaves of other ethnicity, the utility of Igboesque ways of defining whites. Although derived from the Ibibio *mbakara* (*mb-* plural; *-kara*, to encircle, rule, abuse, master, understand), slaves everywhere in Anglophone America used the term to denote 'white folk'.[53] It was Igbo people who brought the term into English as *buckra*, and perhaps also supplied the social subtext of seeing the white man as 'he who surrounds or governs' or as a 'demon, powerful and superior being'.[54] Or, as a slave saying from South Carolina in the 1770s put it, 'Da buccary no be good fatru' ('That white man is not good, to be sure').[55]

How did Igboized slaves perceive the *buckra*? Monica Schuler has provocatively suggested that, in Jamaica at least, many slaves 'defined slaveowners as sorcerers' because of the slaves' common conviction that sorcery had played a prominent role in their original enslavement.[56] There is good evidence to support such a supposition, at least in terms of the initial interpretation that many West Africans had of Europeans as spirits and *juju*s. For example John Jea, who had been born in 1773 in Old Calabar and then taken to New York as a slave remembered that he and his parents 'were often led away with the idea that our masters were our gods; and at other times we placed our ideas on the sun, moon, and stars, looking unto them, as if they could save us'.[57] In general, however, one may suggest that many of the slaves saw the *buckra* in Igboesque terms, that is, as *eze* (masters) or as little kings. As a missionary resident in Onitsha in the 1850s explained, '*Eze* literally means "Master", and is applied to kings and to those who are in an important office'.[58] Just as *eze* were spiritually and materially powerful beings who could lord it over the people and yet were subject to the *omenani* or customs of the place, so slaves saw their masters as cruel and yet bound by customary law. Furthermore, slaves everywhere routinely addressed not just their owners but all *buckra* with the ritual salutation of some variation of 'master', whether 'massa', 'mossa', 'marster', or 'marse'. It may well be that Igboized slaves appropriated familiar political terms to make sense of their masters' formal powers over them, even as they were coerced into signifying their own subordination.

One may also see how an Igboesque political consciousness contributed to the importance of resistance rather than rebellion in the slave worlds of the British Americas. It is perhaps not without significance that successful slave revolts – whether in seventeenth-century Palmares, among the Maroons of eighteenth-century Jamaica, in St. Domingue in the 1790s, or in

Bahia in the 1830s – tended to occur in areas with relatively few Igbo. By contrast, in places such as the Chesapeake and western Jamaica, where there was a strong Igbo presence, slaves tended to resort to resistance within small-scale communities to force the *buckra* to abide by unwritten but well-known plantation customs. Such customs (Igbo *omenani*) varied from place to place but shared many core elements; these included two days off, abroad spouses, 'negro daytime', basic rations, and individual compounds. The growth of plantation customs also contributed to the shift from corporal punishment to systems of discipline and incentives.[59] In the more marginal areas where planters routinely subdivided their slave holdings into plantations, farms and quarters, Igbo concepts of localism, dual division and segmentary social relations would have been adaptive for Igboesque communities, with the incidental consequence of discouraging large-scale revolutionary movements.

Igboized slaves drew on other Eboan African institutions to forge their own power ways and regulate their own lives. The best known (and perhaps least understood) was the common Anglophone slave masquerade, *jonkonu*. Generally given a Gold Coast provenance, this slave social fact was more likely an artifact of Igbo people in the diaspora.[60] This is suggested by the association of *jonkonu* (the 'root' version, that is) with 'gambys', or box-drums, instruments that Matthew Lewis in 1815–17 called 'Eboe drums'. *Jonkonu* is also associated with cow-horn and other animal masks as well as distinctive peaked-hat masks, many of which are nearly identical to mid-twentieth century Kalabari ones. Moreover, the development of *jonkonu* in its Afro-Caribbean form seems to have occurred between 1750 and 1830 when arrivals of Igbos were at their greatest. Such evidence points, therefore, towards Igboland as the primary source of *jonkonu* in Anglophone America.[61]

Two important institutions in historical Igboland were *njokku* (or *ifejioku*), the 'Yam spirit cult', and the yam-associated *okonko* (men's clubs). The latter was the southern Igbo secret society equivalent of the Efik *ekpe* society. Nineteenth-century sources attest to animal- and ragman-maskers in Bonny and Elem Kalabari, and these appear very similar to 'root *jonkonu*' and not unlike the twentieth-century northern Igbo *Omabe* and *Odo* masquerades.[62] It is likely that diasporic Igbo combined these essentially shared traditions into a creole institution. Whites came to call the Christmas-time masquerade 'John Konnu' because that is what the slaves chanted or yelled during the visitation of *njokku*; the rest of the year it may have served as a kind of men's club. So-called 'root' *jonkonu* was a male preserve whose leader wielded a whip or stick in association with fierce animal-masked others. From an Igboesque perspective, we can imagine that what slaves got was an annual visitation by *njokku* in *mmuo* (fearsome masking); those who participated as maskers gained honour and prestige within the slave community. To those enslaved, therefore, *jonkonu* may have been an internal means of establishing status and hierarchy among the slave men independently of any of their relations, occupational or otherwise, with whites, or even with women. The slaves then masked its importance by turning it into a Christmas-time buffoonery for the *buckra*'s viewing. During the rest of the year, though, it may have had a much more serious purpose.

Another important Afro-Caribbean slave artifact, the system of 'doctoring' called 'obeah', points finally towards an Igbo presence in the ideological domain of slave community-culture. Igbo slaves drew on ancestral ideological resources to make sense of their new world and in the process 'Igboized' slave religious traditions throughout British America.

Because of its association with Jamaican slave communities, Afro-Caribbean obeah, like *jonkonu*, has tended to be given an Akan provenance.[63] This may, however, be misleading, for the functions of obeah men and obeah women in the third quarter of the eighteenth century were similar to those of the *ndi obea* (or *dibia*) of pre-colonial Igboland. In the West Indies, as Edward Long explained in 1774, obeah men were 'consulted upon all occasions in order to revenge injuries and insults, discover and punish thieves and adulterers; to predict the future, and for the conciliation of favour'.[64] As in Igboland, therefore, obeah men (and sometimes women) in the Caribbean were diviners, doctors, and petitioners who specialized in finding out why things happened in daily life and in determining what needed to be done to placate the gods in given situations. In short, they were *juju*-men *par excellence*.

In historical Igboland, the *dibia* or *obea* was the person, usually a man, who could communicate directly with the spirits. Known across Igboland and the heavily Igboesque coastal settlements as powerful and dangerous, and thus both feared and respected everywhere, such 'doctors' provide the most common link between the visible and the invisible worlds. Privy to secret information, purportedly including a separate ritual language, and often idiosyncratic in their own lives (and thus thought to be gifted or 'touched'), *dibia* combined their sacred knowledge of the spirit-world with a practical pharmacological knowledge. The latter presumably required them to spend time in the forest collecting herbs, to divine what ailed individuals, to determine the necessary remedies, and then to apply them. Not only were 'Oboe doctors, or Dibbeah' able to 'cure diseases by charms'; they could 'foretell things to come, and discover secrets' as well.[65]

The various magical and religious characteristics of *dibia* seem to have changed very little in Igboland between the 1750s and the 1920s. In southern Igboland, an 'Ibo chief' told P.A. Talbot in the 1920s that 'With our people a native doctor is called Onye *Dibia*. All know witchcraft, but some are good and only make medicine to help men. Others can make both bad and good medicine and yet others only busy themselves with bad ones...Every Onye *Dibia* has great power, because everyone fears to offend him on account of his medicines.'[66] Seventy years earlier, at Onitsha, it was said that 'the doctor, or priest, called *Dibia*, is another person of consequence, and is very much feared by the people. He has a great sway over the people, from his pretension to be able to foretell things to come, and discover secrets'.[67] At Bonny in the early 1800s, *dibia* were said to combine the sacred and the profane and through their powers held 'the populace in the most absolute awe and subjection'. The author of such remarks, Hugh Crow, also emphasized the curative medical abilities of *dibia*, and wrote that although 'they apply certain remedies, chiefly decoctions of herbs and cupping, which they perform with a small calabash, after having made incisions, they depend upon charms, in a great measure, for relief'.[68] In his vivid description of *dibia* medicine, Crow went on to reveal the role of sacrifice in their curing rites. Thus he noted that, after killing a male fowl by slitting its throat, the *dibia* 'then threw himself into many strange postures, and while muttering some incantations over the sick men, he sprinkled the blood on their heads'. Presumably the *dibia* also applied some physical medicine, for Crow noted that in general *dibia* 'make much use of pod pepper, palm oil and various kinds of herbs for the cure of diseases'.[69]

Remembering his childhood in the 1750s near present-day Orlu in Isuama and within the Nri/Awka cultural ambit,[70] Olaudah Equiano in 1789 provided a description of *dibia* similar to Crow's, although Equiano seemed to conflate the work of *dibia* with that of another major group of ritual specialists, the *atama* or Nri-men. Equiano wrote:

> Though we had no places of public worship, we had priests and magicians, or wise men. I do not remember whether they had different offices, or whether they were united in the same persons, but they were held in great reverence by the people. They calculated our time, and foretold events ... These magicians were also our doctors or physicians. They practised bleeding by cupping, and were very successful in healing wounds and expelling poisons. They had likewise some extraordinary method of discovering jealousy, theft, and poisoning ...[which] is still used by the negroes in the West Indies.'[71]

In short, therefore, the *dibia* or *ndi obea* in historical Igboland and the 'obeahmen' of pre-modern Afro-Caribbean societies were responsible for ascertaining why things happened, remedying or influencing them, and punishing transgressors. They also provided other things such as war-medicine to protect those who would shed human blood. The world of the invisibles was as real to diasporic Igbo as it had been in Eboan Africa, because those hosts of invisibles had also survived the Atlantic crossing. Eboan peoples drew on this ancestral tradition of the *dibia* to make sense of their new world, calling it by the Igbo variant of *obea*, and in the process adding a major Igboesque artifact to the religious bricolage of slaves in British America.

Ethnogenesis

The Igboization of enslaved African-American communities in the era of the transatlantic slave trade, and the essential reality of Igbo as a nation in the diaspora, begs the question of ethnogenesis. In particular, to what extent can we see the construction of 'Igbo' peoples as a function of slave trading? After all, Olaudah Equiano, like hundreds of thousands of others from the hinterland of the Bight of Biafra, first learned to call himself Igbo only after he had been taken out of Eboan Africa. Equiano recognized his countrymen in places as diverse as Barbados, Jamaica and London. In the nineteenth century Koelle's Sierra Leone informants were quite explicit in observing that they never heard the term until they were sent or taken away. Scholars of African history have emphasized the colonial era and the role of European administration in the construction of pan-ethnic or meta-ethnic identities. If Equiano and Koelle's informants are to be believed, however, we perhaps need to look to an earlier era to see the historical creation of 'nations', Igbo included, as an integral part of the process of enslavement and entry into the diaspora.

Conclusion

It is the contention of this paper that the ethnicity of Africans thrown by force or by force of circumstance into the diaspora affected (and effected) the historical development of regional slave cultures in the Americas. The ancestral traditions they brought with them across the Atlantic continued to inform their 'secret lives' in the early slave communities. Assuming that the experience of the Atlantic crossing and adjustment to slavery, painful and traumatic as it undoubtedly was, did not obliterate the identities, memory, beliefs and customs of the Africans forced into the diaspora, it is important to examine how those who survived the crossing drew on ethnic-African material, social and ideological resources to adapt to slavery in their new worlds.

As Monica Schuler has noted for the Caribbean, the natural response to this uprooting of people was for them to associate with others of their own specific ethnicity or nation, that is, for people to 're-group' in order to confront the challenges of being slaves. It now appears that the transatlantic slave trade was not so random and randomizing as was once thought.[72] As John Thornton has shown for the seventeenth century and this author has suggested elsewhere for later periods,[73] the organization of Atlantic slave trading perhaps tended to concentrate rather than disperse African ethnic groups. The vast outpouring of literature in the last twenty years on the numbers, origins and destinations of Africans shipped to the Americas promises to provide powerful new tools to identify and describe the historical significance of particular African ethnicities in the various regional cultures of slaves in the Americas.[74] Moreover, one could argue that, in certain respects, these African ethnicities or 'nations' were a product of the trade in slaves.

When Olaudah Equiano published his memoirs in 1789, he included his Igbo name in the manuscript's title and referred to himself as 'the African'. And when he summarized the first chapter of his life's story, as 'some account of the manners and customs of my country', he specifically wanted his audience to know that,

> They had been implanted in me with great care, and made an impression on my mind, which time could not erase, and which all the adversity of fortune I have since experienced served to rivet and record...I still look back with pleasure on the first scenes of my life, though that pleasure has been for the most part mingled with sorrow.[75]

Equiano's own personal diaspora transformed his identity from that of a member of a particular kindred in a local village-group in 'Eboan Africa' to being one of many 'natives of Eboe'. His forced migration did not make him an outcast, but an exile from his 'own nation'.

ACKNOWLEDGEMENTS

The author wishes to thank James Walvin and Maureen Warner-Lewis for their encouragement and Joseph C. Miller, Paul Lovejoy, and David Richardson for their suggestions and comments on earlier drafts of this article.

NOTES

1. Olaudah Equiano, *The Interesting Narrative of the Life of Olaudah Equiano, Written by Himself*, ed. Robert J. Allison (original edition, 1789; Boston, 1995 edition), pp.54–5. For other examples of Equiano's use of 'my own nation' or similar phrases, see ibid., pp.39, 45, 50.
2. Ibid., p.57.
3. Ibid., p.145.
4. Captain Hugh Crow, *Memoirs of the late Captain Hugh Crow, of Liverpool* (1830; London, 1970 edition), p.26.

5. Matthew G. Lewis, *Journal of a West India Proprietor* (London, 1834), p.129.
6. Ibid., pp.133–4 (emphasis in original).
7. William Balfour Baikie, *Narrative of an Exploring Voyage up the Rivers Kwora and Binue* (1856; London, 1966 edition), p.307.
8. Reverend Sigismund W. Koelle, *Polyglotta Africana*, ed. P.E.H. Hair (1854; Graz, Austria, 1963 edition), pp.7–8. See also Margaret M. Green, 'Igbo Dialects in the *Polyglotta Africana*', *African Language Review*, 6 (1967), pp.111–19.
9. Cf. Northrup, who suggests that 60 per cent were Igbo and Inikori who suggests that only one-third were Igbo; David Northrup, *Trade without Rulers: Pre-colonial Economic Development in South-eastern Nigeria* (Oxford, 1978), pp.60–2; J.E. Inikori, 'The Sources of Supply for the Atlantic Slave Exports from the Bight of Benin and the Bight of Bonny (Biafra)', in Serge Daget (ed.), *De la Traite a l'Esclavage: Acts du Colloque International sur la Traite des Noirs*, 3 vols. (Nantes, 1988), II, p.35. Recently Obichère has suggested that Igbo were not the actual source population, and argues that Idoma and Tiv were, but he offers no real evidence to support this; Boniface Obichère, 'Slavery and the Slave Trade in the Niger Delta Cross River Basin', in Daget (ed.), *De la Traite*, II, p.50. Obichère's argument is also supported by A.E. Afigbo; see Inikori, 'Sources of Supply', p.35n.
10. For discussion of the role of commodity-currencies in the transatlantic slave trade from West-Central Africa, see J.C. Miller, *Way of Death: Merchant Capitalism and the Angolan Slave Trade, 1730–1830* (Madison, Wisconsin, 1988), pp.71–104.
11. C.K. Meek, *Law and Authority in a Nigerian Tribe: a Study in Indirect Rule* (1937; New York, 1970 edition), pp.3–4.
12. Daryll Forde and G.I. Jones, *The Ibo and Ibibio-speaking Peoples of South-eastern Nigeria* (London, 1950), passim; cf. Baikie, who in the 1850s recognized four major groups and six or seven other major sub-groups, with a number of lesser districts or places; Baikie, *Narrative*, pp.308–11.
13. Ebiegberi J. Alagoa and Adadonye Fombo, *A Chronicle of Grand Bonny* (Ibadan, Nigeria, 1972), pp.3–16; Ebiegberi J. Alagoa, *A History of the Niger Delta: an Historical Interpretation of Ijo Oral Tradition* (Ibadan, Nigeria, 1972), pp.123–71; G.I. Jones, *The Trading States of the Oil Rivers: a Study of Political Development in Eastern Nigeria* (London, 1963), pp.9–48.
14. Elizabeth Isichei, *A History of the Igbo Peoples* (London, 1976); idem, *A History of Nigeria* (London, 1983); A.E. Afigbo, *Ropes of Sand: Studies in Igbo History and Culture* (Ibadan, Nigeria, 1981); M. Angulu Onwuejeogwu, *An Igbo Civilization: Nri Kingdom and Hegemony* (London, 1981); John N. Oriji, *Traditions of Igbo Origin: a Study of Pre-colonial Population Movement in Africa* (New York, 1990); Don C. Ohadike, *Anioma: A Social History of the Western Igbo People* (Athens, Ohio, 1994).
15. See David Eltis and David Richardson, 'West Africa and the Transatlantic Slave Trade: New Evidence on Long Run Trends', in this volume.
16. On losses before shipment from the coast, see Miller, *Way of Death*, pp.379–442; Inikori, 'Sources of Supply', pp.31–2. Northrup suggested that about 1 million slaves were shipped from the Bight; Northrup, *Trade without Rulers*, pp.54–7.
17. The total African export figures for 1470s–1699 are based on Paul E. Lovejoy, 'The Volume of the Atlantic Slave Trade: A Synthesis', *Journal of African History*, 23 (1982), pp.478, 480–1; for 1700–1809 based on Richardson, 'Slave Exports', p.17; and for 1811–1870, on David Eltis, *Economic Growth and the Ending of the Transatlantic Slave Trade* (New York, 1987), pp.249, 250–2. The Bight of Biafra estimates for 1470s–1600 are arbitrary (simply an average of 200 per year for 100 years), but reflect Pereira (c.1508); Alonso Sandoval, *De Instauranda Aethiopum Salute* (1627; Begotá, 1956 ed.); Northrup, *Trade without Rulers*, pp.50–1. For the 1600–1659, it again is arbitrary, simply an average of 500 per year for 60 years, but reflects Johannes M. Postma, *The Dutch in the Atlantic Slave Trade 1600–1815* (Cambridge, 1990), pp.1–25, 56–83, 106–25. For 1660–1699 the number assumes increases from 1,000 to 4,000 a year over four decades and is based on Northrup, *Trade without Rulers*, pp.52–4; Postma, *Dutch in the Atlantic Slave Trade*, pp.106–25. The figures for 1700–1809 are from Richardson, 'Slave Exports'; for 1811–1870 from Eltis, *Economic Growth*.
18. Alagoa, *Niger Delta*, pp.10–16; Jones, *Oil Rivers*, pp.12–13. The fact that the twentieth-

century 'complexity of the language map of the Niger Delta' (Alagoa, *Niger Delta*, p.16) largely mirrors a similar complexity in the seventeenth century powerfully supports Hair's thesis of the 'ethnolinguistic continuity' of the Guinea Coast; see P.E.H. Hair, 'An Ethnolinguistic Inventory of the Lower Guinea Coast before 1700: part I', *African Language Review*, 7 (1968), pp.47–73 and part II, *African Language Review*, 8 (1969), pp.225–56.

19. Pereira wrote: 'ha outros negros que ham nome Jos e possuem grande terra e sam jente belicosa e comem os homees...Rio dos Ramos...A jente desta terra sam chamados Jos...Rio de Sam Bento...Rio de Sant 'Ilefonso...Rio de Santa Barbara...Rio Pequeno...estes quatros Rios...sam abitados d'aquelles povoos a que chaman Jos...Rio Real...A jente d'este Rio sam chamados Jos; estes e os de que atras falamos, todos sam huus e todos comem carne humana...', cited in Hair, 'Ethnolinguistic Inventory, part II', p.250n. See also Alonso Sandoval, *De Instauranda*, p.94; and also the listing of Ijo and non-Ijo groups in Jones, *Oil Rivers*, pp.12–13.

20. Numbers from Richardson, 'Slave Exports', p.17. The Bight of Biafra numbers that he gives, however, are only the British and French trades. I would guess that the smaller European national slave trades, including the Brandenburgers, Danes, Swedes and, after 1750, the Dutch, as well as the 'Portuguese' (Brazilian) and Spanish (Cuban, Puerto Rican, Louisiana) trades all would have drawn slaves from Calabar. The point is that the numbers should be considered a conservative estimate, and perhaps 10 to 25 per cent too low.

21. The era was best defined by David Brion Davis, *The Problem of Slavery in the Age of Revolution 1770–1823* (Ithaca, 1975). The general Igbo reputation for being 'bad' slaves who tended to run away or shirk work must have played a role in the social relations of slavery in that era, when so many Igbo were flowing into British colonies.

22. This was based on 'oral traditions and corroborative material evidence (captured sacred tusks)' collected by Robin Horton, presumably in the 1950s; cited in Hair, 'Ethnolinguistic Inventory, part II', p.252n.

23. Perhaps this led to the modern distinction between the 'true' and 'affiliated' Kalabari. The traditions acknowledge that Elem Kalabari also subjugated peoples like the Engenni by force of arms; see Alagoa, *Niger Delta*, pp.139–40.

24. Alagoa, *Niger Delta*, pp.138–9. In fact, as the slave trade expanded into the interior, the slave trade places shifted coastwise, from Bile and New Kalabar eastward to Bonny, and later, Opobo.

25. In the twentieth century, Ndoki and Ibani used the phrase 'Amina mina' ('brothers') to refer to each other; Alagoa and Fombo, *Grand Bonny*, pp.7–16, 74; Baikie, *Narrative*, p.438; Oriji, *Traditions of Igbo Origins*, pp.157–9. Baikie (*Narrative*, pp.314–15) related that in Igboland 'the greatest or worst of evil spirits, is named *Kamallo*, possibly equivalent with Satan. His name is frequently bestowed on children, and in some parts of I'gbo, especially in Isuama, Kamallo is worshipped. No images are made, but a hut is set apart, in which are kept bones, pieces of iron, &c., as sacred. Persons make inquiries of this spirit, if they wish to commit any wicked action, such as murder, when they bring presents of cowries and cloth to propitiate this evil being and render him favourable to their designs'. He also wrote that '*Kamallo* means "one going about everywhere and in all directions"'.

26. Alagoa, *Niger Delta*, pp.153–7.

27. Ibid., pp.154, 156–7; see also Baikie, *Narrative*, p.337; Crow, *Memoirs*, p.212; Richard M. Jackson, *Journal of a Voyage to Bonny River on the West Coast of Africa*, ed. Roland Jackson (Letchworth, 1934), p.68; Alexander Falconbridge, *An Account of the Slave Trade on the Coast of Africa* (1788; New York, 1973 edition), p.51. Drawing on classical Greek mythology to interpret Bonny practices, Crow described the seven-year sacrifice as 'a propitiatory offering to Boreas, the god of the north wind' (*Memoirs*, p.83).

28. Alagoa, *Niger Delta*, p.141.

29. Richard N. Henderson, *The King in Every Man: Evolutionary Trends in Onitsha Ibo Society and Culture* (New Haven, 1972).

30. For an explanation of 'iron bars' as a money of account, see Elizabeth Donnan (ed.), *Documents Illustrative of the History of the Slave Trade to America*, 4 vols. (Washington, D.C., 1935; reprinted New York, 1965), IV, pp.69–84.

31. See Major Arthur G. Leonard, 'Notes of a Journey to Bende', *Journal of the Manchester*

Geographical Society, 14 (1898), p.191.

32. Baikie, *Narrative*, pp.309–10.
33. Kenneth O. Dike and Felicia Ekejiuba, *The Aro of South-eastern Nigeria, 1650–1980* (Ibadan, Nigeria, 1990), p.132; Francis Arinze, *Sacrifice in Ibo Religion* (Ibadan, Nigeria, 1970), p.37. The closest thing to 'chance' in 'traditional' Igbo ontology (at least in the mid-twentieth century) was accidentally bumping into particular types of spirit, *udo*, which are said to be 'wicked' and 'like electric wire' and unable to 'consider bona fide transgression [of any kind]'. Arinze, *Sacrifice*, pp.13–14.
34. For *ichu aja*, see Arinze, *Sacrifice*, pp.37–8, 57, 83.
35. Jackson, *Voyage to Bonny River*, pp.83, 89.
36. Equiano, *Narrative*, p.11; see also Arinze, *Sacrifice*, pp.42–4.
37. For the importance of vultures, see the proverbs in Northcote W. Thomas, *Anthropological Report on the Ibo-speaking Peoples of Nigeria*, Vol.II, *English-Ibo and Ibo-English Dictionary* (1913; New York, 1969 edition), pp.157, 382; Arinze, *Sacrifice*, p.44; John E.E. Njoku, *A Dictionary of Igbo Names, Culture and Proverbs* (Washington, D.C., 1978), p.78. For the historiography of the slave acquisition mechanism(s) in Igboland, see Jones, *Oil Rivers*; Northrup, *Trade without Rulers*; John N. Oriji, 'The Slave Trade, Warfare and Aro Expansion in the Igbo Hinterland', *Transafrican Journal of History*, 16 (1987), pp.151–66; Obichère, 'Slavery and the Slave Trade'.
38. Walter Rodney, *A History of the Upper Guinea Coast 1545–1800* (Oxford, 1970).
39. See, for example, Simon Jonas in the various accounts connected with Baikie's expedition in the 1850s. For the presence of Igbo in early nineteenth-century Sierra Leone, see Northrup, *Trade without Rulers*, pp.231, 235–9.
40. David Geggus, 'Sex Ratio, Age and Ethnicity in the Atlantic Slave Trade: Data from French Shipping and Plantation Records', *Journal of African History*, 30 (1989), p.42.
41. For general patterns in sugar production, see David Watts, *The West Indies: Patterns of Development, Culture, and Environmental Change since 1492* (Cambridge, 1987), pp.232–3. My hypothesis has to be evaluated ultimately by reference to distributions of shipments of slaves from Biafran ports to specific destinations in the Americas. The Du Bois data set will provide information on this in due course, but, unfortunately, it was not available at the time of writing this paper.
42. See Richardson, 'Slave Exports', p.13, for coastal variations in slave shipments. Richardson's numbers show that from 1750 to 1807 the Bight of Biafra supplied some 894,000 slaves, or 44 per cent of the 2 million slaves shipped from Africa in British vessels in this period. In the 1780s, the region accounted for over 60 per cent of the British trade.
43. For a theoretical discussion of ancestral and common traditions in the context of small-scale societies in equatorial Africa, see Jan Vansina, *Paths in the Rainforests: Toward a History of Political Tradition in Equatorial Africa* (Madison, Wisconsin, 1990), pp.71–100, 249–63. For *bricolage*, see Claude Levi-Strauss, *The Savage Mind* (1962; Chicago, 1966 edition), pp.16–22.
44. Cf. David Hackett Fischer, *Albion's Seed: Four British Folkways in America* (New York, 1989), pp.7–11, and his discussion of the domains of vernacular culture and his typology of folk ways.
45. See Stacy G. Moore, '"Established and Well Cultivated": Afro-American Foodways in Early Virginia', *Virginia Cavalcade*, 39 (1989), pp.70–83; Robert L. Hall, 'Savoring Africa in the New World', in Herman J. Viola and Carolyn Margolis (eds.), *Seeds of Change: a Quincentennial Commemoration* (Washington, D.C., 1991), pp.161–9.
46. Isichei, *History of Nigeria*, p.28. Cf. Western Bantu 'gumbo' for H. esculentus; Lorenzo Dow Turner, *Africanisms in the Gullah Dialect* (Chicago, 1949), p.194; Joseph E. Holloway and Winifred K. Vass, *The African Heritage of American English* (Bloomington, Indiana, 1990), p.29.
47. Moore, 'Afro-American Foodways', pp.79–80.
48. On the last point see Mark Wagner, 'The Introduction and Early Use of African Plants in the New World', *Tennessee Anthropologist*, 6 (1981), pp.112–23.
49. See Equiano, *Narrative*, pp.36–7; V.A. Oyenuga, *Agriculture in Nigeria: an Introduction* (Rome, 1967), pp.134–9; Barry Floyd, *Eastern Nigeria: a Geographical Review* (New York,

1969), pp.174–7; L.C. Uzozie, 'Agricultural Land Use in the Nsukka Area', in G.E.K. Ofomata (ed.), *The Nsukka Environment* (Enugu, Nigeria, 1978), pp.155, 170–1. For historical sources, see Jean Barbot, *A Description of the Coasts of North and South-Guinea* [1678–1682], in Awnshawn Churchill and John Churchill (eds.), *A Collection of Voyages and Travels* (London, 1732), p.379; Captain John Adams, *Sketches Taken during Ten Voyages to Africa, Between the Years 1786 and 1800* (1823; New York, 1970 edition), p.53; Crow, *Memoirs*, pp.146, 252–3, 258; Richard Lander and John Lander, *Journal of an Expedition to Explore the Course and Termination of the Niger*, 2 vols. (New York, 1832), II, pp.174, 201, 246; R.A.K. Oldfield, 'Mr. Oldfield's Journal', in Macgregor Laird and R.A.K. Oldfield, *Narrative of an Expedition into the Interior of Africa, by the River Niger*, 2 vols. (London, 1837), I, pp.374, 386–7; Captain William Allen, *A Narrative of the Expedition Sent by Her Majesty's Government to the River Niger in 1841*, 2 vols. (London, 1848), I, p.251; Reverend John C. Taylor, 'Journal of the Rev. J.C. Taylor at Onitsha', in Reverend Samuel Crowther and Reverend John C. Taylor, *The Gospel on the Banks of the Niger* (1859; London, 1968 edition), pp.367–8.

50. It is unlikely that Thomas Jefferson, who started growing okra in his garden in 1809, was, as Moore suggests, 'among the first in Virginia to grow this foreign plant'; Moore, 'Afro-American Foodways', pp.79–80. In fact, in the 1790s and 1800s Jefferson suddenly became interested in the African plants that his slaves knew about; see Edwin M. Betts (ed.), *Thomas Jefferson's Garden Book, 1766–1824* (Philadelphia, 1944), passim.

51. Fischer, *Albion's Seed*, p.9.

52. For an analysis of the implications of the separate realities for the continuing relevance of things African, that is, for the importance of the 'substrate' influence in Historical Creolization in the Eighteenth-century Chesapeake, see my ' He Is an African But Speaks Plain": historical creolization in eighteenth-century Virginia', in Joseph E. Harris, Alusine Jalloh, Joseph E. Inikori, Colina A. Palmer, Douglas B. Chambers and Dale T. Graden, *The African Diaspora*, Walter Prescott Webb Memorial Lectures, No.30, (eds.) Alusine Jalloh and Stephen E. Maizlish (College Station, Texas, 1996), pp.100–33.

53. Elaine M. Kaufman, *Ibibio Dictionary* (California, 1972), p.223; Turner, *Gullah Dialect*, p.191. This was true for places as diverse as eighteenth-century Philadelphia, the Chesapeake, the Carolina lowcountry, Jamaica, Barbados, and the Leeward Islands.

54. Turner, *Gullah Dialect*, p.191; *Oxford English Dictionary* (compact edition), p.288; cf. Captain Becroft and J.B. King, 'Details of explorations of the Old Calabar River, in 1841 and 1842', *Journal of the Royal Geographical Society*, 14 (1844), p.261, on the Cross River above Old Calabar. Interior Igbo did not have a common term for 'white folks' until after the 1850s (or even later); see Taylor, 'Journal at Onitsha', pp.251, 261, 281; Thomas, *Anthropological Report*, II, pp.104, 299; Njoku, *Dictionary of Igbo Names*, pp.3–4. The various terms included *oibo* (stranger), *onye oicha* (white-coloured person), and *beke* (light-skinned) or *nwambeke* (children of Baikie, the 1850s Niger explorer).

55. James Barclay, *The Voyages and Travels of James Barclay, Containing Many Surprising Adventures and Interesting Narratives* (n.p., 1777), p.26. It is curious that Mande *toubab*, Akan *abroni*, or Western Bantu *mundele* did not seem to resonate with slaves in the Americas. This is especially so of *mundele*, since Kongo and Angolan peoples were widely distributed. By comparison, Igboesque *buckra* was fairly commonly adopted, even where, as in South Carolina, there were few Igbo.

56. Monica Schuler, 'Afro-American Slave Culture', *Historical Reflections*, 6 (1979), pp.132, 124, 131.

57. Monica Schuler, 'The Life, History, and Unparalleled Sufferings of John Jea, the African Preacher [1815]', in Graham R. Hodges (ed.), *Black Itinerants of the Gospel* (Madison, Wisconsin, 1993), p.90.

58. Taylor, 'Journal at Onitsha', p.264. The locals routinely called Taylor *eze* or master.

59. Cf. Genovese's thesis of 'paternalism'; Eugene D.Genovese, *Roll Jordan Roll: the World the Slaves Made* (New York, 1974), passim.

60. Edward Long originally attributed the custom to a Fante caboceer named John Conny in the 1720s, but the widespread distribution of *jonkonu*, especially after 1750, suggests that such an explanation was, at best, unlikely and, at worst, fanciful; see Judith Bettelheim, 'The

Afro-Jamaica Jonkonnu Festival: Playing the Forces and Operating the Cloth' (unpublished Ph.D. thesis, Yale University, 1979), pp.7–20; Orlando Patterson, *The Sociology of Slavery: an Analysis of the Origins, Development and Structure of Negro Slave Society in Jamaica* (1967; Rutherford, New Jersey, 1969, edition), pp.238–9, 243–4; Mullin, *Africa in America*, pp.70, 326n; Michael Craton, 'Decoding Pitchy-patchy: the Roots, Branches and Essence of Junkanoo', *Slavery and Abolition*, 16 (1995), pp.15–31. Sterling Stuckey suggests a Yoruban or Fon influence, from the Egun masquerade, overlooking the fact that neither ethnic group was numerically important to the British trade; see Sterling Stuckey, *Slave Culture: Nationalist Theory and the Foundations of Black America* (Oxford, 1987), pp.68–73. Others, such as Frederick Cassidy, argue for a possible Bambara or Ewe derivation; see Craton, 'Decoding Pitchy-patchy', pp.38–9. Patterson (*Sociology of Slavery*, p.245) recognized that Igbo *Mmo*, Yoruba *Egugun*, and Ga *homowo* were most like Jamaican *jonkonu*, but again, the proportion of Yoruba and eighteenth-century Ga (who if enslaved would have been sent from the Bight of Benin) in the British trade was small.

61. Bettelheim, 'Afro-Jamaican Jonkonnu', pp.12–13, 20. Bettelheim goes on to write (pp.45–6) that 'This Kalabari peaked hat is so close in style to those worn in Jamaica that one is tempted to make certain assumptions. Yet, the region of Kalabari demonstrates as varied a culture history as does Jamaica and any firm conclusions are impossible'. For various historical descriptions, see Roger D. Abrahams and John F. Szwed (eds.), *After Africa: Extracts from British Travel Accounts and Journals of the Seventeenth, Eighteenth, and Nineteenth Centuries Concerning the Slaves, their Manners, and Customs in the British West Indies* (New Haven, 1983), passim. See also Judith Bettelheim, 'Jamaican Jonkonnu and Related Caribbean Festivals', in Margaret E. Crahan and Franklin W. Knight (eds.), *Africa and the Caribbean: the Legacies of a Link* (Baltimore, 1979), pp.80–100.

62. See Philip A. Oguagha, 'Historical and traditional evidence', in Philip A. Oguagha and Alex I. Okpoko, *History and Ethnoarchaeology in Eastern Nigeria: a Study of Igbo–Igala Relations with Special Reference to the Anambra Valley* (Cambridge, 1984), pp.268–9; Uche Okeke, 'The Art Culture of the Nsukka Igbo' and Chike Aniakor, 'The Omabe Cult and Masking Tradition', both in Ofomata (ed.), *Nsukka environment*, pp.271–2, 286–306. See also Augustine Onyeneke, *The Dead among the Living: Masquerades in Igbo Society* (Nimo, Nigeria, 1987).

63. Patterson (*Sociology of Slavery*, pp.185–6) attributes it to Twi and Ga *obeye*. See also Mullin, *Africa in America*, pp.175–86.

64. Long's account was from his experiences in the West Indies in the 1750s and 1760s, cited in Mullin, *Africa in America*, p.175. See also Albert J. Raboteau, *Slave Religion: the "nvisible Institution" in the Antebellum South* (Oxford, 1978), p.34.

65. The citations are from Crow, *Memoirs*, p.226; Reverend Samuel Crowther, 'Appendix II: a Few Notices of Onitsha, Idda, and Gbegbe, and of the Overland Route to Abbeokuta', in Crowther and Taylor, *Gospel on the Banks of the Niger*, p.435.

66. P. Amaury Talbot, *Tribes of the Niger Delta: their Religions and Customs* (London, 1932), p.131. For how *dibia* were consulted for any misfortune, theft, illness, as well as for every birth and death in central Igboland in the 1930s, see Margaret M. Green, *Ibo Village Affairs* (1947; New York, 1964 edition), p.54. Just as importantly, *dibia* also made 'war-medicine'.

67. Crowther, 'Appendix II', p.435.

68. Crow, *Memoirs*, pp.211, 225.

69. Ibid., p.227.

70. For recent and convincing evidence on Equiano's origins, and the location of his natal village east of the Niger, see Catherine O. Acholonu, 'The Home of Olaudah Equiano – A Linguistic and Anthropological Search', *Journal of Commonwealth Literature*, 22 (1987), pp.5–16; idem, *The Igbo Roots of Olaudah Equiano – an Anthropological Research* (Owerri, Nigeria, 1989), especially her map p.9. Cf. the early guess, based on less convincing evidence, that Equiano's home was west of the Niger, among the 'Ika' Igbo (now generally referred to as 'Anioma'). G.I. Jones, 'Olaudah Equiano of the Niger Igbo', in Philip D. Curtin (ed.), *Africa Remembered: Narratives of West Africans from the Era of the Slave Trade* (Madison, Wisconsin, 1967), pp.60–9.

71. Equiano, *Narrative*, p.12. The ellipsis omits a couple of sentences about how they called

these specialists 'Ah-affoe-way-cah, which signifies calculators or yearly men, our year being called Ah-affoe'. This is problematical, but may be related to the annual New Year festival (*ife-njokku*) as the root-word *afo* is the Igbo word for 'year'. The term *dibia* or a close variant of *obia* apparently was universal in and around Igboland; see Koelle, *Polyglotta Africana*, p.28; Thomas, *Anthropological Report*, II, pp.27, 303.

72. Cf. Sidney Mintz and Richard Price, *The Birth of African-American Culture: an Anthropological Perspective* (Boston, 1992), originally published as *An Anthropological Approach to the Afro-American Past* (Philadelphia, 1976) and the essay by Morgan in this volume.

73. John Thornton, *Africa and Africans in the Making of the Atlantic World, 1400–1680* (Cambridge, 1992); Douglas B. Chambers, '"He Gwine Sing He Country": Africans, Afro-Virginians and the Development of Slave Culture in Virginia, 1690 to 1810' (unpublished Ph.D. dissertation, University of Virginia, 1996).

74. Schuler, 'Slave Culture', pp.123–4, 126–8; Thornton, *Africa*, pp.98–125, 183–205.

75. Equiano, *Narrative*, p.15.

'Of a nation which the others do not Understand': Bambara Slaves and African Ethnicity in Colonial Louisiana, 1718–60

PETER CARON[1]

The French North American colony of Louisiana, parts of which were first settled in 1698, is an interesting and unique example of early eighteenth-century life in a non-English North American colony, especially as it was lived by the several thousand African slaves imported in the 1720s. Comprising fewer than a dozen isolated settlements along the Gulf Coast and on the banks of the Mississippi River, Louisiana experienced a sharp increase in immigration of West Africans which only lasted thirteen years from 1718 yet had a profound affect on the social and economic development of the colony.[2] By the end of the African slave trade to the colony in the early 1730s, Africans made up over half of the total population of the colony's largest settlement and capital, New Orleans.[3] Between 1719 and 1731, the Louisiana colony was the final destination for just over 5,000 Africans. Captives arrived from various points along the West Africa coast including Cabinda, Whydah, Cape Lahou, Cape Apollonia, Bissau, Albréda, Gorée and Saint Louis.[4] Many were sold to plantations along the Mississippi River from New Orleans to Natchez. Thorough and detailed examinations of contemporary events at and near these ports may eventually make it possible to offer more specific conclusions about the geographic origins and cultural backgrounds of Louisiana's African slaves than has been possible in other New World slave societies. As a result, Louisiana may provide for historians a rare opportunity to explore the complexities of African political and social structures in the New World as well as the African contribution to the social and economic development of a part of North America that is often neglected. As an example of an approach which stresses the value of wedding local histories in Africa and in the New World, this essay will focus upon Senegambia since that region accounted for roughly one-half of all the African captives brought to French Louisiana between 1719 and 1731.[5]

The Atlantic slave trade brought together Africans of distinct and varied religious, social and linguistic backgrounds in the hostile and oppressive environment of New World slavery. Louisiana was no exception and the colony had an ethnically, linguistically and religiously diverse African population. Numerous ethnic groups lived in areas that fed the transatlantic slave trade, and individuals from many of these ethnic groups were brought to Louisiana. Approximately 2,000 were shipped from ports along the West Africa coast from Portentic in northern Senegal to Cape Appolonia several hundred kilometres to the south. An additional 2,000 came via the port of Whydah on the Slave Coast, and approximately 300 more departed from Cabinda. We have only a small number of observations relating to the ethnicity of slaves in Louisiana in˙ 1720–50. Despite the geographic diversity of Africans arriving in the colony, a disproportionate number of those to whom an ethnic label is attached were described as Bambara or belonging to the Bambara nation.[6]

Between 1720 and 1750, few African slaves in Louisiana were identified by nation. In fact, prior to the late 1730s most estate inventories did not even identify individuals by name.[7] Though there were more than 3500 Africans living on plantations along the Mississippi river in the 1720s and 1730s, few were ever identified by either name or nation before the late 1730s. Thereafter, inventory records began consistently to note both.[8] Despite the anonymity of individual Africans in early French colonial Louisiana, the ethnonym 'Bambara' appears much more frequently than other designations. It is, of course, possible that large numbers of ethnic Bambara from the region of the Niger bend were captured and transported to the Senegambian coast, whence, having been bought by Europeans, they were shipped to Louisiana. It is possible, too, that Bambara were especially prone to trouble in Louisiana and thus came to the attention of colonial officials. That said, it is also important to treat with caution descriptions of slaves' ethnicity given by Louisiana officials such as Michel Rossard, registrar and royal notary of the colony in this period. It is, for example, not at all clear that when Rossard recorded a slave as being Bambara that this meant the same to Frenchmen as it did to the individual whose national or ethnic identity it was intended to describe. In other words, eighteenth-century meanings of the term Bambara are neither obvious nor certain.[9]

In searching for the origins of Senegambian captives brought to Louisiana, it is easy to confuse the labels which contemporary Europeans used to describe Africans with the ethnic origins of those individuals. How both Europeans and Africans adopted, used and changed ethnic terminology in the New World depended in large measure on how ethnic labels were applied in Africa. We must begin, therefore, by exploring the complex and often deceptive phenomenon of ethnic identification before we can attempt to reach back into their African past to uncover the true geographical or ethnic origins of Louisiana slaves.

Perhaps not surprisingly, Europeans tended to understand Africans in European political terms. This has to be taken into account when examining the terminology employed by eighteenth-century European observers to describe Africans.[10] Contemporary European descriptions of African political groups and alliances were often misleading because European conceptions of nation and race were not fully shared by the African groups to whom they were applied.[11] Using contemporary European labels of ethnicity can, therefore, lead to confusion in historical studies of slavery and the African diaspora because such labels do not always accurately describe the ethnic origins of African captives. Indeed, uncritical use of definitions of African ethnicity may create confusion for scholars of New World slavery and may even result in erroneous conclusions being drawn about the ethnic and cultural heritage of American slaves.

Though it may seem at first a trivial point, the implications of variations and shifts in ethnic labels and meanings are potentially enormous. Some ethnic labels have been applied to African captives which did not accurately describe any particular ethnic or language group. This is true of the designation 'Bambara' and exemplifies the problems of using eighteenth-century European classifications of Africans. Understanding how ethnic labels were applied and, more particularly, how they relate to the origins of African slaves must be central, therefore, to the study of community development and African identity in New World societies.

Despite the problems of identifying slave ethnicity and nation, such terms have provided the framework within which some historians of slavery have sought to suggest that common ethnic heritage between African slaves necessarily implied cultural homogeneity in the New World.[12] However, the framework becomes imprecise, unstable and often simply unusable once one begins to explore eighteenth-century definitions of ethnicity and nation. 'Bambara', for instance, is an example of a generic label sometimes employed exclusively as an ethnic designation in modern slave historiography in the United States, even though, in Senegambia in the 1720s, it was a generic term for slave and was used to describe non-Muslim captives more often than to identify precisely the ethnic heritage of individuals. Similarly, 'Guinea', 'Sénégalais', 'Mina' and other generic labels cast large nets, even though the meanings of such words varied between regions and over time. For example, 'Guinea' could mean a slave from almost anywhere on the West African coast; 'Sénégalais' was a catch-all geographical phrase; and 'Mina' was used to describe any slave from the region extending from Elmina on the Gold Coast to the Bight of Benin. Other examples include 'Igbo', which referred to slaves from the Niger

Delta, and 'Congo', which often meant any person from the Kongo empire or any captive purchased between 'Cap Lopès [and] le Cap Nègre'.[13]

A word used to identify a captive's 'nation' (or 'pays') did not always correspond to his or her ethnicity. Moreover, even shared ethnicity between captives did not necessarily imply a shared culture.[14] Ethno-labels were often little more than rough geographical pointers. Colonial Louisiana notary records and inventories contain a number of references to obviously generic or geographical African origins such as 'nation Congo', 'nation Sénégal', or 'nation Guinée'.[15] Furthermore, it should be noted that such labels were invariably determined by the captors rather than the slaves, and they should, therefore, be used primarily as a guide to the geographical point of embarkation or, in some cases, the point of capture of slaves rather than as a description of their ethnic origin. Nevertheless, French colonial officials insisted on re-interpreting African communal associations in terms of national allegiance and tended to identify groups of Africans by their 'nationality'. For example, in 1728 a fifteen or sixteen-year-old youth brought aboard the ship, *La Renée Françoise*, was identified as 'de nation Cap Apollonie'.[16] In cases such as these, ethno-labels were obviously improvised by Europeans with apparently little or no knowledge of African geography. A remarkable example of European misunderstanding of African ethnic groups is provided by the case of a slave named Benjamin, who was shipped to the French Caribbean in the late eighteenth century and was identified as 'un Congo de nation Poulard'.[17] 'Congo' referred to the large geographical area along the central African coast while 'Poulard' was a far more specific reference, usually to someone from Senegambia.[18] Though there is no equally absurd example for Louisiana, Benjamin's case nevertheless highlights European ignorance of African ethnicity and geography.

Ethnic labels varied according to national or geographical perspectives. As the involvement of Europeans in the slave trade increased in the eighteenth century, so too did their knowledge of Africa. And as Africans from hitherto unaffected regions fed the insatiable appetite of European slavers, new peoples – and with them new ethnic terms – entered the vocabularies of Europeans. A French merchant trading in Senegal in 1723 meant something different when he used the term 'Bambara' than a Muslim slave trader from, say, Futa Toro. To the French trader, Bambara was an abstraction. It could mean a ethno-linguistic group, or not. What mattered most, however, was not the accuracy of the label, but whether it influenced the price that might be obtained for the captive. To a Muslim slave trader, on the other hand, identifying a captive as Bambara – meaning, in this case, non-Muslim – may have been a way of avoiding, if not exonerating, his complicity in the enslavement of a fellow Muslim, an activity clearly forbidden by Islamic law. In addition, both of these definitions or interpretations of Bambara probably differed from that used by an enslaved African who may have used the term to identify himself or herself with a group for whom the definitions ascribed by their enslavers held little or no relevance. In the New World, as in Africa, what was perceived by Europeans as an ethnic or national label could, on occasions, be a reference to a religious designation. At other times, it may have referred to a slave's geographical origin or his or her social condition in Africa (i.e. whether slave or free).[19] In whatever context the ethnonym was used, as James Newman has noted, 'virtually everywhere on the continent, group boundaries, even religious ones, were flexible and permeable. The notion of rigid and unchanging "tribes" belongs to the minds of others; it is not evident in the actions of Africans'.[20] Thus, in addition to referring to the ethnic-linguistic group Bambara (or Banmana, Bamana, and Bamanakan), the term 'Bambara' was variously used in the eighteenth century to refer to a slave, especially at Galam and on the island of Gorée; to a captive from east of the Senegal river; to a slave soldier; to the ethnic group of an individual's captor; or to a pagan or a non-Muslim.[21] The variety of meanings was further complicated by the nature of ethnic Bambara society in the eighteenth century. Like other expansionist military states, the Ségu Bambara kingdom depended on captives to augment and replace its members. According to Richard Roberts, the *ton*, or military and social unit that formed from the bachelor's age set, 'reproduced laterally, by incorporating young men taken as captives into the ranks of the ton itself'.[22] Young men of ethnic groups other than Bambara were therefore forcibly assimilated into Bambara society with the result that, in a sense, not even all 'Bambara' were ethnic Bambara. Though the young men who constituted the warrior class spoke or learned to speak Bamanakan,[23] it is not certain that they would have constituted a homogenous cultural or linguistic group even if transported together as slaves to the Americas. In any case, since the Ségu Bambara state was expanding from 1712, it is far from certain that these soldiers of the Ségu army would have been enslaved in large numbers. On the contrary, in fact, it seems more likely that they would have been enslaving others.

   Bambara was perhaps most often used as a generic term to describe people of an, at best, vaguely defined group or geographic region. In a monograph published in the late eighteenth century, Moreau de Saint-Méry described Africans known as Bambara as coming from points to the east of Senegal. In his description of African ethnic groups, he characterized Bambara slaves as 'amenés de plusiers centains de lieus à l'Est de l'Afrique et vendus avec lui [les Bambara de l'Est], sous la dénomination générique de Bambara, que ce mot sert à indiquer un grand corps sans graces. Le sobriquet qu'il a aux îles, est celui de *voleur de dindes* et *voleur de moutons*, dont il est tres-friand'.[24]

Saint-Méry's characterization of Bambara as thieves is coincident with the appearance of Bambara in a number of criminal cases in Louisiana.[25] More recently, Philip Curtin has suggested that the term 'Bambara' could be interpreted as 'a general designation for all Malinke-speaking peoples, or even of all people from east of the rivers'.[26] Curtin claims that ethnic Bambara slaves, by which he means captives from the Niger bend, did indeed constitute a large percentage of exports from the Senegambia after the 1680s. Significantly, Curtin goes on to note that an exception to this pattern occurred after 1721 when warring factions in the Kingdom of Ségu united to defeat a common enemy, the Ormankoobe. The result was that 'the flow of slaves from the east was sharply cut'. Curtin claims that the next evidence that trade from the east resumed dates from 1733.[27] It is, however, precisely in this period when trade with the east was disrupted that slaves were shipped from Senegambia to Louisiana. This would seem to suggest that most of the Africans sent to Louisiana from Senegambian ports did not originate in the far interior.

Jean-Baptiste Labat, an eighteenth-century travel writer, described slaves exported from the Senegambia in the first half of the eighteenth century as Bambara. Labat's use of the term, however, is not necessarily indicative of the actual ethnic origins of the slaves departing from the region and must be treated with caution. Labat's *Nouvelle Relation de l'Afrique Occidentale* is often cited by modern historians. Published in 1728, much of the information contained in it derives, however, from accounts of visitors to West Africa in the previous century or was borrowed from other accounts. In *Nouvelle Relation*, Labat identified what he described as a 'very large kingdom' situated between Timbuktu and Khasso called Bambara Cana.[28] Historians have sometimes assumed this to be a reference to the kingdom of Marmari Kulibali (1712–25), even though it is more likely that it refers to the kingdom of Kaladian Kulibali in the late seventeenth century. The latter interpretation would be more consistent with the events during the 1680s, the era from which Labat drew much of his information. In a similar account of the region of Lower Guinea, Labat relied heavily on accounts from Willem Bosman and Nicolas Villault de Bellefond, both of whom had visited the coast of Africa between the 1667 and 1702. This period corresponds with the rise of the Bambara state of Kaladian Kulibali, a kingdom described as 'extensive but ephemeral' by Nehemia Levtzion.[29]

Among its various other meanings, Bambara referred to any enslaved individual. The term was used in this fashion by French officials to mean slave on the island of Gorée. There, enslaved blacks were categorized as 'bambaras', to distinguish them from free blacks and mulattoes.[30] This application of the term in Africa dates from at least the 1730s. At the French

Fort Saint-Joseph at Galam, too, Bambara referred to slaves. In 1731, and again in 1734, in addition to the European residents, each *rolle general* at the fort listed 80 and 40 Bambara, respectively.[31] According to Abdoulaye Bathily, Bambara was a term by which one designated domestic slaves permanently employed by the Company at Fort Saint-Joseph who served as guards in the *captiveries* or as cooks, labourers, or perhaps as translators. Furthermore, Bathily claims, all slaves coming from Galam were presented as 'of the race Bambara or of the nation Bambara'. In truth, he argues, 'these slaves were captured in all the lands of the upper Senegal-Niger',[32] or, in other words, from the region near Futa Djallon. Bathily believe that throughout the early eighteenth century the slave traffic through Galam had three principal sources – the Niger valley, the regions immediately neighbouring Galam, and Galam itself – but that between 1720 and 1730 slaves came primarily from the upper Falamé and Futa Djallon. Caravans brought captives taken from the Tenda region (Konyagi and Basari) and from Jallonke in the Fulbé wars of conquest.[33]

Bambara apparently also held a generic meaning for Parisian officials, which may not have been the same as in Senegal. In 1723 Saint Robert, the director of the Senegal concession, was ordered by the company to 'retain 50 Bambara and to leave 20 other Bambara at Gorée, 20 at Arguin, and 5 at Bissau'.[34] It is hard to imagine that a company official in Paris cared whether fifty ethnic *Bambara* were retained, or whether they were fifty Fulbé or fifty Malinké. It is unlikely in any case that he understood the difference. In this case, the official, writing from Paris, was not concerned with the ethnicity of the slaves left at those depots; by 'bambaras' he simply meant slaves.

Slaves or captives may also have been the intended meaning of a reference to the cargo of *Le Duc du Noailles* in 1727. The ship's log notes that 'Les Noirs chargés au Sénégal sont des Bambaras'.[35] Perhaps these captives were, as the phrase suggests, ethnic Bambara. It is equally possible, however, that the phrase meant simply black Africans, perhaps as opposed to Moors. The term was also used generically to mean captured slave soldiers whose use was common in early eighteenth-century Senegal.[36]

There is reason to believe that some of the above meanings associated with the term Bambara, which enjoyed wide currency in Africa and in Europe, were also used in French colonial Louisiana. Indeed, French officials in the New World sometimes added to the confusion of ethnic identification. In a letter in 1731 to Paris in which he expressed his concern over the possibility of an alliance between local Indians and Africans, the Governor of Louisiana, Etienne de Périer, described a conspiracy in which an African came as a secret emissary from the Chickasaws to convince other Africans to join the Anglo-Indian alliance against the French. 'The Indians [French: *sauvages*]', Périer wrote, 'sent one of the *nègres* who had joined them here to tell our *nègres* that they would have their liberty and would want for nothing among the English. This *nègre*,' Périer continued, 'is a Bambara of a nation that the others do not understand'. Périer clearly did not intend to imply that Bambara was the ethnic origin of this black Chickasaw agent; rather he used the term generically, to imply that the agent was black, Senegambian, or even a black slave soldier of the Chickasaw.[37] As one who had served the Company of the Indies for several years in Senegambia, Périer would have been familiar with the term as it was used in the West Africa.[38] Because he served in both Africa and Louisiana, Périer's voice is especially authoritative and cannot be easily ignored. His specific identification of the agent as a Bambara who was not understood by other Africans argues against the existence of a homogenous linguistic group and, even more importantly, indicates that it was normal to group Africans of more than one nation under the umbrella term Bambara.

Bambara also carried religious connotations. Fulbé and other Muslim traders or translators often identified non-Muslim captives as Bambara, by which they meant non-believers or animists.[39] In his early twentieth-century translation of oral histories of the region, Maurice Delafosse wrote that while the Arabic word written by Siré-Abbâs, an historian who recorded Senegambian oral histories in the late nineteenth century, should be translated literally as 'les Berbères' (or barbarians), he also noted that both oral tradition and Siré-Abbâs intended that the word be understood as Bambara. This word, Delafosse explained,

> non pas exactement la valeur d'un nom de tribu à proprement parler, mais l'acception de 'barbares, païens sauvages'. C'est d'ailleurs l'acception que revet communément au Soudan le mot Bambara, dans la bouche des Musulmans; ceux-ci l'appliquent, non-seulment à la tribu des 'Bambara' proprement dits (tribu apparentée de près aux Mandingues et répandue au Sahel, au Kaarta, à Bamako, à Ségu, etc), mais à quantité d'autres peuplades très différents ethniquement des Bambara propres.[40]

It is accepted that in the eighteenth century the term Bambara could refer to a slave's ethnic identity in the sense of his or her ethnic origin. Just as often, however, it could be used for other reasons by slave traders. European and African slavers eager to secure the highest possible price for slaves might apply the label Bambara to a slave or group of slaves without detailed knowledge of their geographic or ethnic origin in the belief that, since Bambara were sometimes characterized as passive, they might earn a higher sale price than others.[41] Whether or not Bambaras actually fetched higher prices is uncertain, but it underlines, nevertheless, the ethnic stereotyping which occurred in both Africa and the New World.

In one of the most famous accounts of early Louisiana, Jean Baptiste Le Page du Pratz, a relatively minor company employee, referred to an alleged slave conspiracy in 1731.[42] Writing several decades after the incident and his own departure from Louisiana, du Pratz alleged that the conspiracy was led by Samba, an African *commandeur* of the concession for which du Pratz was responsible, and that all the Africans of his country would wrest control of the colony from the French and assume power.[43] Samba, a name which means 'second son' in the language of the Fulbé, may have been the same individual who had acted as a translator for the Company and had converted to Christianity.[44] Du Pratz claimed that Samba had not only led a revolt against the French at Fort Arguin in Senegal in 1726, but, deported for that crime, had also plotted to seize the ship *L'Annibal* which in 1727 was said to have carried him to Louisiana.[45] The probability that these incidents were related or that the leader in each case was the same is small. There is no documentary evidence other than du Pratz's own self-serving version to support this contention. Further, it would have been highly unusual in the early eighteenth century to first exile and then spare the life of an African who had led any revolt against the French. This would be especially true of revolts aboard ship. These were not uncommon during this period and in almost every case one or several of the leaders was executed or thrown to the sharks as an example to the rest of the slaves.[46]

On its 1727 voyage, many of *L'Annibal*'s slaves were sold at Cap Saint-Louis in Saint Domingue. One hundred and fifty 'Noirs invendus' were, however, brought to New Orleans by Périer who, coincidentally, was in Saint Domingue on his way to Louisiana to assume his new post as *Commandant*. Had such a notorious figure as Samba been one of the 150 aboard the *L'Annibal*, Périer would doubtless have been alerted to the fact.[47] Yet, several years later, Governor Périer, writing of the same incident in which du Pratz supposedly played such a critical role, mentions neither du Pratz nor Samba, nor, for that matter, any Bambara. Périer, in fact, seems to have doubted the veracity of stories about the conspiracy when in a letter to the Company in July 1731 he wrote that it 'is not at all sure that these blacks [accused of the conspiracy] actually plotted this dark deed, though all the city was alarmed'.[48] Combined with the characterization of the incidents leading up to the execution of several African slaves in 1730 as an ethnically-based conspiracy, the almost mythical, non-historical, treatment of Samba and the imposition of imagined cultural characteristics has clouded our understanding of the historical record.

The persistent identification of Africans by nation in inventories and legal proceedings reinforced for contemporaries and for many modern historians the idea that African slaves recreated New World African national alliances based primarily on ethnicity and, by extension, language. One should not underestimate the influence of ethnicity on the lives of Africans in the Americas. But historians cannot invent ethnicities where records of them do not exist nor should they allow contemporary European assumptions about African ethnicities to distort the lens through which we must necessarily view early African captives in New World societies.

One recent scholar has argued that Bambara slaves 'arrived in Louisiana in large numbers' and that 'they were truly Bambara'.[49] Although a number of slaves in Louisiana were identified as Bambara, it is not at all certain that they were, in fact, 'truly Bambara'. The source of some of the confusion is based on slave testimonies. Under questioning a number of slaves did indeed identify themselves as Bambara and this has led historians to conclude that if they themselves say so, then they must be ethnic Bambara. Yet there is reason to believe that they were not from the region of the Niger bend. Why, then, would some identify themselves as Bambara?

There are several explanations to account for a slave's alleged self-identification as Bambara, even if the slave in question were of another ethnicity. First, as has already been suggested, the names and nations assigned to slaves were often arbitrarily assigned by captors or buyers. Second, the method by which European slave traders identified particular ethnic groups was based on information supplied by African traders and often supplemented by only the vaguest notion of African politics. Third, events in the New World could encourage a slave to identify with one African community over another and to assume the ethnic identity of that group. This is suggested by Barth, by Rodney (in the case of the Mandinga), and by Reis (in the case of nineteenth-century Mâle or Muslims in Brazil).[50] For Louisiana's Africans, Bambara may not have referred to an ethnicty *per se* but instead to a group identification of another sort. Lastly, Africans often spoke through translators whose own interpretations could easily mix with, and conceivably contradict, the words of the slaves themselves.

An example of translations failing to express accurately the sentiments of individuals is provided in September 1729 when several Africans identified as Bambara were questioned before the Louisiana Superior Council. For three of the interrogations the Council used a Frenchman named Jean Pinet to translate.[51] Pinet was a gunsmith who had lived in Senegal and was married to a woman who may have been a Senegambian mulatto.[52] By November 1729, however, the Council had begun to employ an African named Malene to translate for a slave who was also identified as Bambara. Why Pinet was not used in this last case is unclear. He was still alive in 1731 and appears from census records to have owned six slaves.[53] What is important, however, is that Pinet appears to have spoken a language which was understood by the first three Africans brought before the Council in September 1729. These 'Bambaras' were probably from the Galam area, even if they had not had direct contact with the French there or served as slaves, and probably spoke a language of the coastal region rather than Banmanakan, a language of the far interior with which Pinet was unlikely to have been familiar. Nevertheless, Pinet's identification of the Africans for whom he interpreted as Bambara could easily have been based on his own knowledge of Senegal, though his conceptualization of the individual's *nation* would have differed from the African, Malene, who acted as translator for another Bambara in November 1729. Again, it is important to remember the context and meaning of the term 'nation' to eighteenth-century Frenchmen such as Pinet and to remind ourselves that the word did not necessarily carry any explicit territorial meaning and was not synonymous with 'ethnicity' which is a modern construct. The term 'nation' could be, and was, used in a variety of ways depending on the background and purposes of individual writers or speakers.[54]

Just as Europeans ascribed a 'national identity' to some slaves, so slaves disembarking in the New World were often given new names by ship captains, slave traders, or owners. In many cases, these help to obscure the ethnic, religious or geographic origins of slaves. Interestingly, modern historians have accepted that names such as 'Sans Souci' given to slaves by their owners were not their original ones, yet have also gone on to assume that when a slave is identified as 'de nation Bambara' this is probably accurate.[55] If, however, one of the most important representations of an individual's identity – his or her name – could be changed, so too could his or her ethnicity.

Modern historians have attempted to determine the African origins of New World slaves from inventory records and from interrogations of slaves accused of running away, conspiracy, and petty crimes, whether real or imagined. A transcript of a slave interrogation could typically begin, as it did for a slave accused of marronage in 1741, 'Interrogé de son nom, age, qualité et demeure'. As recorded, the slave 'a dit le nommé Pierrot nègre Esclave de Chaperon de nation Nago'.[56] Of course, some of the information gathered during such interrogations is suspect. In the majority of cases the slave's identity was probably already known and it was therefore likely that the preliminary questions as to name and 'nation' of origin were not asked. Instead, information of this sort was probably simply entered by the recorder on the basis of evidence given by the slave's owner. Often in interrogations of slaves, the circumstances of the case are outlined in the opening statements. The questioning then follows. There is little, however, to indicate that this was the actual order in which 'interrogators' obtained information or even if questions relating to the nationality of slaves were asked. A slave incorrectly identified as Bambara, Mina or Ibo upon arrival in Louisiana would not have had an opportunity to correct the error. This is particularly so during interrogations when any attempt by a slave to challenge the 'nationality' ascribed to him or her by European or African traders sometime earlier could be interpreted as a form of deception and carry severe, even mortal, consequences. As a result, it is likely that information concerning a slave's ethnicity can be as misinterpreted in Louisiana to colonial officials as it was misrepresented by traders in Africa.

Despite the caution with which one must approach the term Bambara, it nevertheless offers a vital clue as to the actual geographical origins of Senegambians sent to Louisiana. While we clearly cannot take French use of the term at face value, neither can we discard the term entirely. When understood within the context of Senegambian history, Bambara is still a valuable key to unlocking the origins of Senegambian captives brought to the Americas in the 1720s. It is not my intention, therefore, to dismiss or disregard the ethnic labels attached to individuals or groups of Africans but, rather, to re-assess the significance of those labels in a manner consistent with their eighteenth-century usage, meanings and implications.

Simply put, the problem is as follows: if Bambara did not necessarily refer to an ethnic group, then how do we explain the disproportionately large number of Africans identified as Bambara in eighteenth-century Louisiana? In addition, what did the term mean to Senegambians in Louisiana? It is likely that individuals identified as Bambara were of Senegambian origin. Moreover, it is probable that most were non-Muslims from the littoral rather than the far interior and may have been slaves in Africa of the Fulbé or even the French prior to their sale and shipment to Louisiana. For further evidence to support these suggestions, however, we must look more closely at the history of Senegambia, particularly in the period of the late 1720s when five ships carried some 2,000 slaves to Louisiana.

For many decades prior to the 1720s, religion in Senegambia was both a force which divided many people and an umbrella under which they united. Religious affiliation, most notably Islam, united peoples of different regions, villages, and lineages in the face of common enemies. But, if Islam was an umbrella, it was a porous one for despite their profession of faith in Islam and their public expressions of unity, the peoples of Senegambia remained divided throughout the eighteenth century. Serious divisions existed between the emerging theocratic states of Futa Djallon, Futa Bundu and Futa Toro, and even between individual villages.[57] Religion could unify people across regions, class, language and geographical origin, but it could also provoke deep divisions along the same or similar lines. It could be, and was, a divisive force which segregated peoples and communities, sometimes causing conflict between members of the same ethnic or linguistic group. The degree to which Senegambia was disrupted by

political, economic and ecological upheaval is important to the discussion
of Louisiana slaves for three reasons. First, it calls into question the
assumption that most of the slaves exported from Senegambia during this
period came from the far interior or, more specifically, from near the Niger
bend. Second, the level of commitment to Islam, which was forced upon
many, may not have been so great even while hostility toward Islam,
especially for those captured and enslaved in the *jihads*, may have been
significant both in Africa and in the Americas. Finally, the enslaved
Senegambian population was ethnically heterogeneous, and so were those
exported as captives. Taken together, these three factors are important for
our understanding of the early Louisiana slave population because even
though the largest numbers of captives brought to the colony came from the
Senegambia their common geographical origins, religious unity and shared
languages did not necessarily imply that in Louisiana they developed any
political alliances or even cultural affinities.

Within the crescent formed by the Senegal river as it winds through the
region from the Futa Djallon highlands to the coast there are more than one
hundred ethnic groups and sub-groups. Most belonged to a large yet vague
cultural zone known as Mande. Yet, according to Wondji, 'each ethnic
group, speaking a language distinct from those of its neighbors, [was] aware
of its individuality'.[58] Among the major groups involved in the
Senegambian struggles of the 1720s were the Jallonke Fulbé, Sissibe,
Mande Juula (Jaxanke), Timbo, Soso, Sereer, Malinke, Bobo and Fulbé in
the Gambia River basin as well as related peoples from south of the
Casamance river such as the Kasanga, Papel, Beafada, Bijago, Nala and
Balante.[59] These representative examples are sufficient to show the great
variety of ethnic and linguistic differences in eighteenth-century
Senegambia. Even more importantly in the present context, these various
groups were surely represented among the slaves arriving in Louisiana.

In the first decades of the eighteenth century non-Muslim *ceddo*
(warlord states) of Waalo, Kayor and Baol controlled the coastal region of
the Upper Guinea coast between Senegal and Guinea-Bissau. In the mid-
1720s, both Kayor and Baol, whose rulers and *tyeddo*[60] armies were
especially hostile to Islam because Islam offered 'an alternative source of
political power', were themselves embroiled in civil wars as competing
factions vied for political control of the region.[61]

Futa Toro, like the northern Wolof state of Waalo and the Soninke
Kingdom of Gajaaga, was the object of invasions by Moroccans on an
almost annual basis beginning around 1720.[62] Adding to the political
disruption caused by these invasions and severe grain shortages between
1723 and 1725, the leadership of Futa Toro was in dispute until Samba
Gelaago Jegi assumed the position of *Satigi* in 1725. He and his mercenary

allies captured and enslaved their rivals, selling some to European factors; many were probably Fulbé and some may have been Muslims. Some of these individuals could easily have been identified as non-Muslims or Bambara. Since Islamic law proscribed the sale of Muslims by fellow Muslims, the network of slave traders extending to the coast may have labelled Muslim captives non-Muslim (or Bambara) for fear that their captives might not otherwise be purchased.[63]

The history of Senegambia in 1720–35 was marked by periodic civil and ecological disruption. The latter included drought, infestations of locusts, and famines and served to limit severely the numbers of slaves transported through the region from the interior in the 1720s and 1730s. The same events also led, however, to the displacement of people within the region, leaving them vulnerable to kidnapping, organized slave raids and sale.[64] In the seventeenth century there was a steady flow of captives from the region beyond the confluence of the Sénégal and Falamé rivers, but in the eighteenth century this flow of captives was periodically disrupted, especially during the 1720s when slave shipments to Louisiana were at their height.

The French fort at Galam was the principal nexus of slaves transported both from the interior and from the region immediately surrounding Galam. Beginning in late 1728, Senegambian exports began to rise, though there is reason to doubt that Galam itself was the primary source for the increase. Throughout the summer of 1729, at least three French ships, *Le Saint-Louis*, *Le Saint-Michel* and *La Néréide*, were moored near Gorée hoping to complete their purchase of slaves. There were, however, delays in shipments expected from Galam. The captain of *La Néréide*, Contault Dentuly, wrote in June that his ship and *Le Saint-Michel* were hoping to receive slaves from Galam because at that time 'there were only blacks for *Le Saint-Louis*'. On 23 October, however, the captain of *Le Saint-Louis*, Breban, wrote that he was still awaiting his captives and went on to note that 'we have learned from a courier from Senegal that the *barques* from Galam have descended without captives'.[65] Despite this all three ships eventually managed to sail for America with apparently full loads of slaves, *Le Saint-Louis* sailing with 380 slaves, *La Néréide* with 203, and *Le Saint-Michel* with at least 350. It is unlikely that these slaves came from the interior since expectations of slave deliveries from Galam were low by 1729; as Breban wrote in his log in 1729, 'the 6–800 captives from Galam are lost this year'. Moreover, shipments of slaves from Galam were small at other times in the 1720s; in 1720, for example, only 260 slaves had been dispatched from the port. Overall, therefore, it seems highly unlikely that slaves forwarded from Galam constituted more than a small fraction of the 1,400 or so slaves exported each year in 1729–31 from Senegambia on French ships. It seems that these captives came for the most part from sources much closer to the coast.

The rise in French slave shipments from Senegambia after 1724 may have been the result of increased religious warfare in the region. The drought which struck the region in 1723 appears to have hindered the supply of slaves reaching markets at Gorée and other places along the Senegal coast in the following year; fewer than 500 were shipped from Senegambia in French ships in 1724. The drought conditions which again struck the region in 1729 and 1730 did not, however, have the same effect as in 1723–24, because in the later years the captives were of more local origin and the impact of drought on movements of slaves from more distant sources was therefore less severe. On balance, the slaves shipped by the French after 1724 were probably primarily of Senegambian origin (i.e. the littoral) rather than from the Niger bend.[66] More specifically, it is likely that a large proportion came from areas near or bordering Futa Toro, Futa Bundu and Futa Djallon where the majority of the fighting occurred. This suggests that captives would largely have been non-Muslim Mandinka from Bambuk; partially Islamicized Soninke from Gajaaga; Muslim and non-Muslim Fulbé residing throughout the entire region; and persons from smaller ethnic groups.

Amid the ecological disruptions of the 1720s, Muslim Fulbé and their allies launched from about 1725 a series of *jihads* against their neighbours. They captured and enslaved non-Muslims, including non-Muslim Fulbé, as well as rivals who were Muslims or Muslims whose faith did not measure up to the standards of the jihadists. At the same time, non-Muslims captured and enslaved Muslims and non-Muslims alike. Many of these individuals would have been men and either full or part-time soldiers. In addition, bands of slave raiders generated further supplies of slaves throughout Senegambia.[67] European merchants purchased the captives arising in these various ways, shipping them to the Americas without regard to ethnicity or religion. Added to these captives were slaves brought from much further inland, traditionally from the Niger bend region. These captives were brought to the coast by Senegambian middlemen where they were then purchased by Europeans factors for shipment overseas. The trade from the Niger bend, however, was irregular during the 1720s and the number of captives originating from this source, as we have seen, was probably relatively small.

A combination of economic and political conditions made slaves coming from the Niger bend to Senegambia less attractive to both European and African traders than individuals captured more locally. Drought and famine, exacerbated by war, had a negative impact on the scale of slave shipments from the interior in the 1720s.[68] In an important analysis of the grain trade, Searing has argued that a critical link existed between the harvest of grain and the commerce in slaves. 'The harvest of slaves and gum arabic, sought by Atlantic merchants,' Searing argues, 'was directly related to the harvest of grain. In the simplest sense, this relationship existed because the ability of Atlantic merchants to export slaves depended directly on their ability to feed them from the moment of purchase until they departed for the Americas.'[69] This argument is, of course, consistent with the suggestions made here that in 1723–24 and again in 1729–31 political and ecological impediments militated against the shipment of large numbers of slaves from the Niger bend and reinforces the claim that the captives exported by the French in these years came from areas closer to the coast.

Even though Senegambia accounted for almost half of all the African slaves brought to Louisiana in the 1720s and early 1730s, it is not necessarily the case that this common origin would translate into the foundation of an ethnic, linguistic, or other community in the French colony. While it is tempting to assume that slaves from the same geographical region of Africa would develop mutual affinities once transported and re-settled in the New World, it would be premature to make this assumption in the case of slaves shipped to Louisiana. Separated from their families and living in a strange environment, slaves would have organized their communities and sub-communities according to a variety of factors. These include, among other things, shared (or similar) culture, language, religion, personal preferences and residence. Even Africans of the same ethnic group may not have found common ground in the New World if there was something in their past or their enslavement which mitigated against such bonding. For example, Fulbé captives arriving in Louisiana were not necessarily bonded by their common condition or even as members of the same linguistic group. Non-Muslim Fulbé who had been victims of *jihad* may not have associated with Muslims, Fulbé or otherwise, regardless of their mutual condition. The same reasoning would apply to other slaves from Senegambia thrown together on Louisiana plantations.

In an interesting and revealing passage in his *Histoire de la Louisianne*, du Pratz advised that for domestics and for *commandeurs* he chose only Sénégals ('who are called amongst themselves, *Djolaufs*') because of their 'fidelity and gratitude'.[70] He also characterized Sénégals as having 'plus de fidélité & l'esprit plus penetrant que les autres, & sont par consequent plus propres à apprendre un metier ou à servir; il est vrai qu'ils ne sont pas si robustes que les autres pour les travaux de la terre, & pour resister à la grande chaleur'.[71]

Du Pratz also wrote that it seemed as if Sénégals, whom he also described as the 'most black', were 'born leaders' ('nés pour commander'). Though speculative, it is interesting to compare these characterizations with those attributed to Muslim slaves in English North America.[72] It is possible, given his name, du Pratz's own preference for Sénégals (or Djolaufs), and his cultural characterizations, that du Pratz's own *commandeur*, Samba, whom we encountered earlier, may have been a Muslim, perhaps Wolof, Fulbé, or Tukulour.[73] Du Pratz also claimed that, in the case of Sénégals, once they were made servants 'one sees them sacrifice their own friends to serve their masters'. If true, this raises the intriguing possibility that the 'own friends' of these Sénégals, as du Pratz imagined them, could have been non-Muslims in disharmony with Muslim Sénégals.[74] It is certainly possible that some of those shipped from Senegambia may have retained an antipathy towards fellow captives forged during political upheavals in Africa. There is as yet, however, little more than vague suggestion that Muslims and non-Muslims from Senegambia continued their conflicts in Louisiana.

The death in 1751 of a slave named Marboux illustrates the importance of appreciating how Senegambian political and religious divisions affected New World African communities and how those basic divisions may have changed over time. Marboux's death arose out of a confrontation between himself and another slave, François, a confrontation that may have had a meaning for Africans beyond what French officials were willing to understand or were even capable of understanding. In April 1751, Marboux, whose name was probably derived from *marabout* (a spiritual leader and religious adviser in Senegambia), was fatally stabbed by François with a small knife which Marboux wore around his neck. The judge in the case, Jean Baptiste Raguet, decided that the stabbing was accidental and that François was intoxicated at the time, but there may have been more to the incident than this. As with many cases dealing with conflicts between individual slaves, whites rarely cared to investigate too deeply. But at a hearing held several days after the event, four slaves named Pierrot, Jean, Pierre Birame, and Pierre testified that they witnessed the stabbing. All, like François, were baptized Christians.[75]

Marboux's origins are unknown, though his name strongly suggests that he was a Muslim. The term 'marabout' or maRabu – from the Arabic morâbit – referred to Islamic scholars or saints who were religious and political teachers and leaders in Senegambia. Marabouts were also consulted by the local population and often provided them with amulets, or small leather pouches in which verses from the Qur'an were placed. These were designed to protect the wearer from harm.[76] The death of Marboux may have been an accidental stabbing as the Superior Council ultimately ruled, but it is possible that religious differences may have created antagonism between the men involved in the incident. The questions raised by the incident resonate loudly when seen in the context of Senegambian religious strife and underline the fact that relationships between Bambara, Muslims, Christians, and captives brought together from geographically and culturally dissimilar regions contributed to the cultural world of transplanted Africans. Much still remains hidden, however, behind ethnonyms, Christian names and nicknames which have little bearing on or resemblance to the original identities of the individuals who carried them as reminders of their enslavement.

This essay has sought to suggest that the national or ethnic labels of slaves in Louisiana were flexible and subject to different meanings and interpretations depending on the speaker, the language and the context of usage. Ethno-labels alone cannot be used as a precise indication of African origin, and in any case terms such as 'Bambara' can be useful only if understood within the contexts of West African history. Slaves from the same ethnic group were often identified by different labels such as Fula, Poulard, and Fulbé, while others with little or no relation to each other could fall under the umbrella of labels such as Bambara, Mina, or Congo. As Africans consolidated their communal affiliations within the larger French and Indian communities of Louisiana, the significance of group identifications changed still further. Ethnicity is a complicated phenomenon and one little understood, especially in the context of a slave system that often purposely attempted to sever individuals' links with their past.[77]

Ethno-labels remain important pieces of evidence relating to African slaves' origins, but they cannot be accepted without question. For historians, the problem with terms such as Senegal and Bambara, Igbo and Mina, or Congo and Angola is that one can rarely be certain what the words meant in the eighteenth century and how their meanings differed through time and between individuals. Clearly, ethnic labels did not always mean the same thing to all people. It is likely that in many cases the word 'Bambara', as used by Africans in Louisiana, meant a group of Louisiana slaves who identified themselves as from Senegambia and who were initially distinct from Muslims and later perhaps from Christians.

Bearing in mind the permeability of ethnic groups and boundaries in the western Sudan and the inaccuracy of Senegambian ethnic labels as used by European observers, accepting definitions of Bambara – and, by extension, other ethnonyms – that are based upon assumptions of colonial officials is highly problematical. What at first glance seems to have been a community of ethnic Bambara slaves among the Louisiana population was in all probability something different. In fact, it is unlikely that a community of ethnic Bambara formed the core of the African creole community in eighteenth-century Louisiana. Rather, many Senegambians – ethnically, religiously, and, perhaps, linguistically heterogeneous – either identified themselves or were identified by others as belonging to a group collectively known as Bambaras. For the individuals included, however, the term referred to something other than an explicit reference to their geographical origins or to their African social or language group. Perhaps, as Bathily suggested, many Bambaras were slaves in Senegambia before being captured and sent to Louisiana. Equally possibly, they may have been non-Muslims of many different ethnic groups captured in *jihads* and sold to European slavers.

In all probability, the Bambara in colonial Louisiana comprised all of the above groups as well as some ethnic Bambara (or Banmana) from the Niger bend. Whether they 'became' Bambaras while in Africa or purposely chose to identify themselves with others who were called Bambaras after arriving in the New World, the African identity known as 'Bambara' was probably far more complex than most historians of the Americas have been willing to acknowledge. The presence of a group of individuals who identify themselves as Bambaras is perhaps most interesting in what it suggests about the presence and significance of Senegambian Muslims in colonial Louisiana. The term Bambara – comprising a group of peoples from Senegambia distinct from, and probably antagonistic toward, Muslims – poses important historical questions with profound implications for the cultural formation of creole communities in French North America. These questions will remain unanswered, however, if historians continue to accept uncritically the lexicon of eighteenth-century French colonial officials.

The Bambara phenomenon – when examined alongside other African ethno-national groups such as Igbo, Mina, and Congo – can extend our understanding of African ethnic and cultural re-grouping in the New World. It is a key to helping us unlock the identities and communal development of New World Africans, an enterprise which rests on a clear and precise understanding of local histories in both Africa and the New World interpreted within the broader framework of an Atlantic perspective. In examining other ethno-labels such as Congo and Mina, historians must determine who applied the label, if possible why, and then decide what significance the application of a common label has for group identity. It is a tall order, but one which is essential if we are accurately to identify the origins of Africans in the Americas.

NOTES

1. Versions of this paper were presented at Tulane University in 1994, the Louisiana Historical Association Conference in Houma, Louisiana, in March 1995, and at a symposium on The African Diaspora and the Nigerian Hinterland held at York University, Ontario, Canada, in February, 1996. I would like to thank Carl Brasseaux, Angela A. Caron, Emily J. Clark, Katy Coyle and Gwendolyn Midlo Hall for reading early versions of the paper, and Paul E.

Lovejoy, Philip D. Morgan, Patrick Manning, and especially Sylvia R. Frey for their helpful comments on later versions.

2. See Daniel H. Usner, *Indians, Settlers, and Slaves in a Frontier Exchange Economy: The Lower Mississippi Valley before 1783* (Chapel Hill, North Carolina, 1992); Gwendolyn Midlo Hall, *Africans in Colonial Louisiana: The Development of Afro-Creole Culture in the Eighteenth Century* (Baton Rouge, Louisiana, 1992).

3. 'Recensement general des habitations le long du fleuve – 1731', Louisiana, Historical Collection, Records of the Superior Council 1718–1769 (hereafter LHC, RSC). After 1731, only one ship – *Le Saint Ursin* in 1743 – was recorded as having brought slaves directly from Africa, but slaves may have been smuggled into the colony from the Caribbean in the 1750s in small numbers.

4. Jean Mettas, *Répertoire des Expéditions Négrières Françaises au XVIIIe Siècle, Vol.I, Nantes and Vol. II, Autres Ports*, eds. Serge and Michèle Daget (Paris, 1978–1984).

5. Senegambian ports accounted for some 45 per cent of the Africans brought to Louisiana between 1718 and 1731, with Whydah accounting for 40 per cent and other points along the coast including Cabinda 15 per cent. Unfortunately, data relating to ethnic composition of Louisiana slaves prior to the 1750s do not exist. The relatively small sample of existing references prior to 1750 makes impossible any estimate comparable to that made by David Geggus for Saint Domingue. Even for Saint Domingue, Geggus cautions that definitive conclusions about the ethnic composition of slaves on eighteenth-century sugar plantations cannot be drawn from surviving records because the available sample of records was heavily weighted toward the late eighteenth century. After 1769, Louisiana was no longer a French colony. Consequently there is no easy way to compare slave ethnicity in the two colonies. David Geggus, 'Sex Ratio, Age and Ethnicity in the Atlantic Slave Trade: Data from French Shipping and Plantation Records', *Journal of African History*, 30 (1989), pp.23–44.

6. LHC, RSC records, Baptismal records of the Cathedral of Saint-Louis, ANC C13A. See also Hall, *Africans in Colonial Louisiana*, esp. ch. 1, 2. The number is large only in comparison with other ethnicities. From all recorded references to African nations (including ethnically-based names, i.e. Louis Congo) during the period 1720–50, the number of individuals identified as Bambara is less than twenty-five persons. No other ethnic label appears more than three times.

7. See, for example, the estate inventories for Pierre Manade, Bechemin Corbin, and Joseph Paris-Duvernay (LHC, RSC 1728100601, 1736012301, LHQ 21 (October 1938), p.987), as well as the estate sale for M. Bruslé (LHC, RSC 1728091701). Of the eleven slaves sold by Bruslé only three were identified by name. Exceptions were for Africans baptized with Christian names or for individuals being tried for crimes. In the Sacramental records of the Saint Louis Cathedral at New Orleans more than 300 Africans were baptized in the 1730s. The vast majority of these, however, were infants and they almost invariably took the name of one or the other of their godparents, often white French.

8. See, for example, the estate inventory of le Marechal d'Asfeld, LHC, RSC 1738012401.

9. See Stephan Palmié's review of Gwendolyn Hall's book in *Africa*, 64 (1994), pp.168–71.

10. See, for instance, Geggus, 'Sex Ratio', pp.34–9.

11. For a discussion of the meanings associated with the word 'nation' in eighteenth-century Europe, see E.J.Hobsbawm, *Nations and Nationalism Since 1780: Programme, Myth, Reality* (Cambridge, 1990, 2nd edition), pp.14–45.

12. Stephan Palmié, 'Ethnogenetic Process and Cultural Transfer', in Wolfgang Binder (ed.), *Slavery in the Americas* (Würzburg, 1993). Palmié discusses the relationship of 'tribal affiliations' with *naciones* in Cuba and cautions against a direct transfer of ethnic labels.

13. Roseline Siguret, 'Esclaves d'indigoteries et de cafeières au quartier de Jacmel (Saint-Domingue), 1757–1791', *Revue Française d'histoire d'Outre Mer*, 55, no.2 (1968), pp.224–5. For Igbo involvement in the transatlantic slave trade, see the essay by Chambers in this volume.

14. Frederick Barth criticized the once popular notion that a race equals a culture equals a language, and even that a society equals a unit which rejects or discriminates against others;

see R.B. Le Page and André Tabouret-Keller (eds.), *Acts of Identity: Creole Based Approaches to Language and Ethnicity* (Cambridge, 1985), p.208.

15. As an example of a generic application of the term Congo, see ANC C13A 9, fo. 267–8, Louis Congo.
16. Mettas, *Autres Ports*, p.698.
17. Gabriel Debien *et al.*, *Les Origins des Esclaves des Antilles* (Extraits du Bulletin de l'Institute français d'Afrique Noire – B, 1961–1967), pp.241, 243. Debien cautions, 'On ne sera donc jamais trop prudent dans les identifications ethniques, et ce ne sera qu'à des conclusions très générales qu'on pourra aboutir'.
18. Benjamin conceivably could have been a Peul from northern Cameroon.
19. For example, in Brazil Mâle referred to Muslims while Mina meant any captive taken from the Bight of Benin; João Jose Reis, *Slave Rebellion in Brazil: The Muslim Uprising of 1835 in Bahia*, translator, Arthur Brakel (Baltimore, 1993).
20. James L. Newman, *The Peopling of Africa: A Geographic Interpretation* (New Haven, 1995), p.6.
21. See Philip D. Curtin, *Economic Change in Precolonial Africa: Senegambia in the Era of the Slave Trade* (Madison, Wisconsin, 1975), pp.178–9; James F. Searing, *West African Slavery and Commerce: The Senegal River Valley 1700–1860* (Cambridge, 1993), p.107; Maurice Delafosse, *Siré-Abbâs-Soh, Chroniques du Fouta Sénégalais: Traduits de Deux Manuscrits Arabs Inédits* (Paris, 1913 edition).
22. Richard Roberts, *Warriors, Merchants, and Slaves: the State and the Economy in the Middle Niger Valley, 1700–1914* (Stanford, 1987), p.34.
23. The Banmana people spoke a Mankdekan language called Bamanakan or Bamana which is closely related to Malinke and Maninka. In more recent times this language is also called Bambara. See Barbara F. Grimes (ed.), *Ethnologue: Languages of the World*, Electronic Ethnologue Database, 12th edition.
24. M.L.E. Moreau de Saint-Méry, *Description Topographic, Physique, Civile, Politique et Historique de la Partie Française de l'Isle de Saint-Domingue*, 2 vols. (Philadelphia, 1797), I, p.27.
25. A case in which several slaves identified as Bambaras in 1729 did indeed involve the theft of livestock; in this case a heifer and some chickens. LHC, RSC 1729090503, 05,06; 1729111601.
26. The rivers would presumably be the Senegal and Falamé; Curtin, *Economic Change*, pp.178–9.
27. See also Daniel H. Usner, 'From African Captivity to American Slavery: the Introduction of Black Laborers to Colonial Louisiana', *Louisiana History*, 20 (1979), pp.25–48.
28. Jean-Baptiste Labat, *Nouvelle Relation de l'Afrique Occidentale*, 3 vols. (Paris, 1728), III, p.334.
29. Adam Jones, 'Semper Aliquid Veteris: Printed Sources for the History of the Ivory and Gold Coasts, 1550–1750', *Journal of African History*, 27 (1986), pp.215–35; Nehemia Levtzion, 'The Bambara States', *Cambridge History of Africa, from c.1600 to c.1790*, ed. Richard Gray (Cambridge, 1975), IV, p.175.
30. Searing, *West African Slavery and Commerce*, p.107.
31. Abdoulaye Bathily, *Les Portes de l'Or: Le Royaume de Galam (Sénégal) de l'Ere Musulmane au Temps des Négriers (VIIIe–XVIIe Siècle)* (Paris, 1989), pp.259–60, 284.
32. Ibid., p.267.
33. Ibid., p.264.
34. Hall, *Africans in Colonial Louisiana*, p.68.
35. Mettas, *Autres Ports*.
36. Martin A. Klein, 'Servitude among the Wolof and Sereer of Senegambia', in Suzanne Miers and Igor Kopytoff (eds.), *Slavery in Africa: Historical and Anthropological Perspectives* (Madison, Wisconsin, 1977), pp.335–63.
37. 10 December 1731, New Orleans, Périer to the Company of the Indies, C13A, 13, 63–4.
38. Marcel Giraud, *A History of French Louisiana: The Company of the Indies, 1723–1731*,

vols., translator, Brian Pearce (Baton Rouge, Louisiana, 1987), V, p.54.

39. Levtzion, 'Bambara States', p.171.

40. The Arabic word is translated by Delafosse as 'païen' or pagan; Delafosse, *Siré-Abbâs-Soh*, p.200.

41. Bathily, *Les Ports de l'Or*, p.265.

42. Le Page du Pratz actually dates the conspiracy to 1730; Jean-Baptiste Le Page du Pratz, *Histoire de la Louisianne*, 3 vols. (Paris, 1758), III, pp.304–17. The incident which led to the execution of several Africans actually occurred in 1731. ANC C13A, letter from Périer, f. 85, 21–28 Juillet, 1731.

43. Le Page du Pratz does not indicate from what country Samba came. Hall speculates that Samba was Bambara and that the conspirators spoke that language, but cites no documentary evidence of this; Hall, *Africans in Colonial Louisiana*, pp.107–8.

44. Michael Gomez, 'Muslims in Early America', *Journal of Southern History*, LX (1994), no.4, p.685; LHC, RSC 1728071001. There were many Africans in the colony named Samba and it is not at all certain which one was the Samba to whom du Pratz referred. Samba was a fairly common name in Senegambia, but it is also a Kongo name; John Thornton, 'Central African Names and African American Naming Patterns', *William and Mary Quarterly*, 3rd series, 50 (1993), pp.736–7.

45. Du Pratz, *Histoire*, III, p.315. For an account of du Pratz's version of the conspiracy, see Hall, *Africans in Colonial Louisiana*, pp.107–11. There are many inconsistencies in du Pratz's version, but easily the most glaring is his assertion that Samba was involved in the revolt aboard the ship *L'Annibal*. Hall suggests that Samba came to Louisiana in 1726 aboard the *L'Annibal*. A revolt did, indeed, occur aboard the ship, but not until its 1729 voyage and on this voyage the ship did not go to Louisiana. Records of the 1726 voyage make no mention of a revolt or conspiracy. In the unlikely event that Samba was detained for almost three years in Senegal before being exiled, then he was not the Samba who acted as interpreter for the Company in 1728. Neither Samba nor any Bambaras are mentioned in logs for either voyage. See Mettas, *Autres Ports*; LHC, RSC 1728071001.

46. See, for example, Mettas, *Nantes* and *Autres Ports*. After a revolt aboard the ship *L'Affriquin*, the two leaders were to be made an example to the others. They were executed and their corpses were hung from the mast. Other examples include *Le Courrier de Bourbon* bound for Grenada and Louisiana in 1723. A plot was uncovered after the crew threatened to torture two female captives, one from Gorée and the other from Senegal. The leader of the plot, a forty-five-year-old 'sorcier', was hanged from the mast and shot. During another especially grisly journey aboard *Le Dauphin*, the crew put down two revolts. After overcoming the slaves involved in the first, the leader was hanged from the mast as an example, shot, then thrown to the sharks. Other references are made in ships' logs to slave revolts. Often slaves were killed in revolts, as in the cases of *L'Aimable Renotte* in 1730, when 33 died and *Le Neptune* in 1729 when three died. On occasion slaves were thrown overboard alive as befell a slave involved the second revolt aboard *Le Dauphin* on its fateful 1723 voyage.

47. Mettas, *Autres Ports*, lettre de Périer, du Cap, 8 fevrier 1727.

48. Périer to Company, C13A 13, f.85, 21–28 juillet 1731.

49. Hall, *Africans in Colonial Louisiana*, p.43.

50. Walter Rodney, 'Upper Guinea and the Significance of the Origins of Africans Enslaved in the New World', *Journal of Negro History*, 54 (1969), p.335. For the relationship of Mâle to Muslim, see Reis, *Slave Rebellion in Brazil*; Frederick Barth, *Ethnic Groups and Boundaries: The Social Organization of Culture Difference* (Boston, 1969), p.14.

51. LHC, RSC 1729090503, 05, 06.

52. ANC C13A 11, f.349.

53. *Recensement-1731*, LHC.

54. Hobsbawm, *Nations and Nationalism*, p.17.

55. LHC, RSC, 1741011602.

56. LHC, RSC, 1741011101 (translated: 'Asked his name, age, quality, and residence. Answered "Pierrot, black slave of Chaperon, of the nation Nago"'). See also slave interrogations LHC,

RSC 1729111601, 1729090503.

57. Michael A. Gomez, *Pragmatism in the Age of Jihad: the Precolonial State of Bundu* (Cambridge, 1992), pp.52–73.
58. C. Wondji, 'The States and Cultures of the Upper Guinea Coast', in B.A. Ogot (ed.), *UNESCO General History of Africa*, 5 vols. (Paris, 1992), V, p.368. Most Africans captured in this area would have spoken a language in the Western Atlantic branch of the Niger-Congo family. This family includes, for example, the languages Diola, Serer and Wolof, Coniagui and Baga (in modern Guinea), Temne, and Foulfoulde (Fula, Peul) (Green, *Languages of Africa*).
59. Wondji, 'States and Cultures', pp.368–97. Wondji discusses at length the difficulty of producing an historical synthesis when describing peoples and societies that did not belong to large political states.
60. *Tyeddo* refers to non-Islamic rulers and the paid or slave soldiers in their armies (Martin A. Klein, 'The Impact of the Atlantic Slave Trade on the Societies of the Western Sudan', in Joseph E. Inikori and Stanley L. Engerman (eds.), *The Atlantic Slave Trade: Effects on Economies, Societies, and Peoples in Africa, the Americas, and Europe* (Durham, North Carolina, 1992), p.35).
61. Searing, *West African Slavery and Commerce*, p.80.
62. Ibid. Moroccan forces also attacked northern Senegalese kingdoms in the 1670s and, for a brief time, controlled Waalo, Futa Toro, Jolof, and Kajoor (Klein, 'Servitude among the Wolof and Sereer of Senegambia', pp.344–5).
63. In addition to the Bambara label, a significant number of Muslim names appear in Louisiana colonial records. In the 1720s and 1730s, these Muslims could have only come from the Senegambia. For more on the presence of Muslims in Louisiana, see Peter Caron, 'Problems and Approaches to the Study of the African-American Slave Community: Louisiana, A Case Study' (unpublished MA thesis, Tulane University, New Orleans, 1996).
64. Klein, 'Servitude among the Wolof and Sereer of Senegambia', pp.343–9.
65. Mettas, *Nantes* and *Autres Ports*.
66. Bathily, *Les Ports de l'Or*, p.282.
67. Not all captives would have been taken from among refugee populations, nor were all commoners. There are several examples of educated or wealthy Senegambian Muslims captured and sold into slavery in the eighteenth century. The earliest known, Ayub b. Sulyman (Job Ben Solomon), a native of Bundu, was kidnapped in 1731 by Mandingos during a voyage to the coast to sell slaves of his own. He was brought to Maryland though he eventually returned to Africa several years later. Allan Austin, *African Muslims in Antebellum America: A Sourcebook* (New York, 1984), ch. 2.
68. Ibid., pp.278–82. The region referred to as the interior has a vague meaning in the eighteenth century. Here the expression refers to the area around the Niger bend approximately 1000–1500 kilometres from modern Dakar.
69. Searing, *West African Slavery and Commerce*, p.46.
70. Djolaof may be a corruption of Djola or Wolof both of whom came from the Senegambia, Djola from the southern or Casamance region and Wolof from northern Senegal (Greenberg, *Languages of Africa*).
71. Du Pratz, *Histoire*, III, p.344.
72. See, for example, Ayub b. Sulyman and other Muslims in Austin, *African Muslims*, p.80.
73. Du Pratz's characterization of Sénégals is echoed in Saint-Méry's account published forty years later in which he describes Sénégalais as having 'des marques d'une espèce de supériorité'; 'intelligent, bon, fidèle, ... reconnaissant, excellent domestique'; '...très-sobre, très propre à la garde des animaux, discret & sur-tout silencieux'. Saint-Méry also described the Yoloffes as 'voisins des Sénégalais', and 'leur couleur noire, est plus foncée que celle du Sénégalais'; Saint-Méry, *Description de la Partie Française de Sainte-Domingue*, p.27.
74. Du Pratz, *Histoire*, III, pp.344–5.
75. LHC, RSC 1751041401; 1751041601; 1751042301; 1751050101
76. The Mâle slaves who rebelled in Brazil in 1835 carried amulets to protect themselves from injury. Amulets and talismans were quite popular in both Africa and among the black

Brazilian population in the first third of the nineteenth century; Reis, *Slave Rebellion in Brazil*, p.98.

77. Perhaps the best example of this effort to disassociate Africans from their past is to be found in the naming processes practised by many New World owners. See Ira Berlin, 'From Creole to African: Atlantic Creoles and the Origins of African-American Society in Mainland North America', *William and Mary Quarterly*, 3rd Series, 53 (1996) no.2, pp.251–88; Allan Kulikoff, *Tobacco and Slaves: The Development of Southern Cultures in the Chesapeake, 1680–1800* (Chapel Hill, North Carolina, 1986); Thornton, 'Central African Names and African American Naming Patterns', pp.727–42; John C. Inscoe, 'Carolina Slave Names: An Index to Acculturation', *Journal of Southern History*, 49 (1983), pp.527–54; Cheryll Ann Cody, 'There was no "Absolom" on the Ball Plantations: Slave-naming Practices in the South Carolina Low Country, 1720–1865', *American Historical Review*, 92 (1987) pp.563–96.

The Cultural Implications of the Atlantic Slave Trade: African Regional Origins, American Destinations and New World Developments

PHILIP D. MORGAN

In the early modern era, an increasingly integrated and cohesive Atlantic world began to emerge. The Atlantic was the first ocean in the history of the world to be regularly crossed, and the lands that bordered it came to have a common history. Over time, a variety of links, bonds and connections drew the territories around the Atlantic – that vast 'inland sea' – more closely together. People, goods and ideas circulated in ever wider and deeper flows between the pan-Atlantic continents. Changes in one corner of the Atlantic world had repercussions in others; even seemingly local and provincial developments invariably had Atlantic dimensions. Diverse and heterogeneous, this Atlantic world became one – a unitary whole, a single system.[1]

Slavery was a central feature of this emergent Atlantic system. It was the cornerstone of a vast Atlantic labour market which, though inelastic and inefficient, nevertheless functioned as one. Of course, the institution of slavery varied enormously from one locale to another, but it was no curious abnormality, no aberration, no marginal feature of this world. Few Atlantic peoples before the late eighteenth century found servile labour embarrassing or evil; rather, slavery was fundamental and acceptable, bearing an ancient pedigree to be sure, but readily adaptable to a variety of needs and circumstances. Prior to 1820 two to three times as many Africans as Europeans crossed the Atlantic to the New World. Much of the wealth of the Atlantic economy derived from slave-produced commodities in what was the world's first system of multinational production for a mass market. Slavery defined the structure of many Atlantic societies, underpinning not just their economies but their social, political, cultural and ideological systems. If slavery then must be situated squarely at the centre of the

Atlantic world, it also must be considered as a single sphere of inquiry, encompassing Europe, Africa and the Americas. Slavery must be viewed in its full Atlantic context.[2]

At the heart of Atlantic slavery was the slave trade, a vast co-ordinated system for the forced migration of Africans often from hundreds of miles in their homeland interiors to virtually every corner of the Americas. Both Europeans and Africans participated in the trade, and four continents were deeply influenced by it. The best studies of the trade, beginning with Philip D. Curtin's seminal *The Atlantic Slave Trade*, have sought to explore 'whole institutions and whole processes, seen in the large and separate from the mere national subdivisions'. Since, as Curtin put it, 'the institutions of the slave trade were common to the Atlantic community', an Atlantic perspective is the only way to understand fully what was the largest inter-continental migration then known to the world. Curtin's book is still the best place to start for an understanding of the Atlantic slave trade. Indeed, in many ways, it has still not been superseded.[3]

The book that perhaps has done most to build on Curtin's insights is John Thornton's lavishly praised *Africa and Africans in the Making of the Atlantic World*. Thornton describes his work as an attempt to assess the 'migration of Africans to the Americas and to place this assessment in the growing field of Atlantic history'. He argues, among other things, that randomization was not a function of the middle passage; rather, slave ships drew their entire cargo from only one or two African ports, and their catchment areas were homogeneous. Thus, 'an entire ship might be filled, not just with people possessing the same culture, but with people who grew up together'. Once in the Americas, most slaves 'on any sizeable estate were probably from only a few national groupings'. Therefore, Thornton continues, 'most slaves would have no shortage of people from their own nation with whom to communicate'. In Thornton's view, particular African national groups tended to dominate particular slave societies in the Americas; Africans in the New World often shared common languages and cultures that helped them survive in a hostile setting. In most parts of the Americas, it is now contended, slaves perceived themselves as part of communities that had distinct ethnic or national roots.[4]

Thornton's book ostensibly ends in 1680, but he and others are willing to argue that ethnicity or nationality was central to slave life beyond the seventeenth century. In a general text designed by Thornton and others for the college student and informed reader, the concept of nation as an ethno-linguistic entity serves as the key social force driving the development of slave life well beyond 1680. One or two African nations in most New World settings, it is argued, dominated most slave societies. Gwendolyn Hall credits transplanted Bambara as the central players in Afro-American culture in Louisiana. 'The Louisiana experience,' she observes, 'calls into question the common assumption that African slaves could not regroup themselves in language and social communities derived from the sending cultures.' Mervyn Alleyne believes that 'one African ethnic group (the Twi) provided political and cultural leadership' among Jamaican slaves; he also thinks that 'entire functioning languages' and 'entire religions', not just general cultural orientations or religious beliefs, were carried to Jamaica. Michael Mullin has argued that 'ethnicity', which he sees as a euphemism for tribalism, was particularly important among Anglo-American slaves, especially in the West Indies. Thus, for Mullin, Coromantee was 'the most conspicuous and important nationality in Anglo-America'. In short, an orthodoxy seems to have emerged that sees slaves as forming identifiable communities based on their ethnic or national pasts.[5]

This essay will explore this emerging paradigm in two ways. First, it will examine evidence from the latest and most comprehensive analyses of the Atlantic slave trade, especially in so far as these bear on the question of African ethnicity and nationality. Second, it will explore three key issues raised by the slave trade material and Thornton's (and others') arguments. Throughout, this study will aim for the widest angle of vision, the broadest transoceanic framework, seeking to see the Atlantic as a single, complex unit of analysis, and trying to break out of the national boundaries traditionally set for the study of slavery, whether African or American.

Exciting new material is beginning to emerge from an extraordinarily important project sponsored by the W.E.B. Du Bois Institute for Afro-American Research at Harvard University. With David Eltis, David Richardson and Stephen D. Behrendt at the helm, this project is compiling information on all known individual voyages drawn from the records of all the major European and American slaving powers. To date, records exist on almost 27,000 voyages, extending from the late sixteenth to the late nineteenth centuries. When complete, the project will have information on well over half of all the ships that made a transatlantic slave voyage. This project has already compiled the largest data set for the study of the long-distance movement of peoples before the twentieth century. As a result of this project, and the work on which it builds, we now know more about the forced migration of Africans than the voluntary migration of Europeans in the early modern era.[6]

The brief of this study is limited: to think about the cultural implications of the project's preliminary findings. Clearly, these thoughts are provisional, because the analyses are available in largely aggregate terms. More refined analyses of smaller temporal and spatial units will add much to the general picture and lead to much more sophisticated conclusions than are presently possible. As much as this author recognizes the necessity of Atlantic history, his expertise is confined to the British–American world, followed by some passing acquaintance with the French and Dutch sectors, an even less nodding awareness of the Iberian zones, and least understanding of the African dimensions of the story.

As David Eltis and David Richardson have argued, the key findings of their consolidated and comprehensive set of data concern neither Africa nor the Americas treated alone, but rather the connections between the continents. In short, Eltis and Richardson and Behrendt are engaged in true Atlantic history. They are able to view the intercontinental flow of people from both sending and receiving poles. From the vantage point of Africa, it is now possible to look outward from each coastal region and trace where the forced migrants went. Most African regions funnelled a majority of their forced emigrants to one region in the Americas. Thus, three-quarters of those leaving South-East Africa went to South-Central Brazil; two of three Africans from the Bight of Biafra left for the British Caribbean; 60 per cent of the Bight of Benin's emigrants went to Bahia; a half of those leaving Senegambia went to the French Caribbean; a half of West-Central Africa's emigrants went to South Brazil; and a half of the Gold Coast's and Windward Coast's emigrants went to the British Caribbean. To be sure, all the regions of Africa sent slaves to almost all the regions of the Americas, but people tended to flow in one dominant channel. In some cases, there was a subsidiary stream: thus a quarter of the Gold Coast's slaves went to Surinam and the Guyanas; a quarter of the Windward Coast's slaves went to St. Domingue; and a fifth of West-Central Africa's slaves went to the French Caribbean. Nevertheless, the regional African perspective on slave destinations reveals a distinct geographic concentration, or in a few cases two concentrations, in where the slaves went.

Equally striking patterns emerge when the transatlantic links are examined from the more usual perspective of the American regions of disembarkation. What stands out – and these observations are only a variation on the emphases of Eltis and Richardson – are two extremes. First, the two main regions of Brazil – Bahia and the South-Central area – drew heavily on a single region of Africa. In Bahia's case about nine in ten Africans came from the Bight of Benin; in South-Central Brazil about eight in ten came from West-Central Africa. Second, at the other extreme, true for much of the Caribbean and North America, is the absence of a dominant single African provenance zone. No region of Africa, for example, supplied more than about 30 per cent of arrivals to either Cuba, Barbados, Martinique, Guadeloupe, or the Danish islands. Between the two extremes were some major destinations that received about half of their arrivals from a particular African coastal region: St. Domingue from West-Central Africa, the British Leeward Islands from the Bight of Biafra, and the Guyanas and

Surinam from the Gold Coast. In each of these American destinations –
from St. Domingue to Surinam – the other half of their African influx came
from a number of regions. Brazil, then, was exceptional in drawing slaves
heavily from one region, while most other parts of the Americas drew on a
wider mix of African peoples, even if in some cases about half of slaves
came from one region.[7]

These broad summaries of aggregate patterns disguise marked shifts
over time. David Eltis has provided a detailed chronological analysis of the
British trade before 1714. A close, decade-by-decade examination of this
trade reveals that the leading African provenance zones that supplied
Africans to Barbados and Jamaica were constantly changing. In the 1660s
the Bight of Biafra was the leading supplier; in the 1670s the Gold Coast,
Bight of Benin and Bight of Biafra were roughly equal providers; in the
1680s the Bight of Benin was the leader; in the 1690s again the Bight of
Benin dominated the trade, but with strong infusions from West-Central
Africa into Jamaica and from the Gold Coast into Barbados; in the 1700s
and early 1710s, the Bight of Benin and increasingly the Gold Coast were
pre-eminent. David Richardson has explored the aggregate
eighteenth-century British trade. He reveals, for example, that from the
1710s through 1730s British shipments of slaves from Senegambia reached
an all-time high; during the 1760s and 1770s about a third of British
Africans came from the Windward Coast; and from the 1780s through 1807,
the Bight of Biafra and West-Central Africa accounted for about 70 per cent
of British slave exports. A dynamic, diasporic approach indicates how
slaves came from a changing series of African coastal regions. The
aggregate picture masks a fluid, evanescent reality.[8]

The age and sex structure of a migration, just as much as its size and
regional origin, also had a differential impact on both sending and receiving
societies. While long-distance migrations are typically dominated by young
men, variations occurred. One significant finding is that the slave migration,
stereotypically portrayed as heavily male, was not in fact so, when put in its
full Atlantic context. Compared to the trade in indentured servants, the slave
trade comprised a remarkably large number of women and children. As
Eltis and Engerman note, 'a higher proportion of children left Africa than
left Europe'. Indeed, overall, women and children outnumbered men in the
slave trade. The sex and age ratios of the Atlantic slave trade were most
comparable to free, not contractual, migrant flows.

Furthermore, the proportion of women varied quite markedly, both
between African regions of embarkation and American regions of arrival
and over time. Looked at from the perspective of African regions, the ratio
of male to female slaves varied from about 75:25 in upper Guinea to about
55:45 at the Bight of Biafra. From the perspective of American regions,

much larger shares of women were carried to the British areas than elsewhere, with women and men arriving in almost equal numbers in early Barbados and Jamaica, whereas between two and three times more men than women arrived in Cuba and in Brazil. Over time, the share of women among African arrivals fell uniformly across African regions. From one region to the next, the proportion of women dropped by well over 50 per cent from the seventeenth to the nineteenth centuries. After 1810 women constituted a quite small proportion of Africans from every coastal region.

Lastly, the proportion of children also fluctuated widely. West-Central Africa, and to a lesser extent Upper Guinea and the Bight of Benin exported greater shares of children than other African regions. Even more dramatically, the proportion of children entering the transatlantic trade more than tripled from the seventeenth to the nineteenth centuries. After 1810 over a half of those leaving South-East Africa and West-Central Africa, and just under a half of those from Upper Guinea, were children. The rise in the number of children carried in the Atlantic slave trade occurred in all regions, but was most pronounced at the most northerly and southerly extremes of the African coast. From the perspective of receiving regions, South-Central Brazil imported the most children, accounting for a half of all African arrivals; Cuba received 38 per cent, Bahia 35 per cent, and the French Caribbean and North America about 25 per cent. At the other extreme, only about 10 per cent of the slaves who arrived in the British Caribbean were children.[9]

Aggregate, sequential and structural analyses therefore emphasize the complexity of the slave trade. As a way of summarizing their data, Eltis and Richardson single out the regional composition of an African migration, its duration, and its demographic character, which leads them to posit their own dual pattern. Cuba represents one extreme. Its newcomers were drawn from a wide array of African coastal regions; its African influx was fairly short-lived, lasting about eighty years (from 1790 to 1867); and the African arrivals comprised many children and few women. For all these reasons – the relative absence of a shared background, the short span of the slave-trading connection, and the youthful and predominantly male character of its immigrants, which militated against family life and the transmission of culture – the 'Cuban African population had the potential for the greatest loss of culture and language specific to particular African regions'. At the other extreme, Eltis and Richardson argue, was the British Caribbean, where most immigrants came from just two coastal regions (three out of five newcomers came from the Bight of Biafra and the Gold Coast), where African immigration lasted about twice as long as Cuba's, and where women were twice as numerous as Cuba's arrivals. Eltis and Richardson therefore conclude that 'the opportunities for family formation and the perpetuation of language and culture were likely stronger [in Barbados specifically, and the British Caribbean more generally] than anywhere else in the Americas'.[10]

In several ways the preliminary findings of the Atlantic slave trade project seem to lend support to the emerging paradigm propounded by Thornton and others. Eltis and Richardson emphasize that 'the distribution of Africans in the New World was no more randomized than was its European counterpart'. With the exception of Bahia and Minas Gerais, they conclude that 'the African part in the re-peopling of South and Central America was as dominated by West-Central Africa, as was its European counterpart by Iberians'. In the Caribbean, they continue, 'West Africa was as dominant as was West-Central Africa in South America'. Even where the mixture of African peoples was greatest, African regions tended to supply slaves in sequence, therefore minimizing the mixture at any one time. In short, they conclude, 'the picture of a confusing mix of African cultures with all the attendant barriers to establishing African carryovers to the New World needs revising'. Revisionism then is widespread. My question is simple: is it justified? Was the slave trade markedly less random than we once thought?[11]

To answer these questions, three central issues must be explored. First, how homogenous or heterogenous was the Atlantic slave trade seen from the vantage points of African coastal regions and American destinations? Second, is it best to focus attention on ports, seeing Atlantic slaving vessels largely visiting one or at most two African ports and then delivering their forced migrants to one American port? Finally, and most importantly, what do we mean by ethnic and national identity in the early modern era and what implications has this for New World cultural development? These questions will be addressed from an Atlantic perspective, thinking not just of Africa or America separately; but rather viewing them as linked or interconnected continents. The Atlantic was a bridge as well as a barrier; the lands ringing this ocean were joined as well as sundered by the sea.

The Europeans on the African coast were engaged in a highly competitive trade. To be sure, certain parts of the coast tended to be dominated by one power, as Eltis and Richardson and others have pointed out. In the eighteenth century the British dominated slave exports from the Bight of Biafra; the French held the upper hand in trade with Senegambia; and the Portuguese controlled shipments from most of the region south of Zaire. But domination was never absolute and was always under challenge. Thus, although the Portuguese based in Brazil certainly dominated trade with the Bight of Benin – just over half of all slave voyages that arrived in Benin set out from Bahia – yet French ships accounted for a fifth of all slavers, and the Dutch, English and later Spanish were at various times significant players on the 'Slave Coast'. As much as one might say that Bahia dominated the Bight of Benin trade, nevertheless almost a half of the slavers arriving there were non-Bahian. Furthermore European slavers always encountered shifting fortunes along the coast. In the early eighteenth century the British acquired about a sixth of their Africans from Senegambia but by the 1750s less than half that proportion; in the 1720s the Dutch West India Company dramatically turned from the Bight of Benin to the Gold Coast for its main source of slaves, and, with the era of free trade, the Dutch again shifted their centre of gravity westward to the Windward Coast; as the Dutch moved westward, the French moved eastward, and by the middle of the eighteenth century they had relocated their slave-trading energies from the Bight of Benin to Central Africa.[12]

Even within a single African coastal region, marked shifts often occurred in the peoples forcibly expelled. The complex competition for trade was as much among Africans as among Europeans. The supply of slaves to the Bight of Benin, for example, changed drastically from the eighteenth to the nineteenth centuries. Down to the late eighteenth century, when the Oyo were a principal supplier of slaves to the Slave Coast, peoples from the north and west of Oyo – Nupe, Borgu, Hausa, and various Ewe-speaking peoples – were readily available. In the nineteenth century, after the collapse of the Oyo empire, Yoruba-speaking peoples dominated the flow leaving Bight of Benin ports, while the emergence of the Sokoto Caliphate in the Central Sudan generated a growing secondary stream of Hausa slaves. By the early nineteenth century 'there were at least two demographically distinct components of the trade at the Bight of Benin', notes Paul Lovejoy, 'one that brought males from the distant interior to the coast and another that siphoned off slaves (men, women and children) from the coast itself'. Thus it is somewhat misleading to say that Bahia received virtually all its slaves from the Bight of Benin, if by this is meant to imply some uniformity over time. The ethnicity of those leaving the Slave Coast and arriving in Bahia changed drastically over time.[13]

The relationship of coastal ports to hinterlands grew more complicated over time, which again enhanced the increasing diversity of peoples shipped across the Atlantic. Over time, for example, the region known as West-Central Africa came to cover a wider range of coastline and drew on an increasingly expanding hinterland, extending hundreds of kilometres from the coast. At least three, sometimes four, distinct commercial networks drew slaves from the interior toward the Atlantic shores. The mix of peoples flowing from that region grew more, not less, heterogeneous. Different ports within a single coastal region might draw upon different and fluctuating streams of peoples. Thus, along the early nineteenth-century Bight of Biafra coast, Igbo-speakers dominated slaves shipped from Bonny,

Ibibio-speakers comprised 40 per cent of slaves shipped from Old Calabar, and slaves from much further inland – Nupe, Kakanda, and Hausa, for example – formed between 5 and 25 per cent of the exported slaves from various Biafran ports.[14]

If the lens focuses primarily on the American side of the Atlantic, the emphasis again ought to be on heterogeneity. This is so because, as Eltis and Richardson have noted, the 'geographic concentration of arrivals in the Americas is much less than that of African departures'. Even if attention is directed to the places that received most Africans – a band stretching from about Cuba in the north to Central Brazil in the south – such American destinations encompass a much wider span of landscapes, climates, and environments than the coastline of West and West-Central Africa. If attention broadens to all the places in the Americas that received Africans – from New York in the north to Buenos Aires in the south – then the geographical diversity is staggering. New World slavery knew no limits; it penetrated every economic activity, every type of settlement, every setting. American slaves lived in temperate highlands as well as in tropical lowlands, on large continental plains and on small mountainous islands, on farms as well as on plantations, in cities as well as in the countryside; they worked in fields and in shops, in manual and skilled occupations, in civilian and in military life, up trees and down mines, on land and at sea.[15]

Even when the lens zooms to a single region or city, such as Rio de Janeiro centred in South-Central Brazil, which, as noted, drew heavily on West-Central Africa for its slaves, heterogeneity still seems the most accurate description of its African residents. This may seem a ridiculous proposition, for on the face of it Rio seems the perfect place to find homogeneity. At least two-thirds of Africans living in nineteenth-century Rio traced their homelands to West-Central Africa. As Mary Karasch puts it, the 'Central Africanness' of the city's slaves is fundamental to an understanding of their culture. Yet Karasch stresses Rio's 'extraordinary ethnic diversity'. Slaves from West-Central Africa were from three distinct sub-regions. The first, Congo North, supplied 'thousands of ethnic groups' to Rio, and in certain decades – the 1830s and 1840s, in particular – the ethnic mix from Cabinda, the central port of Congo North, was especially notable. Second, although slaves from Angola came from a more restricted area than the Congos, they still comprised numerous ethnic groups and at least two major linguistic groups: the Kimbundu-speaking populations of Luanda and its hinterland; and the Lunda-Tchokwe of eastern Angola. Finally, the third important port and sub-region was Benguela in southern Angola, whence came Ovimbundu and Ngangela peoples among others. So, the West-Central origins of most Rio slaves was in fact a congeries of peoples, languages and cultures. Further, important as Central Africa was to

Rio's slaves, as many as a fifth to a quarter of the city's Africans could trace their heritage to East Africa. The so-called Mocambique nation became one of the largest in the city. Finally, although West Africa was the least important source of Rio's slaves, so-called Minas and Calabars were prominent in the city. Rio, then, was truly a babel of African peoples.[16]

Just as the new paradigm tightly links one African region to a single American society, so the new orthodoxy sees slave ships connecting one African port to a single American destination. In some ways, this is a valuable perspective. One of the most exciting features of the Du Bois Institute project is its capacity to follow a ship (and perhaps, in the future, individuals) from a port in Africa to a port in the Americas. Preliminary analysis from the project reveals the importance of a small number of African ports. Two-thirds of African slaves shipped from known points, rather than from broad coastal regions, left from just twenty ports. Ranking the ports that shipped the most slaves, three of the top five – Cabinda, Benguela and Luanda – were in West-Central Africa. About two-thirds of departures from the Bight of Benin were from Whydah. Indeed, as Eltis and Richardson note, 'probably well over one million slaves left from Whydah, making it the single most important oceanic outlet for slaves in sub-Saharan Africa'. Similarly, almost 80 per cent of all slaves in the Bight of Biafra region left from just two outlets, Bonny and Calabar. The concentration of African departures from just a few sites is notable.[17]

Nevertheless, some caution is in order. One cannot accept uncritically the stated African destinations of ships clearing European ports. Further, ships designated as having boarded their slaves at a particular port did not always obtain all their slaves even from the coastal region of that port. The African point of embarkation may have been simply the last port of call. In 1744 a Dutchman at Elmina on the Gold Coast reported that most of his countrymen purchased their slaves on the Windward Coast, sailing on to Elmina only when their slave cargo was still deficient. From detailed records of over fifty free-trade Dutch ships from the 1740s through the 1780s, about three-quarters of all slaves were acquired before the ship reached the Gold Coast. Even on the Gold Coast itself, the Dutch drew fairly diversely. Elmina was their major port of call, but slaves from various Dutch trading stations were often taken by small boats to Elmina. One statistical record from the mid-1720s to mid-1750s indicates that Elmina provided only one-third of the Gold Coast slaves; ports from Axim in the west to Accra in the east supplied the other two-thirds. Similarly, in the sub-region of West-Central Africa known as Congo North, slave traders sometimes picked up slaves along the entire coast even if they then called them Cabindas after the central port of the region.[18]

These cautionary notes should not be exaggerated. It was unusual for a ship to purchase slaves in more than one coastal region. The major exceptions were ships that bought in the Gold Coast and Bight of Benin chiefly before 1720, and ships that touched at various points of the Windward Coast on their way to the Gold and Slave Coasts. Probably no more than a fifth of the Gold Coast ships went on to the Bight of Benin, even before 1720; and Gold and Slave Coast ships normally (with perhaps the exception of the Dutch) bought only a few slaves before reaching their major markets. Coastal trading was common, so slaves would come from a range of fairly proximate places rather than from a single port. Nevertheless, there were exceptions. For example, Whydah seemed to be able to supply all its prospective purchasers, without ships having to trade elsewhere, and the same appears to have been the case at various ports on the Gambia.[19]

In another sense, however, whether a ship landed at one or two or more African ports is somewhat beside the point; rather, the real issue is the complexity of networks deep within Africa that funnelled slaves into nodal points on the coast. Joseph Miller has written a brilliant study of just such networks for West-Central Africa. As he points out, the whole region consisted of over 1,000 kilometres of coastline and a slaving hinterland that by the early nineteenth century extended 2,500 kilometres inland. Overall, slaves were drawn from locales within a region of 2.5 million square kilometres, an area larger than the United States east of the Mississippi River. In most of the central market places in the interior of West-Central Africa, traders dispatched slaves in sizeable caravans that marched at best 150 kilometres a month. As the moving frontier zone of slaving violence advanced eastwards, a complex fan of trade routes, ever more extensive and convoluted, radiated out into the interior. The sequence of multiple sales that attended transfers of slaves between their place of seizure and the coast could divert the flow in almost any direction. As slaves plodded westward, many died and others were added, so that by the time they reached the coast the caravans were indeed a motley crew. The process was, in Miller's words, an 'agonizing progress toward the coast that lasted months if not years'. The actual port of embarkation was therefore just one link in a highly complex chain. No other slaving hinterland was large as West-Central Africa's, but then again no other coastal region supplied as many slaves to New World.[20]

The Du Bois Institute project is able to rank not just African ports of embarkation but American ports of disembarkation; once again, the concentration is notable. Eltis and Richardson rank the top seventeen American ports, descending to St. George's in Grenada, the lowest ranked on their list with a known importation of less than 50,000 slaves. The top two ports are Brazilian – Rio de Janeiro on Guanabara Bay which received over 800,000 slaves, and Bahia (presumably primarily Salvador) which received almost 700,000. Directly below these two are many Caribbean ports, the most important of which in descending rank order are Cap Francais in St. Domingue with 350,000 known arrivals, Bridgetown in Barbados with 340,000, Havana in Cuba with 210,000, and Kingston in Jamaica with 190,000.[21]

Most slave ships probably had a single destination, but whether most slaves were sold and remained in the vicinity of their point of disembarkation seems somewhat more problematic. The whole question of Africans' subsequent movements within the Americas is complicated. Much more is known about the first place of landing than the Africans' final destinations. Just as the African port of embarkation is easier to document than the complex chain that led from interior to coast, so it is infinitely easier to record slaves landing at an American port than it is to trace their later movements.

At certain times, a lively re-export trade in slaves unquestionably arose in various American ports. The British sometimes landed slaves in their Caribbean islands before taking them to the North American mainland. After 1763, slaves were commonly re-exported from most British islands in the eastern Caribbean. Equally well known is that Jamaica was a major re-exporter of slaves. Over the course of the eighteenth and early nineteenth century, Jamaica imported over 800,000 Africans and transshipped about 200,000. A British slave trade of sorts persisted for a quarter of a century after abolition when over 20,000 thousand slaves were shipped from the older islands to the newer colonies, especially Trinidad and Demerara. Smaller European slave-trading nations engaged in much re-exporting. Many slaves imported by the Danes were transshipped. The Dutch were well known for landing slaves at islands like Curaçao and afterwards reshipping them to the Spanish–American mainland ports. Some slaves were transshipped from Curaçao to other Dutch colonies in the Caribbean or Guiana. War or market conditions sometimes forced a ship to alter its course and make more than one landing. With the growth of the Dutch free trade, Johannes Postma notes, the restless search for the most profitable markets often led to more than one landing. Before the direct trade to Cuba developed in the nineteenth century, Cuban and other Spanish Caribbean planters regularly purchased slaves in the well-established markets of Jamaica and Dominica. A robust inter-island and island-mainland trade existed in slaves as in much else.[22]

But the forced migration of Africans in the Americas was not just confined to transshipment; far more consequential were the long marches on American soil, sometimes in stages, far into the interior. In many ways, then, America may be conceived as a mirror image of Africa: ports on either side of the Atlantic were funnels for large slaving hinterlands that fanned out across the land. As Miller points out, 'Even the ships headed to a single Brazilian captaincy must, finally, be understood as moving through no more than an intermediate stage in a complex redistribution to further destinations.' Rio received more slaves than any other New World port because it supplied Minas Gerais, was a route of access to São Paulo, and constituted a smuggling station on the way to the estuary of the Plate. Salvador was the second ranked largest port for slaves because many of those Africans continued south to Minas Gerais and north to Pernambuco and the Amazon. Slaves who had already been transshipped from various Caribbean islands to Cartagena and Portobello then faced further journeys to Colombia or Peru. Slaves landed in the Rio de la Plata went overland to Tucuman and then onto the silver mines at Potosi. Africans who arrived in Virginia after the early eighteenth century or South Carolina after the late eighteenth century were usually destined for the piedmont or even further inland. The American trek from port to places of residence was often as long and agonizing as the African march from point of capture to the coast.[23]

Movement both within Africa and the Americas complicates not just the notion of port to port correspondences but also the conception of homogenous peoples being swept up on one side of the ocean and set down *en masse* on the other. Because many African slaves came in tortuous and convoluted ways from the interior to the coast, whatever ethnic identity they originally had was undoubtedly in flux. Furthermore, it is often impossible from a late twentieth-century vantage point to reconstruct what, if anything, that ethnic identity might have been. Miller's description of the functioning of the Angolan slave trade – 'individuals being kidnapped, sold, resold, and captured again in the course of repeatedly disrupted lifetimes' – leads him to conclude that their so-called ethnic origins probably meant 'very little'. In addition, when Philip Curtin assembled a number of different samples of contemporaneous opinion on the ethnic distribution of the eighteenth-century Senegambian slave trade, what is most impressive is that three-quarters of the exported slaves occupy the 'non-ethnic' category. Only about 17 per cent of the slave exports from Senegambia were Wolof, 5 per cent Fulbé, and 3 per cent Sereer. Most slaves seem to have come from east of the heads of navigation – by way of Gajaaga and the Gambia – and cannot be assigned to a specific ethnic group.[24]

Even more fundamental, how aware were people of belonging to an imputed ethnic and cultural tradition? Whether the search is for a pan-African culture, broad regional cultures – as in Thornton's tripartite division of West and Central Africa into something akin to Caesar's Gaul – or more localized ethnic cultures, the same problem inheres: are we not in danger of adopting the hermeneutics of the observer? Do we not fall into the trap of denying the social and cultural worlds created by local actors, of seeing similarities where the actors were aware only of difference? Consider, for example, the eighteenth-century use of the term Yoruba. As Robin Law has pointed out, originally the name designated only the Oyo, being the term by which the Hausa of northern Nigeria referred to the Oyo kingdom. Before the nineteenth century, he continues, 'the name Yoruba was not used to designate the larger group of which the Oyo form part ... It must, indeed, be doubtful whether the various "Yoruba" groups were conscious of forming, on linguistic or other grounds, any sort of unity or community.' Similarly, David Northrup, writing of pre-colonial South-Eastern Nigeria, observes that 'the largest unit of identity for most inhabitants does not appear to have been the primary ethnic unit such as Igbo or Ibibio, but rather the smaller dialect or cultural group'. Indeed, Igbo-speakers enslaved in the early nineteenth century had apparently never heard the name Igbo in their homelands. Or consider the farmers of the central highlands of West-Central Africa, many of whom were shipped to Brazil; they became known as the Ovimbundu because they shared similar linguistic traits, but, notes Miller, 'none of them in the eighteenth century would have claimed much unity'. Ethnicity, in so far as it existed, was clearly very localized in precolonial Africa.[25]

In fact, a distinct danger exists in applying terms such as ethnic group and nation indiscriminately in African and African-American studies. Thornton adopts rather uncritically early modern European usages by talking of 'countries' or 'nations' and even of 'national loyalty', which are not just imposed taxonomies but anachronistic ones. As Karen Fog Olwig notes of Danish West Indian slaves, they 'did not seem to identify strongly with nations, so when asked the name of his nation, a slave often responded "with the name of the place where he lived in Guinea"'. Similarly, while ethnicity can be used to stand for some kind of group (*ethnos*), it is often a residual term applied when too little is known about some group to be able to label it more precisely. The ethnic lexicon of New World planters and slave traders – and they must be distinguished – is often mysterious. As David Geggus has pointed out in the Francophone context, the labels 'Mine' and 'Caramenty' obviously derived from the ports of Elmina and Kormantin 'situated close together on the Gold Coast, but the sex ratios and morbidity levels of these two sets of slaves suggest that they were drawn from quite different, perhaps distinct' locales. Many ethnic labels were affixed inaccurately. Primarily on the basis of scattered references to large numbers of Bambara in early Louisiana, Gwendolyn Hall argues that they served as a charter group, but, as Philip Curtin had earlier noted, Bambara was a catch-all term. Some early Louisiana slaves doubtless were Bambara, an ethnic group, generally non-Muslim, who comprised the dominant people of the new kingdoms of Segu and Kaarta in the eighteenth century.

But the word also meant, in Senegambian French, any slave soldier serving in Senegal, and it could be taken as a very general designation for all Malinke-speaking peoples, or even of all people from east of the Senegal and Gambia rivers. Curtin authoritatively declares that, 'The "Bambara" slaves shipped west as a result of eighteenth-century warfare or political consolidation could be dissident people who were ethnically Bambara, or they could just as well be non-Bambara victims of Bambara raiders.' The term was more geographical than cultural.[26]

In the New World, so-called African ethnic or national identities were often convenient reconstitutions or inventions. Nor could these identities easily remain pristine in the pluralistic Americas. Analysis of the national origins and mating patterns of the Trinidadian slave population in the early nineteenth century – one of the most African slave populations at that time – reveals that the population of about 14,000 was drawn from an wide range of territories, extending from Senegambia to Mozambique. Early nineteenth-century Trinidad was also unusually urban and had relatively small slave-holdings. In this newly settled society, most African slaves – and thus about half of all slaves – did not live in families. The fortunate Africans who found partners generally found other Africans, but not often from their own ethnic group or even region. Ethnic identity, Barry Higman concluded, dissolved rapidly as a result of extensive inter-ethnic marriage.[27]

Just as ethnic identities both within Africa and the Americas should be viewed as fluid and permeable, so cultural development in the New World involved borrowing and adaptation, modification and invention. Slaves functioned as *bricoleurs*, to borrow Claude Lévi-Strauss's term, picking and choosing from a variety of cultural strains to create something new. This plasticity was evident in all aspects of slave culture – from the way the slaves wore their clothes, the way they combed their hair, to the way they organized their yards.[28]

The complexity of ethnic cultural development among New World slaves is well captured in a transcription of three African songs – ostensibly from 'Angola', 'Papa' and 'Koromanti' respectively – heard in Jamaica in 1688. In the 1680s Africans from West-Central Africa (including Angola) and the Bight of Benin (where Popo referred to a people as well as to two ports) comprised about three-quarters of all incoming slaves to Jamaica, so it is not surprising that white visitors heard a Papa and an Angolan song. A little more surprising is the Koromanti song, because only 7 per cent of known Africans imported in the 1680s were from the Gold Coast (where the port of Kormantine was located). Koromantis are often associated with early Jamaican slavery, but in the 1660s there were no Africans imported from the Gold Coast and in the 1690s less than one in ten arrivals were from that region. The only decade in the second half of the seventeenth century when the Gold Coast was a major supplier to Jamaica was the 1670s: it contributed a quarter of Jamaica's Africans, but was easily dwarfed by the 60 per cent who came from the Bights of Benin and Biafra. Nevertheless, so-called Koromantis apparently led two Jamaican slave rebellions in 1673 and 1686, which seems to indicate they exercised a power out of all proportion to their numbers.

A musical analysis of the three songs reveals that they were far from ethnically distinctive. Rather, even at this early date in Jamaica's history when Africans were numerous and might be thought to retain a measure of ethnic integrity, the songs showed influences from other African regions. In particular, the 'Angola' song incorporated musical elements from the Akan peoples of the Gold Coast, even though retaining many Bantu features. Again, then, there seems evidence that Gold Coast peoples had undue influence. But the 'Koromanti' song had little Western Kwa (or Gold Coast) features but was rather 'a loosely bundled set of associations centered on West Africa'. In other words, perhaps the Koromanti, clearly a minority among late seventeenth-century Jamaica's slaves, were especially influential because of their adaptability, their pan-West African outlook. At any rate, as early as the late seventeenth century, syncretism and 'a process of interchange and experimentation' had clearly occurred among African musical cultures in Jamaica.[29]

Another conundrum concerning the syncretism of African traditions and the relative contributions of various African peoples is evident in the early formation of Haitian *vodun* or voodoo. The Dahomean or Aja-Fon influence in Haitian voodoo is paramount: it contributed the major deities, ceremonies, and most of the African vocabulary to this New World religion. But from extant records, which begin in about the 1720s, the Aja-Fon seem to have been a minority of Africans in St. Domingue, comprising at most about a fifth of the island's black immigrants. Like the Koramanti in Jamaica, what has to be explained is the undue influence of the Aja-Fon minority in St. Domingue. One possible explanation is that perhaps before 1720 the Aja-Fon were not a minority. Perhaps in the earliest years of St. Domingue's history they were numerous, and constituted a charter group, creating many of the cultural norms for later newcomers. Or perhaps Aja-Fon languages were particularly easy to learn or their pantheon of gods were especially structured, which gave them influence disproportionate to their numbers throughout the eighteenth century.

While the Dahomean influence in voodoo was dominant, other African sources were important. Perhaps most notable were the Kongo strains in voodoo, which is not surprising for at the height of St. Domingue's power Congos formed the largest single ethnic group in the colony's slave population. John Jenzen has noted the presence in Haitian voodoo of various Kongo rituals, associated with *Lemba*, a cult of healing, trade, and marriage relations in seventeenth-century West-Central Africa. Luc de Huesch sees a syncretism of Dahomey's *rada* and Kongo's *petro* divinities in *vodun*. David Geggus has highlighted two religious chants dating from the late eighteenth and early nineteenth centuries which were Kongo in origin and which were sung during an initiation ceremony into a snake cult. Quite why the Kongo influence was secondary and not primary may be explained variously: the low status of Congo slaves based perhaps on their size, the ability of Congos to assimilate, the Congos' relative lack of women which may have hampered cultural transmission, and their prevalence in the mountains rather than on the plains. Secondary or not, what is most notable here, as in Jamaican music, is the apparent joining together of different African cultures in an early New World cultural form.[30]

An 'Igboized' slave culture, Douglas Chambers argues, arose in eighteenth-century Virginia. He bases his argument on the large number of slaves drawn from the Bight of Biafra who entered the Chesapeake Bay in the 1720s and 1730s. These 'first comers', he contends, shaped the material culture of the region: the cultivation of okra, itself an Igbo word; the reliance on sweet potatoes, which were the nearest equivalent to yams, the staple of the Bight of Biafra region; the prevalence of root cellars in Chesapeake quarters, where the slaves stored their sweet potatoes and other goods. Similarly, the Igbo connection is said to explain much of the musical, magical, and ceremonial culture of Virginia slaves: the incorporation of Igbo instruments such as the *gamby* (Eboe drum) and the *balafo* (xylophone); the practice of conjuring and root-doctoring, which allegedly had precise Igboland analogues; and *jonkonu*, a masquerade involving cow-horn and other animal masks, which can be likened to spirit cults and secret societies in the Bight of Biafra region.[31]

Although the Bight of Biafra region was an important source of slaves for the Chesapeake region, it seems rather far-fetched to claim that Virginia slave culture was predominantly Igbo. First, Africans from Upper Guinea constituted 44 per cent of arrivals in the Chesapeake between 1662 and 1713, outstripping those from the Bight of Biafra. Although the Bight of Biafra was a considerable supplier in these early years – providing just over a third of the Chesapeake's slaves – the numerically predominant 'first comers' came from Senegambia and Sierra Leone. The Gold Coast was a significant supplier too, particularly in the first decade of eighteenth century. The Bight of Biafra was the dominant provenance zone in the 1720s and 1730s, but this influx represented a second, not the first, wave. Other influxes, from the 1740s to 1760s, were quite heterogeneous, with Senegambia the dominant zone in the 1740s and Angola in the 1760s. Second, many of the so-called 'Igboisms' in Chesapeake slave life could just as easily be explained as general West and Central African traits; and, as already noted, Igbo identity is itself problematic. Rather than posit a single ethnic influence, syncretism is the real story of Virginia slave culture. Finally, the reason for the notably syncretic character of Chesapeake black life must be sought not just in the scale and timing of the immigration and the enforced mingling of heterogeneous Africans, but in the local context. Africans in Virginia found themselves purchased in tiny lots, dispersed onto widely scattered estates, resident on small plantations, soon surrounded by a majority of native-born slaves, and brought into close contact with whites. All of this was not conducive to the reconstitution of an African ethnic identity.[32]

The foundation of Louisiana's Afro-Creole culture, Gwendolyn Hall claims, rests on the numerical predominance of Senegambia slaves imported to the colony in the early decades of the eighteenth century. Bambaras, she maintains, 'played a preponderant role' in the formation of the colony's slave culture. They 'constituted a language community', mounted rebellions, were accused of a disproportionate number of crimes, and influenced other slaves with their magical beliefs, evident in the widespread resort to *zinzin*, an amulet, or *grisgris*, a harmful charm, both Mande terms. Aside from whether Bambaras were a true ethnic group, the alleged paramount influence of Mande on Louisiana culture needs to be questioned. First, in the early 1720s, as Peter Caron has emphasized, Africans from the Bight of Benin dominated the colony's African population. The contribution of enslaved Aja peoples from the Slave Coast, Caron observes, may have been especially significant given the large numbers of children born to Africans between 1721 and 1726. Further, Caron demonstrates that most slaves from Senegambia came from the coastal areas, not the Niger bend, which is the area of Bambara and Mande influence. In addition, even by the middle of the eighteenth century most Louisiana slaves lived on units of ten or fewer Africans, which inhibited the domination of one ethnic group. For all these reasons and others, such as the much more heterogeneous and larger influx of Africans when Louisiana became a Spanish colony – it seems sensible to emphasize the pluralistic quality of Afro-Creole culture. The Congo influence in folklore and magic, the Fon role in voodoo, the Yoruba origins of shotgun houses, and the many African religious traditions (from Islam to Congo-Christianity to non-universal variants) that infused Louisiana religion must all be recognized.[33]

Cuban Santeria can serve as one last example of a New World neo-African cultural form. Eltis and Richardson, it will be recalled, argued that the heterogeneity of the island's Africans, the lack of women and abundance of children, and the short period of African importation should have undermined the ability of Cuban slaves to maintain regional African cultures. Cuban Santeria seems an unlikely model for such an argument, because one of its major components was a traditional African religion, the orisha worship as practised by the Yoruba. Eltis and Richardson demonstrate that a quarter of Cuba's Africans came from the Bight of Benin, making it the second most important provenance zone for Cuba's Africans (behind West-Central Africa, which supplied about 28 per cent of the island's Africans). Furthermore, at certain times, the Bight of Benin was a dominant supplier; indeed, from 1851 to 1866, Cuba was the only market available for Bight of Benin slaves. Thus, a powerful Yoruba influence in Cuba should not be all that surprising, although perhaps the question should again be, as in the Haitian case, why West-Central African influences were not more dominant than they were.

But a number of other facilitating forces were also at work, which will demonstrate that the process of New World slave cultural development was far from straight-forward. First, there is the issue of ethno-genesis. As already noted, in eighteenth-century Africa there was no overall term for all the heterogeneous Yoruba subgroups, but in Cuba, descendants of Yoruba-speakers and some of their neighbours became Lucumi. 'Just as Apulians, Sicilians, and Calabians all became Italians in the United States,' George Brandon analogizes, 'Oyos, Egbas, Ijebus, and Ijeshas all became Lucumis in Cuba.' Who was primarily responsible for generating this ethnic label – the slaves, the slave traders, or most likely a combination of the two – is unclear, but this emergent ethnic identity was a New World development. Furthermore, what is evident is that while Lucumi culture had a Yoruba focus, it incorporated traits from far afield. People sold by the Yoruba became Lucumi; people of Allada and the Ibo were incorporated within the so-called Lucumi nation. Some Lucumi words and phrases are not Yoruba in origin, and seem to be Ewe or Fon in derivation. Once again, a minority exercised dominion in excess of its numbers.

In the Cuban case, an important – perhaps the most important – reason why Africans were able to retain so much of their regional cultures should be sought in towns. Cuba was a quite urbanized society by New World standards, and urban slaves experienced a less regimented existence than their rural counterparts. They had greater latitude for cultural development. Slaves and freed people created Afro-Cuban *cabildos* or lodges, clubs, fraternities, and dance groups. They drank in taverns with their *carabelas* or shipmates. By the end of the eighteenth century, twenty-one *cabildos* existed in Havana alone. Each had its own ritual centre, its African language, its distinctive drums and drumming styles and its dances. Just as with Jamaican music, an exchange of musical and other cultural styles no doubt occurred across *cabildo* and ethnic lines. These clubs were, in

Brandon's words, 'important centers for the preservation of African religion in Cuba's cities'. One or more Lucumi *cabildos* provided the crucible in which Santeria evolved.[34]

The role of towns in facilitating ethnic identity in the New World points to the importance of context in the formation of slave culture in the Americas. Perhaps neo-African cultural forms in the New World appeared most readily in urban settings, as the example of Cuban Santeria (and Bahian Candomble) suggests. Conversely, the most generic African cultural forms may have been most conspicuous in heavily rural places, such as Virginia. Yet, important as the urban/rural contrast was in moulding ethnic affiliations in the New World, it was far from being the only contextual variable in shaping black cultures in the Americas. The scale of immigration from a particular African coastal region or regions was fundamental to the process of New World ethno-genesis. Equally important was timing: first-comers in some situations, as in the rapid formation of a new language and religion in Surinam, were extremely influential; in other settings, late-comers, as in the Yoruba influx to Cuba, played a vital role. The demographic structure of the immigrant influx – the ratio of men to women, adults to children – was an important key to cultural transmission. Whether planters bought Africans singly or in large groups was another crucial factor in shaping slave life. The size of plantations, the proportion of black to white, and the nature of the economy were yet other features of a New World context that determined the character of a slave culture.[35]

Finally, even after making allowances for all the demographic, economic and social variables that fostered or inhibited ethnic identity among slaves, many unpredictabilities remain. In some cases, particular African minorities were influential in shaping certain slave societies, perhaps because these African minorities were especially adaptable and could incorporate others, or perhaps because some features of their homeland culture were especially attractive to others, or perhaps because of their high status among Europeans. Such might explain the influence of 'Koromantis' in Jamaica. Conversely, in other cases, particular African majorities were surprisingly uninfluential, perhaps because they were too adaptable and were therefore readily assimilated by others, or perhaps because they lacked enough women to transmit effectively their culture, or perhaps because they were located on the margins rather than in the heartlands of their new society, or perhaps because they were viewed negatively by Europeans. Such might explain the relative lack of influence of 'Congos' in St. Domingue.

Overall, Africans in the Americas had to adapt to survive. They had no time for debates about cultural purity or precise roots; they had no necessary continuing commitment to the societies from which they came. They were denied much of their previous social and cultural heritages: the personnel who maintained their homeland institutions, the complex social structures of their ancestral societies, their kings and courts, their guilds and cult-groups, their markets and armies. Even what they brought they ruthlessly jettisoned because it was no longer applicable or relevant to their new situations. No wonder, as Mintz puts it, when we think of the history of African-American slaves, 'we are speaking of mangled pasts'. For that reason, he continues, 'It is not the precise historical origins of a word, a phrase, a musical instrument or a rhythm that matters, so much as the creative genius of the users, molding older cultural substances into new and unfamiliar patterns, without regard to purity or pedigree'.[36]

Whether the focus is on African regional origins, American destinations, or New World cultural developments, the emphasis should be on heterogeneity, on fluid boundaries, on precarious and permeable zones of interaction, on hybrid societies, on mosaics of borderlands where cultures jostled and converged in combinations and permutations of dizzying complexity. A key way in which the many and disparate parts of the Atlantic world were coming together – albeit at unequal speeds – was in the creation of ever more mixed, heterogeneous cultures. The homogenizing tendency of stressing cultural unity in Africa, of emphasizing the non-random character of the slave trade, and of seeing the dominance of particular African coastal regions or ethnicities in most American settings, is at variance with the central forces shaping the early modern Atlantic world. This tendency should be resisted.

NOTES

1. Bernard Bailyn, 'The Idea of Atlantic History', *Itinerario*, 20, no.1 (1996), pp.19–44; Daniel W. Howe, 'American History in an Atlantic Context: An Inaugural Lecture delivered before the University of Oxford on 3 June 1993' (Oxford, 1993).
2. David Eltis, 'Free and Coerced Transatlantic Migrations: Some Comparisons', *American Historical Review*, 88 (1983), pp.251–80.
3. Philip D. Curtin, *The Atlantic Slave Trade: A Census* (Madison, Wisconsin, 1969), p.xvi.
4. John Thornton, *Africa and Africans in the Making of the Atlantic World, 1400–1680* (New York, 1992), pp.1, 195–7.
5. Michael L. Conniff and Thomas J. Davis (eds.), with various contributing authors, *Africans in the Americas: A History of the Black Diaspora* (New York, 1994), pp.53–8; Gwendolyn Midlo Hall, *Africans in Colonial Louisiana: the Development of Afro-Creole Culture in the Eighteenth Century* (Baton Rouge, Louisiana, 1992), p.159; Mervyn C. Alleyne, *Roots of Jamaican Culture* (London, 1988), pp. x, 18; Michael Mullin, *Africa in America: Slave Acculturation and Resistance in the American South and the British Caribbean, 1736–1831* (Urbana, Illinois, 1992), p.160.
6. In addition to the three principal organizers are three associates: Herbert S. Klein, Joseph C. Miller, and Barbara L. Solow. The core data consist of 177 fields of information, including the names of vessels, captains and shipowners, regions and dates of trade in Europe, Africa, and the Americas, and the number, age, and gender of slaves confined on the middle passage. The directors eventually hope to link related information, such as African climatic patterns, slave phenotypes, slave rebellions, and slave prices to the main data-set.

7. David Eltis and David Richardson, 'The Structure of the Transatlantic Slave Trade, 1595–1867' (unpublished paper presented to the Social Science History Meeting, 1995). This is an important paper. Much of my analysis, which sometimes varies from that of the authors, is based on their tables. I owe them a great debt for sharing their information with me.

8. David Eltis, 'The Volume and African Origins of the British Slave Trade before 1714', *Cahiers d'Etudes africaines*, 138 (1995), pp.617–27; David Richardson, 'Slave Exports from West and West-Central Africa, 1700–1810: New Estimates of Volume and Distribution', *Journal of African History*, 30 (1989), pp.1–22; David Richardson, 'The British Empire and the Atlantic Slave Trade 1660–1807', in Peter J. Marshall (ed.), *The Oxford History of the British Empire: The Eighteenth Century* (forthcoming), Table 3.

9. David Eltis and Stanley L. Engerman, 'Was the Slave Trade Dominated by Men?', *Journal of Interdisciplinary History*, 23 (1992), pp.237–57 (quote p.245); David Eltis and Stanley L. Engerman, 'Fluctuations in Sex and Age Ratios in the Transatlantic Slave Trade, 1663–1864', *Economic History Review*, 2nd series, 46 (1993), pp.308–23. For a less persuasive view on this subject, see Joseph E. Inikori, 'Export versus Domestic Demand: The Determinants of Sex Ratios in the Transatlantic Slave Trade', *Research in Economic History*, 14 (1992), pp.117–66.

10. Eltis and Richardson, 'The Structure of the Transatlantic Slave Trade'.

11. Ibid.

12. Ibid.; Richardson, 'Slave Exports', pp.13–14; Johannes Menne Postma, *The Dutch in the Atlantic Slave Trade 1600–1815* (New York, 1990), pp.114–15, 122–3.

13. Robin Law, *The Oyo Empire c. 1600–c. 1836: A West African Imperialism in the Era of the Atlantic Slave Trade* (Oxford, 1977), pp.206, 219–29, 274, 281–2, 303–8; Paul E. Lovejoy, 'The Central Sudan and the Atlantic Slave Trade', in Robert W. Harms, Joseph C. Miller, David S. Newbury, and Michele D. Wagner (eds.), *Paths Toward the Past: African Historical Essays in Honor of Jan Vansina* (Atlanta, 1994), pp.345–70 (quote p.359).

14. Joseph C. Miller, 'The Numbers, Origins, and Destinations of Slaves in the Eighteenth Century Angolan Slave Trade', in Joseph E. Inikori and Stanley L. Engerman (eds.), *The Atlantic Slave Trade: Effects on Economies, Societies, and Peoples in Africa, the Americas, and Europe* (Durham, North Carolina, 1992), pp.77–115; David Northrup, *Trade without Rulers: Pre-Colonial Economic Development in South-Eastern Nigeria* (Oxford, 1978), pp.60–4.

15. Eltis and Richardson, 'The Structure of the Transatlantic Slave Trade'.

16. Mary C. Karasch, *Slave Life in Rio de Janeiro 1808–1850* (Princeton, 1987), pp.xxiv, 8, 18.

17. Eltis and Richardson, 'The Structure of the Transatlantic Slave Trade'; David Eltis and David Richardson, 'West Africa and the Transatlantic Slave Trade: New Evidence of Long-Run Trends', this volume.

18. Adam Jones and Marion Johnson, 'Slaves from the Windward Coast', *Journal of African History*, 21 (1980), pp.17–34, for arguments for not accepting destinations; Postma, *The Dutch in the Atlantic Slave Trade*, pp.120–4; Karasch, *Slave Life in Rio*, p.16. When detailed records on individual voyages are available, the ship often stops at a number of ports: see, for example, Nigel Tattersfield, *The Forgotten Trade, Comprising the Log of the Daniel and Henry of 1700 and Accounts of the Slave Trade from the Minor Ports of England 1698–1725* (London, 1991), and Suzanne Schwarz, *Slave Captain: The Career of James Irving in the Liverpool Atlantic Slave Trade* (Wrexham, Clwyd, 1995).

19. Personal communication from David Eltis, 23 October 1996.

20. Joseph C. Miller, *Way of Death* (Madison, Wisconsin, 1988), pp.7–8, 141–53, 189–203, 223, 224 (quote), 226.

21. Eltis and Richardson, 'The Structure of the Transatlantic Slave Trade'.

22. Richardson, 'The British Empire and the Atlantic Slave Trade', in Marshall (ed.), *Oxford History of the British Empire*; David Eltis, 'The Traffic in Slaves between the British West Indian Colonies, 1807–1833', *Economic History Review*, 2nd series, 25 (1972), pp.55–64; Svend E. Green-Pedersen, 'The Scope and Structure of the Danish Negro Slave Trade', *Scandinavian Economic History Review*, 19 (1971), pp.149–97; Postma, *The Dutch in the Atlantic Slave Trade*, pp.168–9, 226; Franklin W. Knight, *Slave Society in Cuba during the*

Nineteenth Century (Madison, Wisconsin, 1970), p.8.

23. Miller, 'Number, Origins', in Inikori and Engerman (eds.), *Atlantic Slave Trade*, p.89; Patrick Manning, 'Migrations of Africans to the Americas: The Impact on Africans, Africa, and the New World', *The History Teacher*, 26 (1993), pp.279–96, especially p.281; Philip D. Morgan and Michael L. Nicholls, 'Slaves in Piedmont Virginia, 1720–1790', *William and Mary Quarterly*, 3rd series, 46 (1989), pp.211–51; Philip D. Morgan, 'Black Society in the Lowcountry, 1760–1810', in Ira Berlin and Ronald Hoffman (eds.), *Slavery and Freedom in the Age of the American Revolution* (Charlottesville, Virginia, 1983), pp.83–141.

24. Miller, *Way of Death*, p.225; Philip D. Curtin, *Economic Change in Precolonial Africa: Senegambia in the Era of the Slave Trade* (Madison, Wisconsin, 1975), pp.187–8. See also Adam Jones, 'Receptive Nations: Evidence Concerning the Demographic Impact of the Atlantic Slave Trade in the Early Nineteenth Century', *Slavery and Abolition*, 11 (1990), pp.42–57.

25. Richard Rathbone, Review of Thornton, *Africa and Africans* in *Journal of African History*, 34 (1993), 495–6; Law, *Oyo Empire*, pp.5–7; Northrup, *Trade Without Rulers*, p.15; Miller, *Way of Death*, p.28. This subject is treated at much greater length in Sean Hawkins and Philip Morgan, 'Patterns of Cultural Transmission: Diffusion, Destruction, and Development in the African Diaspora' (paper delivered at York University Workshop, 'The African Diaspora and the Nigerian Hinterland', 2–4 February 1996, which the authors hope to publish in a revised form soon).

26. Karen Fog Olwig, 'African Cultural Principles in Caribbean Slave Societies: A View from the Danish West Indies', in Stephan Palmie (ed.), *Slave Cultures and the Cultures of Slavery* (Knoxville, Tennessee, 1995), p.29; Sidney W. Mintz, 'More on the Peculiar Institution', *New West Indian Guide*, 58 (1984), pp.185–99, especially p.189; David Geggus, 'Sex Ratio, Age and Ethnicity in the Atlantic Slave Trade: Data from French Shipping and Plantation Records', *Journal of African History*, 30 (1989), pp.23–44, especially p.35; Curtin, *Atlantic Slave Trade*, p.184, and Curtin, *Economic Change in Precolonial Africa*, p.179 (quote).

27. Barry W. Higman, 'African and Creole Slave Family Patterns in Trinidad', *Journal of Family History*, 3 (1978), pp.163–80. For a contrasting argument in a different context, see Colin A. Palmer, 'From Africa to the Americas: Ethnicity in the Early Black Communities of the Americas', *Journal of World History*, 6 (1995), pp.223–36.

28. Claude Levi-Strauss, *The Savage Mind* (London, 1966); Shane White and Graham White, 'Slave Hair and African-American Culture in the Eighteenth and Nineteenth Centuries', *Journal of Southern History*, 61 (1995), pp.45–76, and 'Slave Clothing and African-American Culture in the Eighteenth and Nineteenth Centuries', *Past and Present*, 148 (August 1995), pp.149–86; Grey Gundaker, 'Tradition and Innovation in African-American Yards', *African Arts* (April 1993), pp.58–71, 94–96; Richard Westmacott, *African-American Gardens and Yards in the Rural South* (Knoxville, 1992).

29. I rely heavily on an excellent article by Richard Cullen Rath, 'African Music in Seventeenth Century Jamaica: Cultural Transit and Transition', *William and Mary Quarterly*, 3rd series, 50 (1993), pp.700–26, although my emphases are a little different, and Rath did not have the advantage of the most recent analysis of the slave trade to Jamaica, which can be found in Eltis, 'Volume and African Origins', p.619.

30. Serge Larose, 'The Meaning of Africa in Haitian Vodu', in Ioan M. Lewis (ed.), *Symbols and Sentiments* (London, 1977), pp.85–116; John M. Janzen, *Lemba, 1650–1930: A Drum of Affliction in Africa and the New World* (New York, 1982), especially pp.273–92; Luc de Heusch, 'Kongo in Haiti: A New Approach to Religious Syncretism', *Man*, XXIV (1989), pp.290–303; David Geggus, 'Haitian Voodoo in the Eighteenth Century: Language, Culture, Resistance', *Jahrbuch Fur Geschichte Von Staat, Wirtschaft und Gesellschaft Latein Amerikas*, 28 (1991), pp.21–51; David Geggus, 'The Bois Caiman Ceremony', *Journal of Caribbean History*, 25 (1991), pp.41–57, especially p.50; David Geggus, 'Sugar and Coffee Cultivation in Saint Domingue and the Shaping of the Slave Labor Force', in Ira Berlin and Philip D. Morgan (eds.), *Cultivation and Culture: Labor and the Shaping of Slave Life in the Americas* (Charlottesville, Virginia, 1993), pp.73–98, especially p.80. See also John K. Thornton, 'On the Trail of Voodoo: African Christianity in Africa and the Americas', *The Americas*, 44 (1987–1988), pp.261–78.

31. Douglas B. Chambers, '"He Gwine Sing He Country"': Africans, Afro-Virginians, and the Development of Slave Culture in Virginia, 1690–1810', unpub.Ph.D. thesis, University of Virginia, 1996; Douglas B. Chambers, '"He is an African But Speaks Plain"': Historical Creolization in Eighteenth-Century Virginia', in Alusine Jalloh and Stephen Maizlish (eds.), *Africa and the African Diaspora* (College Station, Texas, 1996), pp.100–133; and Douglas B. Chambers, '"My own nation"': Igbo Exiles in the Diaspora', this volume. Chambers has broadened his argument to two other regions in his 'Eboe, Kongo, Mandingo: African Ethnic Groups and the Development of Regional Slave Societies in Mainland North America, 1700 1820', Working Paper No. 96–14, International Seminar on the History of the Atlantic World 1500–1800, Harvard University, September 1996.

32. Eltis, 'Volume and African Origins', p.619; Allan Kulikoff, *Tobacco and Slaves: The Development of Southern Cultures in the Chesapeake, 1680–1800* (Chapel Hill, North Carolina, 1986); Philip D. Morgan, *Slave Counterpoint: Black Culture in the Eighteenth-Century Chesapeake and Lowcountry* (Chapel Hill, North Carolina, 1997).

33. Hall, *Africans in Colonial Louisiana*, pp.41, 51, 111–13, 164, 293, 302; Peter Caron, 'The Peopling of French Colonial Louisiana: The Origins and Demographic Distributions of African Slaves, 1718–1735' (paper delivered at Tulane–Cambridge Atlantic World Studies Group, 21–23 November 1996); Peter Caron, '"Of a nation which the others do not understand"': Bambara Slaves and African Ethnicity in Colonial Louisiana, 1718–1760', this volume; John Michael Vlach, 'The Shotgun House: An African Architectural Legacy', in John Michael Vlach (ed.), *By the Work of Their Hands: Studies in Afro-American Folklife* (Charlottesville, Virginia, 1991), pp.185–213.

34. This account rests on Knight, *Slave Society in Cuba*, pp.60–1; Manuel Moreno Fraginals, 'Africa in Cuba: A Quantitative Analysis of the African Population in the Island of Cuba', in Vera Rubin and Arthur Tuden (eds.), *Comparative Perspectives on Slavery in New World Plantation Societies* (New York, 1977), pp.187–201; Herbert S. Klein, *Slavery in the Americas* (Chicago, 1967); Stephan Palmié, 'Ethnogenetic Processes and Cultural Transfer in Afro-American Slave Populations', in Wolfgang Binder (ed.), *Slavery in the Americas* (Wurzburg, 1993), pp.337–33; and most usefully, George Brandon, *Santeria from Africa to the New World: The Dead Sell Memories* (Bloomington, 1993), pp.55, 69 (quotes).

35. Sidney W. Mintz and Richard Price, *The Birth of African-American Culture: An Anthropological Perspective* (Boston, 1992), pp.48–50; for size of purchases, see Stephanie Smallwood, 'After the Atlantic Crossing: The Arrival and Sale of African Migrants in the British Americas, 1672–1693', Working Paper No. 96–13, International Seminar on the History of the Atlantic World 1500–1800, Harvard University, September 1996, and Trevor Burnard, 'Who Bought Slaves in Early America? Purchasers of Slaves from the Royal African Company in Jamaica, 1674–1708,' *Slavery and Abolition*, 17 (1996), pp.68–92.

36. Sidney W. Mintz, 'Foreword', in Norman E. Whitten, Jr. and John F. Szwed (eds.), *Afro-American Anthropology: Contemporary Perspectives* (New York, 1970), p.9, and Sidney W. Mintz, 'Creating Culture in the Americas', *Columbia Forum*, 13 (1970), p.8.

Notes on Contributors

David Eltis is Professor of History at Queen's University, Kingston, Ontario; Research Lecturer at the University of Hull; and Visiting Fellow at the W.E.B. Du Bois Institute for Afro-American Research, Harvard.

David Richardson is Reader in Economic History, University of Hull.

Herbert S. Klein is Professor of History at Columbia University.

Stanley L. Engerman is John H. Munro Professor of Economics and Professor of History at the University of Rochester.

Stephen D. Behrendt has taught at Drake University and Northern Iowa University and is an Honorary Fellow of the W.E.B. Du Bois Institute, Harvard.

Douglas B. Chambers teaches at the Corcoran Department of History, University of Virginia, Charlottesville.

Peter Caron is a graduate student at the Department of History, Tulane University, New Orleans.

Philip D. Morgan is Professor of History at Florida State University.

Index